GUIDES, PHILOSOPHERS AND FRIENDS

STUDIES OF COLLEGE MEN

27- 12783

BY

CHARLES FRANKLIN THWING

Litt.D., L.H.D., LL.D.
PRESIDENT EMERITUS OF WESTERN RESERVE UNIVERSITY
AND ADELBERT COLLEGE

New York
THE MACMILLAN COMPANY
1927

All rights reserved

To
GEORGE HERBERT PALMER
SCHOLAR, TEACHER, AUTHOR,
INTERPRETER OF HOMER,
THIS VOLUME IS DEDICATED
IN GRATITUDE AND AFFECTION

PREFACE

Biographies may be either historical, interpreting a period, or personal, interpreting a man. Of course, each type necessarily includes and uses certain elements of the other. The following sketches are of the second sort: primarily they are concerned with the personal character and services of the subjects themselves. Yet, I venture to believe that they also may serve a bit to present some of the educational movements, to interpret some of the educational facts, and to intimate a few of the many educational problems, of the last half-century.

The personal interpretation is made yet more controlling for a particular reason: each one of the twenty-two men considered I number among my personal friends. For them, if their names are starred in the college catalogues, as most are, I have a heart overflowing with fragrant and grateful memory. For them, if they still continue here, and only one does, my heart is a loving heart. In either case, I can justly and humbly claim, though lacking all other qualities of a biographer, to have one essential element, the element of sympathy.

The volume is in part concerned with college presidents. A few months ago, a book, entitled "The College President," was published. It was a rather theoretical discussion of the chief executive of the American college and university. Possibly, the present volume might be regarded as a sort of application, or personal illustration, of some of the principles, methods, aims, rewards, and perils outlined in the earlier book.

C. F. T.

Western Reserve University,
        Cleveland,
    1st January, 1927.

CONTENTS

ix

I

CHARLES WILLIAM ELIOT

CHARLES WILLIAM ELIOT was born, of distinguished ancestry, in Boston, March 20, 1834; died August 22, 1926. Received A.B. degree, Harvard, 1853; A.M,. 1856. Tutor in mathematics and student in chemistry with Professor Josiah P. Cooke, 1854-58; assistant professor of chemistry and mathematics in Lawrence Scientific School, Harvard, 1858-63; 1863-65, in Europe, student of chemistry and of educational organization; assistant professor of chemistry, Massachusetts Institute of Technology, 1865-69; president of Harvard University, 1869-1909; president emeritus, 1909-1926. Received many honors from many universities. Commander of *Légion d'Honneur;* Grand Officer of the Crown of Italy, 1908; Imperial Order of the Rising Sun of 1st class, 1909; Royal Prussian Order of the Crown (1st class), 1909; Order of the Crown of Belgium, 1919; Grand Cordon of the Order of St. Sava, 1923. Received first gold medal, American Academy of Arts and Letters, in recognition of "special distinction," 1915. Writer of books on chemistry, and on education, capital and labor, war and peace, the conduct of life, and on government.

GUIDES, PHILOSOPHERS AND FRIENDS

I

CHARLES WILLIAM ELIOT

PIONEER, INTERPRETER, ADMINISTRATOR, CITIZEN

In a farewell letter which Lord Grey of Falloden wrote to Walter Hines Page, at the close of his ambassadorship, he said: "I have often thought that the forces behind public affairs are so tremendous that individuals have little real, even when much apparent, influence upon the course of events. But in the early years of the war I think everything might have gone wrong if it had not been that certain men of strong moral conviction were in certain places."[1] In a similar interpretation, one may say of the whole educational process and movement, individuals do have small influence. The tides which bear our little school and college barks are mightier than all the forces of engineer or of pilot. Yet, it is still true that if certain men had not been in their places on

[1] "The Life and Letters of Walter Hines Page." By Burton J. Hendrick. Vol. II, p. 409.

the captain's bridge or elsewhere, in all the educational voyage, many things would have gone wrong. Eliot, like Page, was one of the men who were in their places and helped to make things go right.

Eliot was born 20th March, 1834; he died 22nd August, 1926. At the age of thirty-five, in 1869, he became president of Harvard University, one of the most important of all educational or other offices.

The preceding years of boyhood and of early manhood had well prepared him to undertake the great office. Born in Boston, of the best New England ancestry, bred in a home on Beacon Hill, in which culture and a high idealism of public service were natural, fitting for college in the historic Latin School, entering Harvard in 1849, he graduated four years later in a class which subsequently became historic and distinguished. The influence of Harvard College over him is interpreted in a letter which he wrote to me in the year 1894. In it he said:

"The best thing Harvard College did for me was to give me practice in thinking and acting independently in a crowd of intelligent contemporaries of very various characters and aims. In the retrospect I can see that I got in college a good deal of such practice, some of it being rather trying at the time. Secondary advantages were, some scholarly instruction in Latin, some advanced work in mathematics, under an inspiring but incomprehensible teacher, and some study of chemistry in Professor Cooke's private laboratory—the last opportunity being a per-

sonal favor and not a part of the College system. All
the rest of the instruction which I received from the
College between 1849 and 1853 was of a very elementary sort. I did the work and got something out of
it; but it was really secondary school work.''

For another quartette of years, 1854-1858, Eliot
was a tutor in mathematics and a student in chemistry. In 1858 he was promoted to an assistant professorship of mathematics and of chemistry, in which
he served for five more years. In 1863 he retired, and
went to Europe, to study further in his old professional field of chemistry, and in the new field of educational methods, forces, and conditions. Returning,
after two formative and fruitful years, he accepted
a professorship of analytical chemistry in the recently
established Massachusetts Institute of Technology.
Here he served four years.

In all this time, at home and abroad, he had been
a student of the new education, as well as a learner
and a teacher of the new chemistry. The educationally progressive party in Harvard College—a party
then becoming strong—realized in the closing years of
the seventh decade of the century that a new type
of president was demanded in and for their College.
In writing and in speech Eliot had interpreted and
argued for a type of the higher education, broader
and richer in contact, more liberal in tone and
method, than Harvard had formerly embodied.
Therefore, the progressive party—in the face of
rather severe opposition, however—elected Eliot, the

disciple of the new education and its apostle, president of Harvard University in 1869. For forty years he held the office, a length of term equalled by few college executives. In 1909 he retired. He was at once chosen president emeritus.

This simple academic record is made yet more illustrious by effective service in public or semipublic positions. The presidency of the Carnegie Foundation for the Advancement of Teaching, membership in historic societies, such as the American Philosophical, the receiving of many honorary degrees, the accepting of significant orders, as The Imperial Order of the Rising Sun (first class), the doing of special work in the cause of international peace, represent highest honors conferred and richest opportunities opened.

His was a life useful in services, noble in honor and honors, as it was notable in length of years. In fact such conditions a long time ago were well summed up by the remark that President Eliot was America's first citizen. Recent years have shown the fuller appropriateness of giving to him the great name. His primacy has received full recognition. He stood alone.

But undoubtedly the greatest of the manifold works of President Eliot was his presidency of Harvard, and the consequent service which through this office he rendered to American education and to the cause of education in the world. He came into the office following five brief terms, beginning with

Edward Everett's in 1845, which was succeeded by that of Sparks, of Walker, of Felton, and of Hill. He came into the office when the United States, after the Civil War, was prepared to accept the highest civil and educational leadership. The nation was eager to transfer the enthusiasms and the allegiances of the war-period to the interests of peace. Scientific discoveries and development had made the times ripe for an enlarged educational curriculum. The increased wealth of the country, too, gave a foundation for progress in all intellectual endeavors. The period was, in its awakened conditions and quickening influences in education, akin to the fourth decade of the same nineteenth century.

Beginning in this opportune time, President Eliot for forty years, without haste and without rest, labored at his momentous task. He broadened the academic and the public conception of education. By the side of the classical tradition was installed the scientific method and equipment. By the side of the sciences were placed the newer humanities, of economics, of government, of literature, of history, and of modern foreign languages. He added to the list of the great scholars and teachers of Harvard—already including Louis Agassiz, Benjamin Peirce, Asa Gray, Child, Lane, Goodwin, Francis Bowen—such philosophers as Palmer, James, Royce.

To the other great departments of human learning and teaching he appointed, as the event has proved, the greatest of historians, of economists, of physicists,

of teachers of law, of language, and of theology. In
his inaugural he said that the choice of teachers is
the most important of all works of the president. "It
is in discharging this duty that the President holds
the future of the University in his hands."[2] The
result has proved with what discrimination he did
this duty. He also made clear to the American community that money invested in the American college
is one of the most effective methods for securing the
elevation of American society, and for the development of a world-civilization. He has in many ways,
direct and indirect, given definitions of the nature,
the content, the forces, and the aims of education,
both higher and lower. Perhaps no better definition
of education has he made than is found in his interpretation of the service of Langdell in the Law
School. Of Langdell, Eliot says:

"He tried to make his students use their own minds
logically on given facts, and then to state their reasoning and conclusions correctly in the classroom.
He led them to exact reasoning and exposition by
first setting an example himself, and then giving them
abundant opportunities for putting their own minds
into vigorous action, in order, first, that they might
gain mental power, and, secondly, that they might
hold firmly the information or knowledge they had
acquired. It was a strong case of education by drawing out from each individual student mental activity
of a very strenuous and informing kind . . . a

[2]"Educational Reform." p. 35.

method which is not passive but intensely active, not mainly an absorption from either book or teacher but primarily a constant giving-forth." [3]

The interpretation thus given of the method of a single teacher of law can be vastly broadened into an interpretation of education itself.

These results, so fundamental, so diverse, apparently so enduring, he achieved by many forces and through many conditions. Of course the most obvious remark is that the part of personality was regnant. But such an interpretation is meaningless without discrimination, even though the personality was forceful, gracious, great-minded, great-hearted, and fine. Generations and traditions of good breeding entered into this personality, traditions which, be it added, have been worthily transmitted to the generations following. Abundance of life rested upon him in body and mind. The abundance was rich without profuseness, virile without being hard, calm without sluggishness, vigorous without restlessness, progressive, buoyant, and optimistic. Seen or heard by a stranger, the manner, the voice, commanded attention, compelled and held interest. The personality reminded one of the familiar remark of Emerson that the dominance of what one is deadens, or deafens, the hearing for what one says, even though the saying be most significant and impressive.

Yet, despite such dominance, Eliot seemed to me to be a selfless personality. The apparent contradic-

[3] "A Late Harvest." pp. 53-54.

tion is striking and impressive. What is the explanation? Does not the explanation lie in the fact that the personal strength, however great, was directed outward and not inward, that the thought, however large and earnest, was given to the exterior and not to the interior subject, that the feeling, though intense, went to the cause and was not occupied about, or by, the personal feeling, that the will, though strong, was applied to the movement and not to the one acting, that, in a word, the man—as say the philosophers—was objective and not subjective? "Look out and not in," was his rule and counsel. This explanation seems to remove the apparent contradictoriness. Such a union of selflessness and of power of selfhood is seldom found. But wherever it is found, it represents tremendous, as well as unique, force, and a force making greatly for the welfare of men. It is found in men as unlike in character and circumstance as Washington and Lincoln.

In this personality the most dominant force always seemed to me, after an acquaintance of more than fifty years, to be the desire to know and to declare the truth. His emphasis on truth prepared the way for his emphasis on liberty. He well incarnated the motto of the college, *Veritas.* His was a scientific mind applied to causes of all kinds. He embodied in himself what he declared to be the primary methods of study and research in a university: "A careful observation of actual facts, an accurate recording of the facts determined, and a just and limited inference from the recorded facts."[4] Prevarications, dissimulations were abhorrent to his whole nature.

At times his desire to make known the truth seemed to be so intense as to take no notice of personalities. His interpretations have been known to wound friends, but this sense of truthfulness has also proved itself quite as often in commendation. Many a young college teacher and freshman student could bear witness to hearing words of encouragement at times when such words had tremendous weight. The love of and loyalty to truth were vitally united with a good will. The community's confidence in his loyalty to truthfulness was general and strong. It is told that one of his colleagues in a subordinate position he had declined to promote, on the ground that the man was not a fit teacher of youth. "Did Charles Eliot say that I am not a fit teacher of youth?" "Yes," was the reply. "If Charles Eliot said that I am not a fit teacher of youth, I am sure I am not."

Such loyalty to truth is disturbing and disrupting. Truth and its testing give trouble, are "annoying," as Lord Balfour once said, in his way, of the German advance of March, 1918. As John Dewey says: "To generalize the recognition that the true means the verified and means nothing else, places upon men the responsibility for surrendering political and moral dogmas, and subjecting to the test of consequences

[4] "Harvard Memories." pp. 65-66.

their most cherished prejudices. Such a change involves a great change in the seat of authority and the methods of decision in society.''[5] But ncne of these things moved Eliot. Truth was chief, foremost, controlling, compelling. On *Veritas* Harvard is founded; through *Veritas* it is nourished; for *Veritas* it is endowed; and to strengthen for doing duties which *Veritas* teaches it ever exists.

In this love for truth were included two qualities often exclusive or contradictory: care for detail and loyalty to principles. President Eliot was one of the two men known to me who best represent this unique and precious combination. His mind was both microscopic and telescopic. I could give many instances of his knowing the apparently trivial in the affairs of Harvard College. But his vision was also regnant and far-off. He had a taste for great causes. He was thus like two outstanding and opposing prime ministers, Salisbury and Gladstone.

In such a union of the remote and of the near went along at least two elements—hard work and exhilaration in hard work. In a chapter in his ''A Late Harvest,'' entitled ''How I have Kept my Health,'' he says:

''I began as a boy to use my mind intently several hours a day. As a college student, I increased the number of hours a day of mental occupation. . . . During the last three years of my college course I did

[5] ''Reconstruction in Philosophy.'' p. 159 f. See ''Source Book in the Philosophy of Education.'' By W. H. Kilpatrick. p. 4.

much work in that little laboratory [6] every week, in addition to attending all the recitations required of my class, and doing well [he was second scholar in his class, consisting of eighty-seven freshmen and eighty-eight seniors] in all the studies of the regular course." [7]

"From the time I became tutor, at the age of twenty, onward, I think I have done per day an unusual amount of mental work, much of which, however, has had a routine or repetitive character, as in all teaching and administration. . . . That I have borne much labor and responsibility without ever suffering even a temporary breakdown seems to me to be due—after the inheritance of a sound constitution —to my possessing a good muscular and nervous system, preserved by open-air exercise and the habit of moderate eating. . .

"It undoubtedly contributed to my endurance of the laborious and responsible life I led as President of Harvard College for forty years that, beginning in 1871, I passed the long summer vacation at or near the island of Mount Desert, devoting, however, part of the time during the first nine years to cruising in a seaworthy sloop along the New England coast from Block Island to Grand Manan. This summer life gave me a strong and wholesome change of air and scene, and also of mental occupation, for I went

---

[6] The Laboratory of Josiah Parsons Cooke, at that time instructor in chemistry.

[7] "A Late Harvest." p. 9.

skipper and pilot. It provided for me and my family during nearly a quarter part of the year a simple, wholesome, natural life in close contact with the ocean, woods, and hills, with opportunity for various excellent kinds of physical and mental activity, and with freedom from the turmoil, noise, dirt, foul air, and nervous tension of city life.

"One result of the balance between my bodily and mental powers has been that I have always been able to sleep well at night, and, since I was seventy, briefly in the daytime also. I could always spend a long evening in stirring debate or in public speaking, and go to sleep, on getting home, without delay or need of any calming process. I could also write diligently all the evening on a subject which greatly interested me, stop at eleven o'clock, and fall asleep the moment I got into bed."[8]

"My own experience has led me to think that strenuous work, done with interest and zeal, usually promotes health and vigor, and is seldom injurious if kept within the limits set by bodily fatigue."[9]

For three-score years and ten Eliot toiled, not "terribly"—as was said of another—but constantly, intensely, calmly, rejoicingly. The mood of joy was especially regnant. The toil made joy, and the joy quickened toil, increasing the forces for toil.

United with the loyalty to truth was another characteristic element, to wit, the desire to minister to the welfare of all the people. Writing of Harvard gradu-

[8] *Ibid.*, pp. 9-12.   [9] *Ibid.*, p. 13.

ates he says, ''They differ strongly on political, industrial, and religious questions, but have a common unifying desire to contribute to the public welfare.'' [10] This desire was dominant in the president. If in his tastes he belonged to the Brahman class, in his principles he embodied the democracy of public service. In his service a prototype may be found in his predecessor, Josiah Quincy, of whom he has written, ''By his speeches and writings and through his personal energy and uprightness [he] became a trusted leader among his contemporaries, although too independent by nature to be always an approved member of any party.'' [11] The eagerness for service is both the cause and the result of the leadership which was invested in him. To this quality, Chief Justice Taft devoted the larger share of his congratulatory address at the ninetieth anniversary:

''The most ambitious and the most difficult task that man has attempted is successful self-government. When people are herded as cattle under the rule of the strongest, the problem is a simple one of force and discipline. The few are intelligent and controlling and are united to keep the many under their will. But when government is based on the electoral equality of all among a people who vary much in conditions of bodily comfort and estate, in natural capacity, in trained intelligence, in self-restraint, in a sense of justice, and in the interest of each in the welfare of all, it is not easy safely to interpret the popular will

[10] ''Harvard Memories.'' p. 8.   [11] *Ibid.*, p. 4.

into effective action, and at the same time secure the just rights of the minority. Experience has proved that parties are indispensable in working out this problem, and, the fewer parties there are, the greater the chance of efficient action toward a desired end. But if the party convention and the party leaders are to be the only exponents of political opinion, party expediency will shrivel all reforms, and progress will cease. In no kind of government, therefore, is independent and courageous non-partisan leadership in economic, social, and political discussion so vital as in a democracy.

"Such leadership does not count numbers in its following. It does not trim its sails to catch the wind of popular acclaim. Its concern is with its facts, its logic, its clearness of vision, its own disinterestedness, its freedom from prejudice, its concern for the common welfare, its power of reasoned statement, its real prophetic faculty. With these, it seeks no census, convention, or primary. It tells the truth to the electors, however unpalatable. It abides the slowly waking but clarified convictions of the people taught by hard experience, and achieves a real advance by the occasional overthrow of party rule. It may not always be right. It may underestimate practical objections to measures it urges; but it promotes discussion on a plane of unselfish patriotic endeavor, and offers to a great electorate, groping for the welfare of the State, a high standard of judgment and a freedom from the self-seeking of groups.

"The number who can succeed to such leadership is small. They must have won the confidence of the public by long service in the sight of men in fields in which they are acknowledged masters. Their influence upon the body politic must be a consequence of their actual and proved achievements for the community in other than the domain of party government.

"Dr. Eliot is a leader and prophet of the people in this true sense. His primacy in all educational reform, his interest in adjusting the equities of the laborer and the capitalist, and the useful candor in which he points out the shortcomings of each, his abiding enthusiasm for the promotion of municipal governments in which the welfare of the citizen is most intimately bound up, his yearning for the enlargement of the lungs of congested cities in parks and playgrounds, his activity in the husbanding and preservation of the National resources, his patient, persistent, consistent advocacy of the reform of the Civil Service, has earnest labor in the cause of international peace, have prompted his lay sermons and made men harken to him.

"He is an individualist. He accepts only what approves itself to him. No mass inclination carries him to a conclusion. He loves liberty and democracy. He loyally yields to the majority when ordered liberty requires such yielding; but he never ceases to advocate a change in the popular verdict, should he deem it unjust. His training in the traditions and freedom of discussion in the town meeting has followed him.

His New England conscience is as erect, as powerful, and as unbending as his stature. His love of religious liberty and resentment at intolerance are part of his being and sensitive to the slightest alarm. Liberal beyond the sympathy of many, in an absence of creed he would cherish religion as the greatest agency in the advance of mankind.

"His life has borne testimony to his deep love for his fellow men, and his constant solicitude for the right solution of their problems. It has given him a pulpit from which he has preached as few men have preached to our people. He has represented no class. He has banished all prejudice. He has subjected every problem to the test of a judicial spirit of inquiry. It is not fulsome to say that he has wielded greater power with the intelligent democracy of this country than any other unofficial citizen of his time." [12]

It may be said by some that more constructive than Eliot's emphasis on truth and on public duty is the interpretation which he put upon the principle of liberty. For Eliot was a mighty believer in liberty. He constantly stood for the "patriot" side. The right to differ he believed in and practiced, both for others and for himself. He was by nature a protestant. Individualism was the prevailing note of the college song. The elective system of studies stands primarily for individualism of interpretation and of

[12] "The Ninetieth Birthday of Charles William Eliot: Proceedings." pp. 19-22.

practice. To him freedom and democracy were
united and uniting forces. For, as he said, "Democracy simply means freedom for each individual to
arrange his training and his life-career so that he can
do his best for the common welfare. You all understand that the variety of human nature is such that
one man's best is very different from another's, just
as one man's mental habits and powers are different
from every other's. With these varieties in human
nature democracy has to deal; and the hopes of democracy depend on whether all these varieties are
developed and made serviceable." [13]

In this trio of fundamental principles, of loyalty
to truth, of the desire to serve the common welfare,
and of the passion for liberty, are to be associated at
least two other elements; they are boldness and patience. The boldness was usually proved by the result
to be sane. The consequences of courageous initiative
justified the initiative. Illustrations of the academic
bravery abound. Perhaps the most significant is
found in the nomination of comparatively unknown
men to positions of great responsibility. Royce, a
young Californian, who grew into a fruitful thinker
and formative teacher; and Langdell, a comparatively inconspicuous, though very able, lawyer of
New York, who became a great professor, a wise
dean, and the founder of a new and subsequently
widely adopted system of teaching law, are moving
illustrations. The reconstruction, too, of the Har-

[13] "Harvard Memories." pp. 36-37.

vard Medical School, in the teeth of opposition, proves and illustrates the boldness of thought and endeavor. In the address which President Lowell made to his predecessor, at the great birthday celebration, one quality, and one quality only, was interpreted. President Lowell said:

"Much has been said, and will be said here, of the many achievements in that long career of service. One may, however, dwell for a moment upon some single pervasive quality which, throughout the trials, the obstacles, and the struggles of these years, he has possessed in unfailing and triumphant strength. That quality, unfortunately rare, is courage.

"From first to last Mr. Eliot has been an educational warrior. Elected President at thirty-five, dealing with colleagues in Faculties and Governing Boards much older than himself, many of them clinging tenaciously to the traditions of the past, he grappled fearlessly with the problems of the time. Undismayed by the opposition of men of weight among the graduates, by the frowns of almost all rival institutions, and by sharp public criticism, he pursued without flinching the end he had in view. Nor did he ever shun reform in a department of the University because it involved for years a serious falling off in the number of students but persisted calmly until public confidence should approve the change.

"Never in education or in public questions did he shrink from taking the unpopular side, but trusted to his faith in the rectitude of his own convictions.

More, perhaps, than ever before is such a quality needed in our leading citizens, and above all is it essential in those who are charged with the training of youth. Like most strong characters he has, no doubt, rated his own courage lightly, for it is an integral part of his vigorous nature; but we who bring him today our tribute of respect may well marvel at its force and its resistless potency." [14]

Two examples of his courage it is proper to cite. In the year 1893, making an address at Salt Lake City, Eliot drew what was interpreted as a parallel between the Pilgrims of Plymouth and the Mormons. The address called out severe and widespread criticism. Almost ten years after, in a speech on labor questions, he commended the "scab" and the "strike breaker" in ways which brought upon him the wrath of the labor unions. The too frequent endeavors to restrict the output of labor received his constant and severe criticism. Yet the labor leaders did invite him to make a speech to them in Faneuil Hall. His criticism, too, of capitalism was hardly less bold than that of labor unionism. His method and mood in meeting criticism in quite a different field, in the field of his booklet on the new religion, including even the title, illustrate his virile and constant courage.

The courage was also manifest in a way possibly yet more significant. President Eliot's dealing with

[14] "The Ninetieth Birthday of Charles William Eliot: Proceedings." pp. 11-12.

the newspapers was significant of his virile boldness. In various personal letters to me, he writes regarding their intellectual and moral weaknesses and
sins. In the year 1898, he says:

"The condition of our newspapers . . . seems to
me a very serious danger for the republic and a
grave source of moral and mental degradation for
the people. As to individual reputations as af-
fected by the inaccuracy and dishonesty of the press,
I suppose that future historians will know enough
not to accept the newspapers' estimates of contemporary personages."

In the same year, in the month of May, when
the madness of the Spanish War was possessing the
people and the papers, he writes:

"I need not say to you that I have made none
of the unpatriotic remarks attributed to me. The
criticisms of the newspapers have absolutely no
foundation. So far as I am concerned their criticism is based on pure invention. The remarks attributed to Professor Norton are also a travesty
of what he really said to his class. The extraordinary indifference of our newspapers to truth is certainly one of the most discouraging features of
American life."

The virtue of moral courage becomes more impressive when put in contrast with certain other elements
in his intellectual and moral constitution. He lacked
the lightness of touch which his colleague, Oliver Wendell Holmes, incarnated, or that personal sympathetic

charm which his kinsman, Charles Eliot Norton, embodied. By solid argument, he convinced his hearer of presumed truth. He had the *gravitas* which Mr. Stanley Baldwin says is one of the great qualities of the English race. But he did not possess that tactfulness which swiftly quickens responsiveness or love. His words sometimes struck to a sensitive conscientious nature a hard blow, which for a time, and for a time only, left soreness. Neither were such thrusts relieved by a sense of humor, that dear possession of college presidents and other administrators.

Lying hard by the virtue of courage, and by the defects which often go along with the virtue, were Eliot's incarnation and practice of patience. He himself would have said that to him the virtue of patience was more important than his boldness or energy. At the beginning of his career, he declared his belief that energy was the quality which he would most need in his forthcoming administration. At the close of his administration he declared to a few friends that he found patience was the more necessary. He once said, when a college association declined to accept his recommendation for the inclusion of music, drawing, and design, in the undergraduate curriculum, "It takes at least thirty years to get a new idea accepted and put into practice. We must try again. In time we shall succeed." [15] In this, as in many instances, however, a period

[15] "Charles W. Eliot." *Museum of Fine Arts Bulletin.* Vol. XXIV, No. 145. p. 64.

shorter than one score years and ten, saw the general acceptance of his purpose. But, to hold great causes in the heart while laboring for a fitting opportunity for the executive will to work, to bear with personalities extreme in either their radicalism or their conservatism, to seek to find ways of making a movement move when it is inclined to hide in the tents of sulkiness, or to stagnate in the bog of either indifference or indolence—such is the duty, the function, and should be the happiness, of a great president. This was the happiness of Eliot. It also was the happiness of a few of his contemporaries.

This happiness had special relationship to his associates of the faculty. In the interpretation of this happiness, a remarkable letter from Professor Palmer gives impressive testimony. After working with the great president for twenty-four years, and upon the twenty-fifth anniversary of his presidency, Professor Palmer wrote, saying:

"I cannot let this memorial day go by without expressing to you my gladness for the twenty-five years that are gone. Twenty-four of them I have spent with you, and every one has made me more deeply your debtor. Without you I should not have known myself; I might have missed my work; and should certainly have conceived it in different terms. No living man has had a larger share than you in shaping my ideals and powers. At the first I saw how significant you were to be for me and—though disliking—I set myself early to study you. My com-

prehension was slow and resisted. Few members of
the Faculty have voted against you more times than
I. But sympathy was growing through the years
when our radical difference of temper was becoming
plain. Smoothly and with no violent change I
passed through distrust, tolerance, respect, admiration, liking, into the hearty friendship—I might say
the love—which makes it a delight to work with you
now, whether in opposition or alliance. Probably we
shall always approach subjects from opposite sides.
You began in chemistry, I in theology. But nothing
can touch my deep affection for you or my gratitude
to the man who more than any other shows me perpetually how to rely on the Eternal for personal
strength.''[16]

Higher and deeper than the relations which man
holds to the immediate in time and space are the
relations which he holds to Ultimate Being. Of
this relation the testimony, written or spoken, is
far less eloquent than the evidence given by works
and service, and by the impressiveness of character.
This relation is more definitely, as well as more com-
monly, interpreted by the word *religion,* and by the
phrase, *the Christian religion.* Eliot was a member
of the church—as were his father and his grandfather and as is his son—which represents the
simplest, some would say the barest, of all the faiths.
Such simplicity throws the believer back on the

[16] *The Harvard Crimson:* Charles William Eliot Memorial
Issue. Vol. LXXX, No. 68. p. 5.

realities.   The realities are best summed up in the
infinite monosyllable, God.   There is a passage in
the Bible which we have usually limited in application to the oppressed and the desolate, ''The Eternal
God is thy refuge and underneath are the everlast-
ing arms.''   The passage, however, belongs quite as
fully and constantly to the strong, to the valiant,
to the victorious.   It belonged to the great president.   Perhaps the fullest expression of his thought
is found in an address, given under the auspices of
the Unitarian churches of Philadelphia, in the year
1914 although by no means is the sentiment confined to this address.

''Mankind needs to worship, needs incitements to
love, reverence, and duty, and a happy spiritual
conception of the universe.   Without these helps,
man cannot possibly be happy in his family, his
labor, or his social order.   Without these conceptions of the finite and the infinite values, man cannot rise in his nature or his life from bad to good,
and from good to better.   No single personality
born in Christendom—and no class of persons—can
reach his best without accepting as his guides in
life the fundamental teachings of Jesus Christ—love
God and thy neighbor, have compassion on the
wronged and the desolate, seek the truth that frees,
and worship God in spirit and in truth.   To live
in this way, it is not necessary to accept any of
the dogmas of the great churches, or any part of
their symbolism or ritualism.   Indeed, much of their

symbolism, ritualism, dogmatism, and ecclesiasticism
is inconsistent with essential obedience to the pre-
cepts of Jesus Christ.

"What then is the renewed Christianity which
these terrible times we are living in cry out for in
the midst of tears and heartbreaking sorrows? It
is a Christianity which abandons the errors and the
unjust, cruel conceptions which the centuries have
piled up on the simple teachings of Jesus. It is a
Christianity which sympathizes with and supports
the aspirations of mankind for freedom—freedom
in thought, speech, and action—and completely
abandons authoritative ecclesiasticism and governmental despotism. It is a Christianity which hal-
lows and consecrates birth, marriage, the bringing
up of children, family life, the earning of a liveli-
hood, and death, and rejects all the aspersions on
the natural life of man which Christianity inherited
from paganism and Judaism. It is a Christianity
which will be the friend and ally of all that is good
and ennobling in literature, science, and art, and
will avail itself without fear of all the new means
of teaching and helping men which successive generations shall discover, and of all the innocent en-
joyments and social pleasures, while resisting effec-
tively every unwholesome or degrading influence on
human society. It is a Christianity which will recognize that the pursuit of happiness in this world
is legitimate for every human being, and that the
main function of government is to protect and fur-

ther men in that pursuit by securing to the community health, education, wholesome productive labor, and liberty."[17] The love of Christ's second commandment was thus made practical.

The relation to Ultimate Being is also comprehended in philosophy, as well as in religion. Eliot was rather a scientist than a metaphysician. He was concerned with the phenomena, and not as the Germans are, with the thing-in-itself. He probably would have smiled at the use of the awkward phrase. Few allusions one finds in his books, and few references would one hear in his addresses, to the schools of philosophy or to their founders or leaders. In the addresses given on his great anniversary, the lack of philosophic or of religious references was worthy of note, and was silently felt by some. This condition finds an impressive illustration in the counsel he once gave to graduates and to undergraduates. Among the items were the comprehensive remarks, "Look out and not in,"—a counsel based, as he declared, on his own practice,—"Avoid to the utmost introspection. Avoid dwelling on your own state of mind." This counsel he gave in various forms, and to many. One may contrast with this advice some words of John Henry Newman, written near the beginning of the "Apologia," in which he says: "Confirming me in my mistrust in the reality of material phenomena, and making me rest in the thoughts of two and two only absolute and luminously

[17] "A Late Harvest." pp. 229-230.

self-evident beings, myself and my Creator.'' [18] In
Eliot, there was no element of the mystic. His
thought was intellectual, exact, definite, and the expression of it, likewise, was devoted to the visible,
the audible, and the tangible, to humanity as a
present force and a future condition.

One chief direct method of his influence over the
academic and general community lay in his writing
and in his speech. His books are rather weighty
than numerous, dealing chiefly with educational
themes, yet dealing with the field of religion, of
public service, and of biography. The religious subjects upon which he wrote were both timely and
of lasting interest. The very titles illustrate the
union of the immediate and the permanent in his
thinking. Among them are ''Progressive Liberalism
in the Closing and Opening Century,'' ''Religion,''
''Twentieth-Century Christianity,'' ''The Crying
Need of a Renewed Christianity,'' ''A Free and
Open Christian Church,'' and ''The Wise Direction
of Church Activities toward Social Welfare.'' Perhaps the most noteworthy and apparently enduring
part of his writings is found in his annual reports as
president. They are models of what the annual reports of a president should be. For, they are interpretations definite in statement of facts, broad
in outlook, free from the temptation to eloquence,
inspiring to the broadest and highest educational and

[18] p. 4. Also quoted in ''The Mystery of Newman,'' by
Henri Bremond (translated by H. C. Corrance). p. 189.

human endeavors. Out of these forty volumes could
be well written a succinct and pregnant history of
the higher education of America from 1869 to 1909.
His addresses, too, likewise concerned education,
though such matters as the civil service, the public health, and the peace of the world, causes dear
to him, were treated, for giving light and leading to
the people.

It is true of Eliot, as it is true of most, that the
written style and the spoken are largely alike. As
Eliot's colleague—for so many years—George Herbert Palmer, says: "Whether words are uttered on
paper or to the air, the effect on the utterer is the
same. . . . As a rule, language once within our control can be employed for oral or for written purposes." [19]   Written, as well as spoken, utterance
offers evidence that the style is the man. Orderly
in arrangement, comprehensive in survey, progressive
in narrative, free from ornament, with paragraph,
sentence, phrase stripped of adjective and adverb,
each page marches on with other pages toward the
desired conclusion. His paragraphs move on like
Macaulay's, yet without Macaulay's declamatory,
periodic constructiveness. Of its type, no better
example is found in American literature.

Of its type, I say: for, in contrast, is found the
style allusive, studded with references and intimations that send the reader's mind to far-off fields

[19] "The Teacher." By George Herbert Palmer and Alice
Freeman Palmer. pp. 77-78.

of thought and of imagination. Contrast, for instance, the directness of Eliot's "Durable Satisfac-
tions" with Matthew Arnold's "Essays in Criticism,"
or with Pater's "The Genius of Plato."

In the largeness and impersonality of interpretation, President Eliot gave credit, ever and everywhere, to the happiness of circumstances and to the
favoring lot in which his life was cast and in which
his work was done. No selfish arrogance touched
him. The great gentleman was fittingly present in
his interpretation of others, as well as of himself.
In his farewell address of the ninetieth birthday, he
said:

"Consider now the sources of my career as a
teacher. Those sources were in the times, in that wonderful period of human history, in which my whole
educational career lay. Think of it! When I was
coming on as a teacher in Harvard, the great prophets
and exponents of experimental science in Europe and
America were taking possession of that great field.
Think how the philosophers of the world were preaching attention to the individual and proclaiming the
immense variety in human nature. Think how James
Russell Lowell told us in 1886 that democracy must
not only raise the average mass, but must give a free
field to all the finest qualities of human nature; for
that is the only salvation for democracy. Think how
Emerson came into power in the days of my youth.
Think how Oliver Wendell Holmes, as a teacher of
anatomy, physiology, and the carrying of contagion,

enlarged the conception of human sagacity, penetration, and discrimination, and combined with that instruction great power of expression in both prose and poetry. Think how Asa Gray, Joseph Henry, Jeffries Wyman, Benjamin Peirce, and Louis Agassiz were the leaders in American science and in methods of teaching science. All that came out of the times when I was a young teacher in Harvard; out of that extraordinary period have come the ideals and the lessons which I have followed all through my active career. Then, as the years went by and the period of combat and persistent effort against opposition passed, and the new structure of Harvard University began to take effect, think how the Divisions and the Faculties gave me the opportunity to see where modern education was going, and where it ought to go. Now and then I could help their labors, especially in the Medical Faculty; but it was the strength of the Harvard Faculties themselves which filled me with strength and what is called leadership. I gave expression and opportunity to their hopes, aspirations, and devotions; and great was the privilege of so doing. You must attribute the successes which I have been privileged to win to the very fortunate circumstances of my life, to the leadership of the extraordinary philosophers and scientists of my time.'' [20]

But there was one further advantage, which President Eliot shared with every president. It was the

[20] ''The Ninetieth Birthday of Charles William Eliot: Proceedings.'' pp. 25-26.

advantage that the field of his influence and work lay in the heart and the mind of youth. It was the American boy and girl in whom and for whom he labored. It was the high school, the academy, the college, and the professional school, which he served. Each institution, through its students, gave the most responsive opportunities. His conception of an enriched curriculum belonged to the pre-college age. His conception of the elective education program belonged to the college age. His conception of the definite and vital course of study belonged to the medical and the law school. The opportunities which youth offered to him, as to every college president in some degree, were indeed of inexpressible richness. It may be added that his living with and for youth helped to give to his own life a permanent sense of youthfulness.

The great college executives of his time, especially of the earlier period—Gilman, the cultured gentleman; Angell, the great democratic president of a great state university; White, the founder and supporter of Cornell, the noble humanist—have all passed away. The immediate associates of his early prime, always excepting the beloved Palmer, have gone. The older Boston historians, the Cambridge poets, the Concord essayists are dead. Eliot remained, and remained for years, to search for and to declare the truth, to serve the common good and to promote the cause of human liberty.

The last years were ways of pleasantness, and all

his paths were peace. The contrast with the earlier period was marked. He himself has said:

"In all the early part of my career as a teacher and an educational administrator I was much engaged in controversy, not to say combat, and that at home as well as outside of Harvard. In all my public appearances during those years I had a vivid sense that I was addressing an adverse audience. Now to-day is a very delightful illustration of a change that has come over my experience. For twenty years past, I should think, I have found myself often in the presence of a favoring audience—of one that wished, at any rate, to agree with me, or, if they could not, regretted that they could not." [21]

These outward signs and symbols of the change in his normal constituency are an intimation of the changes which the years wrought in his character. At the time of his resignation, at a public dinner tendered him in Boston, Bishop Lawrence "traced the development of his character as seen in the changing lines of his face for forty years: at the first austere and cold; then sad from personal sorrow; soon softening and mellowing as he felt the sympathy and growing appreciation of friends and alumni. Suggestions of isolation faded into the background, while friendly, social, and cheerful fea-

[21] "A Late Harvest." From Introduction by M. A. DeWolfe Howe. p. ix. (A quotation from an address by President Eliot, October 11, 1923, at the fiftieth anniversary of his election to the Massachusetts Historical Society.)

tures, even a sense of humor, gained emphasis; the mellow, tender lines grew continually stronger, so that, as he reached threescore years and ten, his portrait revealed a man strong and serene, a lover of truth and of his fellows, full of hope and the spirit of optimism." [22] Those who knew President Eliot personally for the long period will recognize the truthfulness of the lines of the etching. President Eliot himself,—Bishop Lawrence tells,—at the close of the address, remarked "I recognize the truth of much that you have said." [23]

[22] "Memories of a Happy Life." By William Lawrence. p. 296.
[23] *Ibid.*

II
JAMES BURRILL ANGELL

JAMES BURRILL ANGELL was born at Scituate, Rhode Island, January 7, 1829; died April 1, 1916. Received A.B., Brown University, 1849; A.M., 1853. Assistant librarian, Brown, 1849-50; studied in Europe, 1850-53; professor of modern languages and literature, Brown, 1853-60; editor, Providence Journal, 1860-66; president of the University of Vermont, 1866-71; president of the University of Michigan, 1871-1909; president emeritus, 1909-1916. Minister to China, 1880-81; commissioner in negotiating important treaties; member, Anglo-American International Commission on Canadian Fisheries; chairman of Canadian-American Commission on Deep Waterways from Lakes to Sea, 1896; appointed minister to Turkey, 1897, resigned, August, 1898. Regent, Smithsonian Institution. Author: Progress in International Law; The Higher Education; Reminiscences; and many articles in reviews.

JAMES BURRILL ANGELL

LEADER, FRIEND, MAN OF CONCILIATIONS

In his "Remembered Yesterdays," Robert Underwood Johnson quotes a letter from John Burroughs in which the philosophic naturalist says that Matthew Arnold is "a great critic-pedagogue; . . . the outcome of the best English schoolmaster," and that "Emerson is the outcome of the best type of New England clergyman." [1] In Angell of Michigan the characteristics of both the schoolmaster and the clergyman are united. To these two elements, many others also are to be added, elements which have constructive worth.

For, there were in Angell a comprehensiveness of knowledge, a catholicity of judgment, and a variety of service, which, united, make up a unique manhood and a diversely rich achievement. Intending to become a minister and prevented by a weakness of the throat, offered professorships as diverse as civil engineering and modern languages, and accepting the chair of languages, retiring from his professorship to become editor of a leading journal in

[1] p. 340.

the critical Civil War period, resigning from the editorship to take office successively in two universities as president, and punctuating his presidencies with diplomatic service in countries as unlike as China and Turkey,—does any career offer an illustration richer in comprehensiveness and in catholicity? Of course, one might add that his teaching did not cease with his retirement from his chair at Brown. For, while president in Vermont, he taught subjects as unrelated as rhetoric, history, German, and international law. At Ann Arbor he instructed in political economy for a time, and continued to lecture in international law to the end of his presidency.

The causes of such broad ministries, reminding one of Whewell's encyclopedic knowledge, treatises, and foundations, lead one far back, reaching to the beginning of life and of school. These causes touch the sources and forces of education, both formal and informal. In his fifteenth year, he came under the instruction of Henry S. Frieze,—afterward his colleague at Ann Arbor,—in the University Grammar School at Providence. Many years after, he wrote of Frieze:

"Contact with this inspiring teacher formed an epoch in my intellectual life, as in that of so many other boys. He represented the best type of the modern teacher, at once critical as a grammarian and stimulating with the finest appreciation of whatever was choicest in the classic masterpieces. At first, as we were showered with questions such as I

had never heard before, it seemed to me, although
the reading of the Latin was mainly a review to
me, that I should never emerge from my state of
ignorance. But there was such a glow of enthusiasm
in the instructor and in the class, there was such
delight in the tension in which we were kept by
the daily exercises, that no task seemed too great
to be encountered."[2] But the great force in his
formal education was,—as it was to another college
president. Robinson,—President Wayland himself.
In an article, attempting to answer the question
"How I was Educated," Angell writes with special
fullness and gratitude of the worth of Wayland. He
says:

"He had in a wonderful degree two gifts of a
great teacher, the power of analyzing a subject and
the power of simple and happy illustration. He
insisted on the clearest and sharpest definition of
terms before answering a question or engaging in a
discussion, and thus often made the inquirer answer
his own question by an accurate definition, or rendered the discussion superfluous. Withal, he had
the keenest wit and a thorough knowledge of men,
especially of students. He had the happiest way,
often a homely way, of stating an important truth
so that it remained forever fixed in the mind of the
hearer. There was too, beyond all this, a certain
power of personal presence, a force of character, a
moral strength, which lent a tremendous weight to

[2] "Reminiscences." pp. 17-18.

even his commonest words. I have met in my day
not a few distinguished men; but I recall none who
have so impressed me with their power of personality, none who have uttered so many wise words
which I recall every week to my advantage and
help in the duties of my daily life. He was a very
inapt pupil who passed from under Dr. Wayland's
instruction without catching something of his catholic spirit, his passionate love of soul-liberty, and his
earnest Christian principle." [3]

Happy indeed the youth who can come under the
influence of such a teacher as Wayland. Wayland,
Robinson, Woolsey, and Hopkins remain the great
college presidents who also were formative teachers.

The formal education, creative of comprehensiveness and catholicity of power, was aided by the education of "the fellows." Of this type of education,—
overvalued to-day in relation to the more formal
disciplines,—he writes:

"The students, with few exceptions, lodged in the
dormitories, and took their meals in Commons Hall.
They went little into society in the city. They were
thus drawn very close to each other. The enthusiasm
of the more gifted and accomplished scholars was
caught in some degree by nearly all. I remember
that men were divided as Carlyleists or anti-Carlyle-
ists, Coleridgeians or anti-Coleridgeians, and so on,
and that literary, historic, and philosophic theories

[3] "How I was Educated." *The Forum,* Vol. II, January,
1887. p. 457.

were as hotly discussed as the current political questions of the day. Not wishing to be unduly *laudator temporis acti*, I am sure that whoever examines the triennial catalogue of Brown for the years from 1845 to 1852 will see that the college contained within its walls in those years a good number, perhaps an exceptionally large number, of men whose lives have shown that it must have been a high privilege to be intimately associated with them in the companionship of student life. The society of some of them has been one of the chief factors in my own education, both in college and afterward, and one of the chief delights of life. On the whole, I think that any student in Brown University who did not graduate in those days with a mind well disciplined for entering upon any worthy career, was himself greatly at fault." [4]

As one reads such an interpretation of the students of Brown, in the last half of the fifth decade of the last century, one pauses to ask the question, Why, to-day, are there in the American college fewer students, exultantly literary, and giving abounding promise of great position and future distinction in the higher zones of achievement? The answer is, I think, two-fold. First, in the early period the students were a body more carefully selected. They represented a pretty pure Anglo-Saxon breed, coming from a zone of plain living and of high and religious thinking. The present body of college students,—

[4] *Ibid.,* p. 458.

and all commendation be given to them,—are like the yield of the gospel fish-net, composed of all kinds. A bare reading of the names in the catalogues and the class histories helps to answer the question. Such origins and such environments do not furnish personalities which can be easily trained unto greatness. But, secondly, a larger proportion of present graduates enter callings which do not naturally lead to, and eventuate in, personal distinction. At least one half of the members of each class, on leaving college, enter business. Business does not so usually and normally lead to personal distinction as do the professions.

Two students of his time Angell recalls with special pleasure. They are two who afterwards filled with distinction the office of Secretary of State, Richard Olney and John Hay. Near the close of his life he wrote of them, saying:

"Both gave marked promise. Mr. Olney, afterwards Attorney-general and then Secretary of State of the United States, showed the traits of mind which characterize the profound lawyer. For Mr. Hay one would have predicted a brilliant literary future. I have often said that he was the most felicitous translator I ever met in my classes. He wrote verses of unusual merit for an undergraduate. He was modest even to diffidence, often blushing to the roots of his hair when he rose to recite. In the years of his middle life, and especially after the production of his books on Spanish life, written in so picturesque a style, I used in common with many of his friends to regret that circumstances had diverted him from a purely literary career. But we all rejoice now that Providence placed him in the chair of Secretary of State, at a time when he could be of such transcendent service to us and to the Eastern world. As I happened to be on the steamer with him when he was returning from the Embassy at London, I know from my conversation with him on the voyage that he entered on the duties of that high office with hesitancy and misgiving. He said to me, 'I accepted it because it is an office that one can hardly refuse.' " [5] The relation of Angell and Hay continued to the end. While editor, Angell gave to Hay the chance to report Lincoln's great Cooper Union speech for the Providence *Journal*, and, as Hay was entering into the office of Secretary of State, and as Angell was returning from Constantinople, the older man wrote to the younger, saying:

"You and I are apparently in these days walking round like official St. Denis, with our heads under our arms. Only you are so soon to be re-capitated, and with a 'big head' indeed." [6]

I thus write at length of this characteristic of intellectual diversity in Angell. For, it seems to me to be a chief element in his comprehensive greatness.

[5] "Reminiscences." pp. 109-110.
[6] "The Life of John Hay." By William Roscoe Thayer. Vol. II, p. 179.

Yet by its side and linked with it, both as cause and effect, is a quality which I call conciliatoriness. This quality was to many friends quite as evident, in any superficial view, as the element of catholicity. It is the element which John Morley so well sets forth in his great, little essay on Compromise. I remember being a fellow member with Angell on a committee of the American Board of Foreign Missions, serving at a critical moment in the history of that great organization, to consider complex and vital problems. Opinions were divided. Passions in heart and on lip were hot. I recall well the endeavor of Angell toward understanding, unity, harmony, peace. He had the gift of intellectual altruism and of a quiet mood in speech. Personal enmities were remote from his heart and will. In youth he was well trained in making personal adjustments. Near the close of his life he wrote:

"If, as I have sometimes been assured, I have any power of adaptation to the society of different classes of men, I owe it in no small degree to these varied associations of my boyhood." [7]

This conciliatoriness was ever consistent with his primary allegiance to truth itself. He recognized the inevitableness of the fact. Like his contemporary, Eliot, he made *Veritas* more formative and more important than *Artes*.

This conciliatoriness sprang from, and was incarnated in, a character that ever seemed well-bal-

[7] "Reminiscences." p. 4.

anced. Every part of his being was fittingly adjusted
to every other. He was also able to make proper adjustment of personalities, even opposing ones, and to
call out the deeper elements of manhood which unite
individualities. Superficialities separate. Fundamentals unite. The balancing of comprehensive, and
of even antagonistic, qualities in himself helped to
make harmonious relations among men. Master of
himself, he became master of others unto their united
affection and common service. Loving his colleagues
and students, he found, as one ever finds, that love
is the most uniting force among men. Understanding human nature, he used the understanding to
promote good-will among men, and good-will, he
knew, as does no other force, results in the mood of
peace.

This quality of conciliatoriness was also aided by
that indefinable quality of tact, and by that very
definable quality of wit. With both tact and wit,
Angell was greatly endowed. One of the deans of
Michigan, Reed, tells the story of himself, that, when
he "came to Michigan as a Freshman, he once, entering the office of the president, failed to remove
his hat. Dr. Angell excused himself, went into the
outer office and put on his own hat, and returned
to the interview without saying a word. Dean Reed
often said that it was the most diplomatic but effective rebuke which he had ever received."[8]

[8] "Odd Incidents in Dr. Angell's Life Recalled." *The
Detroit News Tribune*, April 2, 1916.

As may be easily inferred, the principle of democracy was bred in the bone of Angell in his youth, and, through all the following decades, never suffered decrease. It began with his experiences on the farm. From early spring till late autumn of two seasons, in his youth, he worked upon that farm, and side by side with the hired men, hoeing his row and mowing his swath. He says: "I now learned thoroughly how much backache a dollar earned in the fields represented. I was also enabled to see how the world looks from the point of view of the labouring man." [9] The results of this early democratic experience were constantly reënforced in later life. With Lord Bryce, he believed that democracy in the State is subjected to perils most serious, both from within and from without; but, on the whole, be believed also with Bryce, that democracy is the best instrument yet developed in and for the governing of men. He appreciated the worth of the simple, individual man embodying fundamental and elemental character. Life's luxuries made to him little or no appeal. Life's accouterments had for him no weight and slight impressiveness. This democracy of interpretation and of relationship sprang from his real love for men as men. Love he gave, and love he received. His associates were to him "beloved colleagues," and "the great company of students," was one of his "great delights." [10] In a letter of the Regents of the University, written to him concerning

[9] "Reminiscences." p. 11.   [10] *Ibid.,* p. 258.

his resignation, it is said that no other person can take his place "in the love of the people."

Angell's own working habits interpret this sense of democracy, and give intimations of the power, of the man himself. In a sketch which he wrote and which was published after his death, it is said: He "had two fads, if one may call them so, and they had to do with the sleep and the exercises of his charges. But he was his own best pupil, for he was diligent in the observance of his rules, which say, 'Plenty of exercise and plenty of sleep.' He was an early riser and always up by six o'clock and breakfast by 7:45. In the old days he took his exercise between these two hours, but latterly he deferred the exercise to a digester, instead of an appetizer. After his breakfast and his home duties he went for his morning walk of about two miles to the postoffice and back, following out an early custom established before the days of free delivery in Ann Arbor. On this walk he did all the errands for his household, marketing and buying whatever was needed for the house. He then went to his office in University hall, where he met his stenographer and disposed of his mail. From 12 o'clock to 1 p. m. he was in his office, where he met the students, such members of the faculty as had business with him and callers, all of whom were given ample time to tell their stories, unless the president had already acquired the information, when he sometimes surprised them with his store of knowledge. They were then diplomatically dismissed and hardly realized just how they reached the outer door, but it was effected successfully. More work at his desk followed his noon meal and then again at his office in University hall, often until dark. The immense amount of fatiguing work which he turned off in a day would surprise a man of many less years. Yet he was apparently never weary or fatigued after hours of close application to some problem." [11]

All these qualities and forces were illustrated, and came to their full flower, in his long and great presidency. After a service of five years at the University of Vermont, he became president of the University of Michigan, in 1871. He retired in 1909. He came to a presidency which had been peculiarly infected with deep, long-continued, and fundamental quarrels, despite the gentleness of his immediate predecessor, Haven. But he also came to a presidency which had been filled for eleven years by Tappan, one of the ablest and most formative in service of all college administrators, but also one of the least tactful and conciliatory. He came to the presidency of the university of a State whose educational and other history had been made great by great men. In this list Woodward and Peirce were among the more notable. What Horace Mann was to Massachusetts in the early middle decades of the nineteenth

[11] "Dr. Angell's Busy Life, as Editor, Teacher and Diplomat as He Told It." *The Detroit News Tribune*, April 2, 1916.

century, in respect to public education, Angell was to Michigan in the later decades, in respect to the higher education. He came into a great tradition, to the greatness of which he was, in turn, to add. In his Commemorative address, given at the semi-centennial of the University in 1887, he indicated five causes for its prosperity. As he named them, they were:

"1. First . . . the broad conception which has for the most part been held with distinctness, of the function and methods of a university. The custodians and administrators of this institution have striven to build on a large and generous plan. . . .

"2. The authorities of the University have been guided throughout its history by the wise principle enunciated early by Superintendent Peirce, that men, not bricks and mortar, make a university.

"3. It has doubtless been conducive to the growth of the University that the founders organized it on the plan of bringing education within the reach of the poor. . . . This has always been, and we are proud of the fact, the University of the poor. From these halls the boys born in the log cabins of the wilderness have gone forth armed with the power of well disciplined minds and characters, to fight their way to those brilliant successes which mere wealth could never have achieved, to the foremost positions in church and state.

"4. We gladly recognize the fact that the success of the University is largely due to the efficient aid

of the schools of the State. . . . The child who enters
the primary school is now stimulated to hope for
the highest education, since the way lies open,
straight, and clear from his school-house to the very
doors of the University. . . .

"5. The loyalty and the success of our graduates
of all departments have also been most helpful to
our rapid growth. More than eight thousand in number, they have gone to all parts of this land and to
foreign lands, speaking with loving praise the name
of their Alma Mater, and illustrating in their lives
the value of the training they had received under
our roof." [12]

To these five causes, which have indeed become
the more fruitful in the generation passing since
he stated them in 1887, is to be added the worth
of the President himself. For Angell embodied several of the greatest forces that contribute, in a president, to the power and place of a university. He
possessed that most manifest of advantages, length
of active service, a service of thirty-eight years,
among the longer in academic annals. Brevity of
service spells plans, well laid, yet utterly failing;
associations, begun in hope, speedily broken; visions,
held before expectant hearts and minds, quickly, and
sometimes rudely, vanishing. Length of service
promises plans achieved, associations consummated,
visions realized. Angell was also able to avoid, above

[12] Commemorative Oration. *University of Michigan Semi-
Centennial,* 1887. pp. 117-181.

most, those embarrassments which almost normally
seem to belong to a State university and its president. These embarrassments he has pointed out.[13]
These embarrassments are a failure to secure con-
tinuity in work through the unexpected failure of
appropriations of the State legislature; opposition
arising, as from the churches, on the ground that a
State university is Godless and irreligious; and the
antagonism of criticism arising from "unintelligent
and mischievous" citizens. Such embarrassments
and opposition, by his mood of conciliation, by his
sense of democracy, by his sincerity, he was able
either largely to avoid, or wholly to dispel. In him,
in fact, were embodied the great qualities of the
great president,—patience (which includes the power
and quality of adjustment to men and to conditions),
intellectual and personal altruism, ability to call out
the respect and love of the people, moral and intellectual understanding, tact, energy, honesty, candor
and frankness.

In his book on "American State Universities and
the University of Michigan," Professor Ten Brook,
at the time that Angell was entering into his office,
said:

"As 'he that girdeth on the harness should not
boast as he that putteth it off,' so his friends should
not boast for him. That President Angell may long
wear the harness, and, together with his co-workers,

[13] "The State Universities of the West." Address at Johns
Hopkins University, February 22, 1893.

accomplish so much for the university that he shall have the best of eulogies in the perpetual remembrances of some thousands of graduates, is the honest and earnest wish with which we take leave of him in this direct narrative."[14]

At the time of his resignation, thirty-eight years after, and also on the day of his death, forty-five years after, it could be said of Angell, in gratitude and exultation, that the prophecy had proved true. To him could be applied the interpretation and the benediction of *"Ecclesiasticus:"*

"Leaders of the people by their counsels, and by their knowledge of learning meet for the people, wise and eloquent in their instructions: . . . honoured in their generations, and were the glory of their times . . . their name liveth for evermore."[15]

[14] p. 281.
[15] *Ecclesiasticus*, Chapter xliv.

III

DANIEL COIT GILMAN

DANIEL COIT GILMAN was born, of good colonial stock, in Norwich, Connecticut, July 6, 1831; died October 13, 1908. Degree of A.B., Yale, 1852; A.M., 1855. Continued studies in Cambridge, New Haven, and Berlin. Librarian, and secretary, Sheffield Scientific School, and professor of physical and political geography, Yale, 1856-72; president of the University of California, 1872-75; first president of Johns Hopkins University, 1875-1901; president emeritus, 1901-1908. First president of Carnegie Institution, Washington, 1901-04; president, American Oriental Society, 1893-1906; member of the Venezuelan Commission, 1896-97; member of Commission to draft new charter for City of Baltimore, 1897; member of board of school commissioners, 1900; vice president of Archæological Institute of America; commissioner of awards, Atlantic Exposition, 1895; president of the John F. Slater Fund for Education of Freedmen; vice president of Peabody Education Fund; member, General Education Board; trustee of Russell Sage Foundation; president, National Civil Service Reform League, 1901-07; trustee, Carnegie Institution.

Author: Bi-centennial Discourse, Norwich, Connecticut, 1859; Inaugural Address, 1876; Life of James Monroe; Introduction to De Tocqueville's Democracy in America; Life of James D. Dana, Geologist; Science and Letters in Yale; Launching of a University. Editor-in-chief of the New International Encyclopedia.

III

DANIEL COIT GILMAN

PRESIDENT OF VISION AND OF SYMPATHY

THE New England boy of Old England ancestry and name, born in the first year of the fourth decade of the last century, before the Victorian Age had begun, of Christian home and nurture, of the education of the town schools and of an historic university, possessed of the best elements of moral and intellectual character, Daniel Coit Gilman became, through diverse experiences, a great president of a great state university, and, as the founder and first president of Johns Hopkins University, attained large place and enduring recognition.

Chief among the constituent elements of his early, as well as of his later, manhood was the instinct and the will to be useful. Such an element was characteristic of a boy and man of his constitution and environment. His vision of the future, and such a vision seemed characteristic, might or might not touch a specific form of usefulness, or might or might not interpret the method of reaching or of using this form. But the fact of the vision and the fact of the general purpose were clear to his prophetic

57

mind, and were ever nestling close and warm to his bosom. At the age of twenty-three, in 1854, from Berlin, he wrote:

"For some things I rejoice to find that my notions grow more and more definite. For instance, in the desire to act upon the minds of men, to do my part, even though it may be but little, for the elevation and improvement of such society as my lot may be cast in. It seems to me I care less and less for money and for fame, but I do desire to use what influence I can for the establishment of such principles and the development of such ideas as seem to be important and right." [1]

Such a general desire was characteristic of the young men of his period and condition. Eager were they in their general atmospheric searchings. To Gilman, as to most, the general eagerness became specific. Writing in the same year from St. Petersburg, he refers to the ministry:

"I look therefore more and more to the ministry as probably the place where I can do more good than anywhere else: that is to say, if I can have a congregation which will let me preach such things as we have talked over so many times in our up-stairs confabs. . . . I told him [Mr. Porter in Berlin] that if I should become a minister I should want to preach about every day affairs—not in the style of H. W. B. if I could get above it, but in a more dignified man-

[1] "The Life of Daniel Coit Gilman." By Fabian Franklin. p. 30.

ner—and that instead of dwelling long and regularly upon such points as original sin and the doctrine of election, I should urge the practical application of the Bible to common events and daily habits. Most of all I told him I should abjure cant, and the 'technicalities' of theology, and that I should make my one great text—'Pure Religion and undefiled is to visit the fatherless and widows in their affliction and to keep himself unspotted from the world.' But I told him I was afraid to begin—lest I should not succeed, and lest if I should succeed according to what seemed to me right principles—proper clergymen who are accustomed to preach upon abstractions would 'read me out of meeting.' I cited Dr. Bushnell, H. W. Beecher and others—but he convinced me that what was objected to in them were unnecessary excrescences, so to speak; in the one case, mystical doctrinal views; and in the other rough, crude and undignified forms of expression—both of which faults are easily avoided. He told me that the kind of preaching I spoke of was the kind now needed— the kind which would be most influential of good— and on the whole he encouraged me to attempt it. I feel more and more desirous to do so, and shall keep on, in all I see and hear abroad, with the examination of every influence now working upon men— churches and schools, politics and literature—and if I can, when I return to America, be useful either as writer or as speaker in promoting the spread of Christian principles, and their application to every matter *great and small,* I shall be delighted indeed.'' [2]

Referring to this period in his reminiscences of thirty years in Baltimore, he interprets a condition, which is significant of certain lacks in the higher education of the middle years of the last century. He says:

''After taking the degree of Bachelor of Arts in Yale College, I was undecided what profession to follow. The effect of the collegiate discipline, which 'introduced' me, according to the phrase of the day, to not less than twenty subjects in the senior year, was to arouse an interest of about equal intensity in as many branches of knowledge. I remained a year at New Haven as a resident graduate. President Woolsey, whom I consulted, asked me to read Rau's political economy and come and tell him its contents; I did not accept the challenge. I asked Professor Hadley if I might read Greek with him; he declined my proposal. Professor Porter did give me some guidance in reading, especially in German. I had many talks of an inspiring nature with Professor Dana—but, on the whole, I think that the year was wasted. The next autumn I went to Cambridge and called upon President Sparks, to learn what opportunities were there open. 'You can hear Professor Agassiz lecture,' he said, 'if you want to; and I believe Mr. Longfellow is reading Dante with a class.' I did not find at Cambridge any better opportunities than I had found at New Haven—but

[2] *Ibid.,* pp. 28, 29, 30.

in both places I learned to admire the great
teachers, and to wish that there were better arrangements for enabling a graduate student to ascertain
what could be enjoyed and to profit by the opportunities." [3]

But Gilman's thought, as the thought of many
young men of the middle decades, who specially desired to make a particular contribution to human
well-being, continued to turn toward the ministry.
So lasting and so strong was his feeling for the great
profession that, in the year 1860, he was, as the
phrase runs, "licensed to preach" by the New Haven
Central Association of Congregational Churches. Of
this important step he writes to his elder brother:

"You are aware that for a long time I have been
considering the expediency of this step. Indeed Mr.
Thompson invited me to meet the New York Association early in the spring, to which (on account of
your connection and his with that body) I was naturally attracted. But I could not then quite see the
way plain to take that step. Lately however it has
been quite clear to me, that while I propose to
remain in the Library, I should have increased opportunities of usefulness by preaching or by being ready
to preach when invited. I do not at present have
any purpose of 'entering the ministry,' and so I have
stated to all with whom I have advised,—but those
in whose judgment I can most trust see nothing in
my present pursuits as Librarian incompatible with

[3] "The Launching of a University." pp. 8-9.

the work of an occasional preacher, and have approved of my engaging in it. When asked by the Association to state my reasons for appearing before them I said candidly that I did not ask for a license in the usual form, as I was not a candidate for the Ministry, and had at the present time no purpose of becoming such,—but I asked that if upon inquiry they thought it would be wise for me to accept such invitations as often come to me, they would formally express their approbation. They first voted an approval of my purpose, and then examined me in all the Chief Doctrines, say for an hour or more, and then voted to give me a license in the usual form.

". . . Before leaving the Association I was invited to preach four times, and have now two more invitations. I declined the former summons, and my mind is not yet quite clear as to what course I shall pursue. . . . If opportunities of increased usefulness present themselves, I certainly ought to rejoice, and I think I shall not be wanting in willingness to improve them; but I feel an unaffected distrust of my power to instruct an audience, which makes me shrink after all from beginning the work for which by intellectual training—by reading, etc., I am not wholly unprepared. As I only desire to be useful I think I can safely go forward with deliberateness, and judge by and by better than at present, what course to pursue."[4]

[4] "The Life of Daniel Coit Gilman." By Fabian Franklin. pp. 36-37.

The ministry did not prove to be the permanent calling of Gilman, but I have ventured to make these long quotations referring to the early purpose, because they represent a type of the development of manhood characteristic of the earnest and purposeful men of those decades. Although the specific purpose changed, yet, as he indicates, the aim or desire to use every talent for the advantage of his fellows, and to follow every opportunity to the full, was mightily dominant.

Cardinal Bourne, in speaking to the Catholic students of the University of Cambridge, in the autumn of 1923, has indicated the duty of the youth to his faith: it is identical with the purpose which influenced Gilman, three quarters of a century before. The Cardinal said:

"If a man had one talent and he cultivated that, he would be a saint. If he had four talents and he did not cultivate one, he would be in danger of condemnation. God had never made anyone a failure. They stood each one alone before Almighty God, and they had to make the best use of their lives."[5]

Gilman had no other purpose than to use all his talents, four, or more, or fewer, in the service of his fellow men. This dominant purpose was incarnated in the personality which bore every mark of distinction.

Many and diverse are the types of the gentleman,

[5] "Cultivation of Talents." Address by Cardinal Bourne. *The Tablet*, November 24, 1923. p. 648.

and these types are present in the scholar and in the college president. The more usual type of the gentleman, especially of him who chances to be the president of a college, according to the common interpretation, is of reserve, of remoteness from one's fellows, of coldness in one's bearing. Gilman, on the contrary, was warm, cordial, energetic, forthgoing, altruistic in mood and manner. Urbanity is the one word that is most descriptive and interpretative. An editor wrote of him, at the time of his leaving California, as "a quiet, perfect gentleman." Youth admired him, children played with him, and for his peers he had a heart responsive, as well as the best of good wills. His face betokened the scholar and the thinker. The forehead was broad, the eyes full with a bright expressiveness, the shoulders slightly stooping, the footstep quick. His whole manner, in office, in home, or on the platform, was of the gracious gentleman. A keen observer was asked about a college president, just beginning his career, in relation to his predecessor. The answer was, "In the new man we feel the lack of distinction." Such a remark could never have been made of Gilman. Affability was his, as well as distinction, and a certain dignified facility in manner which sprang from intellectual alertness and responsiveness. As I think of Gilman, my mind recurs to the beloved and lamented Master of Balliol, Dr. Smith,—"A. L." as he was familiarly known,—the incarnation of graciousness and of emotional altruism.

Distinction of manner was only a visible and outward sign of inward graces and powers. These inward graces and powers, of course, were fundamental.

Among them I first notice a sense of intellectual prudence. His prudence united the secondary moral virtue of caution, and the primary intellectual virtue of foresight. The intellectual foresight was preeminent. Its illustration is seen in the pains he took in examining conditions in the University of California before accepting an election to its presidency in the year 1872. This election was the second made, the first, two years earlier, having been declined.

The general circumstances prevailing in California and in its university, at that time, were complex and difficult. His biographer, Fabian Franklin, says of the conditions:

"Many points of divergence might be suggested in the resulting discussions and controversies, but three may be specially singled out as distinguishing their exponents into (1) those who resented New England assumption of superiority in, if not exclusive possession of, educational ideals, and Puritan assumption of superior righteousness; (2) those who provoked such feelings of resentment; and (3) church bodies and individuals, who deplored any sort of undenominational college and especially a non-sectarian, otherwise 'godless,' State University." [6]

[6] "Life of Daniel Coit Gilman." By Fabian **Franklin.** p. 113.

Of course Gilman, before accepting election, visited California. He held conferences, personal and official. He counselled with presidents of the West regarding the opportunity and the duty. In the consideration of his acceptance of the presidency of the newly established Johns Hopkins, a similar method he employed. He wrote to a trustee of Hopkins, saying: ". . . I hope that a formal and final decision will not be required of me, on your part, until we have met face to face." [7] He also wrote to another, after receiving notice of his election: "They unanimously invite me to come, and I think I shall accept; but I keep back the formal words until I can confer with the Californians. . . ." [8] The prudential foresight, united with discriminations, he outlines in his sketch of his subsequent thirty years in Baltimore:

"I was a close observer of the changes which were introduced at Yale in the fifties and sixties, the grafting of a new branch—'a wild olive,' as it seemed—upon the old stock. Then I had some experience, brief but significant, in California, as the head of the State University, at a time when it was needful to answer the popular cry that it should become chiefly a school of agriculture, and when it was important to show the distinction between a university and a polytechnic institute. Then came a call to the East and a service of more than a quarter of a century in the organisation and development of a new establishment. These are three typical institutions. Yale

[7] *Ibid.*, p. 187.   [8] *Ibid.*, p. 191.

was a colonial foundation, wedded to precedents, where an effort was made to introduce new studies and new methods. California was a state institution, benefited by the so-called agricultural grant, where it was necessary to emphasize the importance of the liberal arts, in a community where the practical arts were sure to take care of themselves. Baltimore afforded an opportunity to develop a private endowment free from ecclesiastical or political control, where from the beginning the old and the new, the humanities and the sciences, theory and practice, could be generously promoted.'' [9]

Caution and prudence are, of course, important virtues and graces. They are not, however, positively constructive. They belong rather to the negative condition and outlook. With them, however, Gilman united a sense of progressiveness. This progressiveness indicated itself in no more moving form than in his power to attract, to inspire, and to promote the interests of young scholars and teachers. He says of the original Hopkins Faculty:

''Those of us who initiated, in 1876, the methods of instruction and government in the new foundation at Baltimore were young men. Sylvester alone had more than three score years to his credit. Gildersleeve and I, now patriarchs, were forty-five years old. Morris was a little older. Remsen, Rowland, and Martin were not thirty years of age. The original Associates, many of whom became leaders in their

[9] ''The Launching of a University.'' p. 4.

several departments of study, Adams, Brooks, Cross, Elliott, Hastings, Morse, Scott, were still younger. All were full of youthful enthusiasm and energy. There were none to say 'This is not our way;' none to fasten on our ankles the fetters of academic usage. Duty, youth, hope, ambition, and the love of work were on our side. Laboratories were to be constructed, instruments and books to be bought, colleagues and assistants to be chosen, regulations to be formulated, conditions of admission, promotion and graduation to be determined, plans of study to be matured.'' [10]

One of his colleagues, who also became a colleague of mine, and was till 1926 the head of the department of Romance Languages in Yale University, Professor F. M. Warren, has written:

"He kept close to his graduate students socially, giving several small receptions for them annually, tempering the wind with alluring femininity, but never failing to call the crowd together near the end of the evening and show it a new book, or to speak briefly about some new investigation. If it were a book we called his manner 'hefting' (the book). Then he would spot us individually any time with something in our line, which we might not have seen. His interest in these matters was most unusual. . . . He was absolutely up to date with his graduates, and constantly seeking to bring them out, interested in their work and success. His eye was always single

[10] *Ibid.*, pp. 47-48.

to his job. He seemed to live on that idea alone:
what he could do to push matters. He would civ-
ilize us all and we needed just that as you know. . . .
After years had gone he was talking—at dinner—
one year I had gone down to lecture, about his own
work, and said 'What I evidently have done is to
"open" things. Practically all these addresses I have
here in print are to "open" one institution or building
or another.' " [11]

His colleague, Dean Griffin, says of him in the same
spirit:

"It is impossible to conceive anything more nearly
ideal than his relations with his official subordinates.
He always spoke of his professors as his 'colleagues,'
and he treated them as such, in very fact, seldom
using words of authority, but taking them into his
confidence, and working with them in the spirit of co-
operation and comradeship. As a consequence, he
secured a kind of service which could not be commanded and could not be bought." With an intimacy
of personal interpretation almost unique Dean Griffin
continues,

"I never knew any one who was more quick to recognize merit, and was more delighted when good
work was done, and was more ready to help forward, in every possible way, any one worth helping.
His nature was too magnanimous to harbor jealousy,
or to act under any kind of unworthy motive. No
one could see him often, and talk with him con-

[11] Personal letter from Professor Warren. June 4, 1923.

fidentially, without learning lessons of honor and generosity and high-mindedness.''[12]

Yet his thought and feeling were by no means limited to the younger scholars and teachers. Marvelous was his power to quicken interest, personal, scholarly, administrative, in all associates. Dr. John K. McLean, President of the Pacific Theological Seminary says:

"He was endowed with an extraordinarily sharp, quick and unerring discernment, first of measures and men, and next of ways and means, not merely as to things in themselves, nor yet as to their latent values—he had all that, and more. With it all was allied the more fruitful sense of how to extract those values, and how, once extracted, to set them into active productiveness. He seemed to grasp the whole at once, at a glance,—the metal in the rock, the particular mode of extracting that special grade or class of metal, of handling it when extracted, with also the ability to set in motion the required means to bring out a final, finished product, and not stopping there, but also to set the tide of this final product at earning its own daily bread."[13] Gilman himself recognized this duty as belonging to the university. In his Phi Beta Kappa address at Harvard in the year 1886, he says:

"Among the offices of a university there is one too often undervalued or perhaps forgotten—the dis-

[12] "The Life of Daniel Coit Gilman." By Fabian Franklin. p. 428.   [13] *Ibid.*, pp. 124-125.

covery and development of unusual talent. . . . The history of civilization declares that promising youth should have the most favorable opportunities for intercourse with other minds, living as well as dead, comrades as well as teachers, governors as well as friends.'' [14]

With this power over, and exercised for, young men was joined an even more unique power in the reconciliation and co-working of men whose theories might be contradictory, and whose personalities were more or less antagonistic. College faculties and boards of trustees are, and ought to be, composed of members of diverse judgments respecting content and method of college instruction and administration. Respecting the fundamental principles of education there should be a common intellectual assent and agreement. But regarding methods, details, applications, freedom should be allowed. Both unanimity and liberty, with the consequent diversity, which characterizes a political party, should also characterize an academic body. Gilman himself says:

''We brought to the council room many prejudices and preferences derived from our previous training and from our personal idiosyncracies. Two of the staff had been professors in the University of Virginia, two had been Fellows in the great English universities, two had received degrees in German universities and others had studied abroad, two had been connected with New England colleges, two had been

[14] ''University Problems.'' p. 93.

teachers in scientific schools, and one had been at
the head of a State university. Our discussions were
free and familiar, as of friends around a council
board. It was rarely, if ever, necessary to 'make a
motion' or to put a question to the vote. By processes
well known to Friends, 'the sense of the meeting'
was taken and recorded.''[15] Consciously or ·uncon-
sciously, Gilman followed the principles of Edmund
Burke in political compromise. But his minor principles were based upon the fundamental principle
lying beneath the phenomena. He united the antinomies in a deeper law.

The rare and beautiful power of conciliation was
born not simply of his penetration or his many-sided
vision, but also of his patience united with enthusiasm.
For, these two virtues and graces, each important
and infrequent in their union, formed a joint force
as important as it is infrequent. For, the man of
enthusiasm is eager to secure results speedily, to
adopt methods which are timely and of present
worth, to adjust himself to circumstances and conditions which promise an early benefit. The man of
patience, in turn, is prone to put off doing, or de-
ciding, "until Thursday of next week," as says the
Spanish proverb. He is in peril of allowing his waiting to lapse into stagnation, and of demanding perfect means and impeccable methods before beginning
a course of conduct, or of laying down a method
of procedure. Gilman, on the contrary, was free

    [15] ''The Launching of a University.'' p. 48.

from the double dangers which beset,—he had happy
enthusiasms held in restraint, and he was neither
the victim nor the agent of impatience. At the age
of seventy-one, in the year 1902, on becoming president of the Carnegie Institution, he wrote to his
family circle of Norwich, saying:

"This is the best opportunity for usefulness that
has ever come to me, and it makes me feel as if I were
forty once more. I see so much to do, and I am so
happy to be a part in the doing." [16]

Yet, throughout his life, he knew that in the development of institutions, as in the processes of
nature, the element of time is fundamental. He was
ever ready, like Ulysses, in Tennyson's poem, to seek
a newer world, and he also was willing to take a
proper time for finding that world. In Franklin's
"Life" it is said of him:

"He was born with a quick and ardent energy
which would carry him over many obstacles, and
with time and discipline he had learned great patience which could bear with long delay and many
drawbacks and yet never lose the end in view. This
was naturally partly due to a sanguine and hopeful
disposition, but the root was still deeper in his un-
shakable faith in God's providence, which soon or
late would prosper all good purposes and bring good
out of apparent evil. When fair prospects were
clouded by misfortune, he would often say, 'The

[16] "The Life of Daniel Coit Gilman." By Fabian Franklin.
p. 401.

Lord reigns,' and found in that strength and courage.'' [17]

The element of patience in the great career has peculiar illustration in his service as a scholar. For, at the present time, too many presidents of colleges are chosen on the basis of their ability as administrators without reference to their worth as scholars. The earlier president was a scholar, as well as an executive. Eliot was a chemist, Andrew D. White, an historian, the elder Angell, a teacher of history and of international law, Patton of Princeton, a theologian, and Wheeler of California, a Hellenist. Gilman, in turn, was a geographer and a librarian. For nine years he served as teacher in the Sheffield Scientific School, giving courses in geography, in history, and in political economy. As a teacher he was enthusiastic, quickening, interested in his students, as they were in him. His worth as a geographer and as an historian received signal evidence in his membership in the Venezuelan Boundary Commission. The learning and training of a scholar gives to the college president the assurance of sympathy with the scholarly work of his colleagues, founds and forms a basis for judgment of the merits of their teachings and researches. The president who is a mere executive is in danger of becoming vain, in both senses of emptiness and ostentation. Through personality and experience, Gilman was made free of this peril.

[17] *Ibid.,* p. 429.

It is not often that full, explicit testimony, regarding a college president, is given by another college president. The infrequency of such testimony becomes the more infrequent when the witness himself has been a professorial colleague of the president about whom he writes. Therefore, the testimony of President G. Stanley Hall, regarding Gilman, has peculiar significance. In his biography, issued not long before his lamented death, President Hall says:

"Gilman was essentially an *inside* president. His interest in the work of the individual members of his faculty did not end when they were engaged, but began. He loved to know something of their every new investigation, however remote from his own specialty, and every scientific or scholarly success felt the stimulus of his sympathy. His unerring judgment of men was triumphantly justified in the achievements of those he appointed; and although in selecting young men he had to walk by faith, he nowhere showed more sagacity than in applying individual stimuli and checks, so that in this sense and to this extent he was a spiritual father of many of his faculty, the author of their careers, and for years made the institution the paradise and seminarium of young specialists. This made stagnation impossible, and the growth of professors there in their work was, I believe, without precedent. . . .[18]

"The new policies which mark Gilman as the most

[18] "Life and Confessions of a Psychologist." By. G. Stanley Hall. pp. 246-247.

creative mind in the field of the higher education
that this country has yet produced may be sum-
marized as follows. First of all, he realized that as
civilization advanced, all critical decisions and new
steps must be made by experts who could command
all the available knowledge in their field and perhaps add something new to the sum of the world's
knowledge. To have made a contribution to this,
however small, marks the real attainment of majority
in our world. Scholarship is a prime condition but
erudition is not enough; each must have had the
unique experience of having contributed some tiny
brick, however small, to the Temple of Science, the
construction of which is the sublimest achievement
of man. In everything else there may be docility
but at some point each must be an authority and
have passed beyond apprenticeship, and be able to
light his own way with independent knowledge. Then
alone is he a real citizen in the culture world of
to-day. Thus intellectual creativeness must be made
the real standard and test of any system of higher
education of to-day. Anything and everything must
be subordinated to this, and Gilman must have had
great satisfaction in realizing that in this kind of productivity the Hopkins University, at least for a decade or two, was the leader and pioneer in this
land. He was never dismayed to be told that this
ideal was 'made in Germany.' It found the warmest
response in every able and original mind in all
academic America, as is abundantly witnessed by the

fact that the Hopkins fashions have been so generally cultivated in later years by all our higher institutions. And although this tradition has been sedulously maintained and so far as possible is ever advancing at Baltimore, the leadership of this institution is now relatively less pronounced only because its ideals have been so infectious in so many other centers.'' [19]

In a specific foundation, it now seems probable that the most outstanding of Gilman's achievements may lastingly be found in the Johns Hopkins Medical School and its affiliated Hospital. The advance of the graduate departments of other universities, and the impossibility of again finding such able scholars as constituted the faculty of the Graduate School of John Hopkins in its early years, have contributed to its declining leadership. But the Medical School is still the first, or, if not the first, one of a distinguished quartette, of schools. Gilman was not a physician, but he was united and coöperative with the medical scholars who founded and who manned that School. Professor Howell, Dean of the Medical Faculty, has said:

''He gave to it on the administrative side an ideal organization which has been the envy of other schools, and which will eventually, I believe, be generally adopted. The central feature of this organization is that it places all power in the hands of a small but representative body, composed of the heads

[19] *Ibid.*, pp. 248-249.

of departments, the president, and the superintendent of the hospital. . . . Our foundations were well laid, and I am sure that the great success of the school, acknowledged everywhere, was a source of the deepest gratification to Mr. Gilman. It may be fairly claimed that it constituted his second great contribution to the educational development of this country. I hope that the future historian of medical education in the United States will not make the mistake of supposing, because Mr. Gilman was not a member of the medical profession, that therefore his connection with this medical school was in any sense perfunctory. On the contrary, it was real, it was vital, and it was continuously maintained." [20]

Gilman's remoteness, combined with his sympathies, may have contributed to the large sanity and wholeness of his interpretation of medical education. Mountains are not seen from their base in their proper meaning and impressiveness. It was perhaps better for the great foundation for him to be *with* the doctors than *of* them.

Throughout his life of seventy-seven years, Gilman was, in respect to the opportunities for service, what might be called the obvious man. His early ambition received full and constant gratification. In early life, at the age of thirty-six, in 1867,—a pregnant age for first invitations to college presidencies,—he was asked if he would consider an election to the presidency

[20] "The Life of Daniel Coit Gilman." By Fabian Franklin. p. 255.

of the University of Wisconsin, an intimation which
made slight or no appeal. Again, at the age of
sixty-six, he was asked if he would be willing to
accept an election to the presidency of the Institute
of Technology. This also he declined. In both early
and late life, he was approached in respect to the
presidency of Yale. To the superintendency of the
New York public schools, he was invited. He served
as the first president of the Carnegie Institution, an
opportunity which, as he said, he deeply appreciated.
For many years, his was the first figure which one
saw when a great university was looking for a worthy
president. This obviousness was especially significant in his election to the Johns Hopkins office.
When the trustees of Hopkins were searching for a
president for their new foundations, they turned for
counsel to three presidents, the most outstanding of
the eighth decade of the last century. They turned
to Eliot, White, and Angell. The method is as
wise as it is infrequent. For, as Gilman's biographer
says:

"In going to the three university presidents above
named, the Trustees were evidently seeking out three
men who had not only shown preëminent success in
the handling of their own problems, but were the
three men most fully representing the idea of progress in American education. Each of them had been
for only a few years at the head of a great university, and each of them was at that time of life
when the full vigor of youth is combined with the

sagacity and the experience that belong to mature manhood.''[21]

Without conference with each other, they each recommended Gilman. Regarding this unanimity, Fabian Franklin adds:

''This unanimity of choice testifies to something more than the eminent fitness of Mr. Gilman for the important post upon which he was about to enter. Of that, of course, no evidence is necessary or can add to that which is furnished by the history of Johns Hopkins. What it does impress upon the mind, however, is the extreme rareness of the qualifications which it was necessary to secure if something truly great and valuable to the country was to be achieved at Baltimore.''[22]

Gilman's own interpretation of his life and career, as expressed to his intimate friends, is found in his phrase that ''he 'opened' things.'' For, he gave, in his brief service in California, an orderly beginning to its great university. He shared with its original trustees the founding of the university which made the name of a Baltimore merchant lastingly illustrious, and he himself established, in his quarter century of service, its great on-goings. He prophesied, in a significant address, the dawn of a university in the Western Reserve. He helped to establish special education for philanthropic work. He early pointed out the value of publications in and to a university. His ideas were as seeds. He

[21] *Ibid.*, p. 194.　　　　　　[22] *Ibid.*, p. 195.

was another Sir Walter Mildmay, founder of Emmanuel College, Cambridge. Of him, his eminent colleague, Gildersleeve, says in a letter written to me not long before his death:

"Months before the opening of the Johns Hopkins University, President Gilman did me the honour of unfolding to me in two long interviews his plans for the new institutions. As the first professor of the University I was closely associated with him in the working out of those plans of far-reaching significance. I have given expression to my appreciation of his large vision, notably in the address which I drew up in behalf of the faculty, sometime before his withdrawal, and at the memorial meeting following his death. Passing years have only heightened my admiration of his great services to the cause of higher education, his resourcefulness, tact, generosity, his rare skill in finding the currents of popular opinion, and in the direction of individual capacities and I regret that I can only reaffirm here, what I have already written concerning the achievements of him who led us so many years along paths which have become national land marks." Gilman's service is a marvelous record of beginnings of institutions which are to go on so long as men think and stand in need of thoughtful, scholarly leadership.

On the retirement of Gilman from the great office of which he had been the great head for twenty-five years, Woodrow Wilson wrote, in behalf of the graduates, a noble interpretation of their appreciation of

Gilman and of his unique service to the higher education.[23]   At that time also Gilman presented, to his successor, Wilson himself as a candidate for an honorary degree, with this citation: "whose vision is so broad that it includes both North and South; a master of the principles which underlie a free government."[24]

Among Gilman's papers was found, after his death, a pledge taken from the "Monologen" of Schleiermacher and printed in Hagenbach's "History of the Church:" "I will keep my spirits without flagging to the end of my days. The fresh courage of life shall never forsake me. What gladdens me now shall gladden me always. My will shall continue firm and my imagination vivid. Nothing shall snatch from me the magic key which opens to me those doors of the invisible world which are filled with mystery, and the fire of love in my heart shall never grow dim. I shall never experience the dreaded weakness of old age. I will treat with noble disdain every adversity which assails the aim of my existence, and I promise myself eternal youth."[25]   This promise was, after the completion of his full career, fittingly fulfilled by Daniel Coit Gilman, the Connecticut boy who became the founder and the great president of a great university, the man of vision and of sympathy.

[23] *Ibid.*, pp. 388-389.

[24] See "The Life of Sir William Osler." By Harvey Cushing. Vol. I, p. 573.

[25] "The Life of Daniel Coit Gilman." By Fabian Franklin. p. 434.

IV

ANDREW DICKSON WHITE

ANDREW DICKSON WHITE, born in Homer, New York, November 7, 1832; died November 4, 1918. A.B., Yale, 1853, A.M., 1856; graduate studies at the Sorbonne and Collège de France and University of Berlin, 1853-54; Yale, 1856. Attaché United States Legation, St. Petersburg, 1854-55; professor of history and English literature, 1857-63; lecturer on history, 1863-67, University of Michigan; member of New York Senate, 1863-67; first president of Cornell, 1867-85. United States Commissioner to Santo Domingo, 1871; chairman, Jury of Public Instruction, Centennial Exposition, Philadelphia, 1876; honorary United States commissioner, Paris Exposition, 1878; United States minister to Germany, 1879-81, to Russia, 1892-94; member of Venezuelan Commission, 1896-97; United States ambassador to Germany, 1897-1902; member of the Peace Commission at The Hague, 1899, and president of the delegation. Trustee, Hobart College, 1866-77, Cornell, 1866-1918; Carnegie Institution for Research, and Carnegie Peace Endowment; officer of the Legion of Honor; received Royal Gold Medal of Prussia for Arts and Sciences, 1902; honorary member of Royal Academy of Sciences, Berlin; president, American Historical Association, 1884-85.

Author: Paper Money Inflation in France, 1876-1896; Battlefields of Science, 1876; Swedish translation, 1877; The New Germany, 1882 (German translation, 1882); Message of the 19th Century to the 20th; The French Revolution, Syllabus of Lectures; The Teaching of History in Our Public Schools; Democracy and Education; "Erasmus;" A History of the Warfare of Science with Theology in Christendom, (French translation, 1899, Italian, 1902, Portuguese, 1910, German, 1899); The Warfare of Humanity with Unreason; Autobiography, 1905.

IV

ANDREW DICKSON WHITE

FOUNDER, DIPLOMAT, AUTHOR, GENTLEMAN

THE remark that an institution is the lengthened shadow of a man, however true in its intent, always seems to me to be an unfortunate metaphor. It is an especially unfortunate figure as applied to a college. For, a shadow stands for darkness, a college stands for light. A metaphor, less impressive but truer, is that an institution is a man raised to his second, or third, or even nth power.

The remark, thus interpreted, may be applied with special truthfulness to Cornell University and to Andrew Dickson White. For, White was at once its founder,—in several meanings of the word,—and also its preserver, its defender, its guide, its inspiring force, its bountiful benefactor. In a word, he was its friend. As a friend, he was constant, wise, thoughtful, self-sacrificing. No friendship, more vital or more commanding, do American academic annals contain. His ideal of a great academic foundation began early. In fact, in his blood there was a strain which led him to feel, from early years, that the building up of good institutions is more honorable than any other work. This idea, he declares, was at the bottom of his efforts to found Cornell, and earlier, as a professor, to aid in the development of the University of Michigan.[1] His subsequent life gave substance to the dream of his youth. His education, at home and abroad, his affluence which enlarged his strength and opened opportunities without enervating his power, his diplomatic experiences, his catholicity of intellect, his wide learning, his calmness of temperament, his acquaintance with many men of many minds, his sympathies of heart and of will, his distinct charm of manner, all contributed to constitute him a founder and a supporter of great institutions.

In the seventh decade of the last century, it was White who, as legislator at Albany, secured the charter for Cornell. This charter indeed, leaving out its financial parts, was written by him. It was he who, in the antagonism of many opposing influences, held Mr. Cornell to his purpose of giving an endowment to the proposed university. It was he who suggested electing trustees for a term of years, and not for life, and who gave special rights to the alumni in the election of trustees. These two methods were among the earliest, if not the first, examples of a method now becoming common. It was he who first made the connection between an incorporated university and the public schools of its State, formal, regular, vital. It was he who caused to be declared, in formal instru-

[1] "Autobiography." Vol. I, p. 6.

ment, that sectarianism as such should have no weight in the election of teachers. It was he who first arranged for a regular body of non-resident professors or lecturers,—and, be it added, this first body of Cornell included Goldwin Smith, Agassiz, and James Russell Lowell. It was he who, among the colleges of the Middle and New England States, first gave to women the right to be admitted on terms as free as those belonging to men. It was he who, in his plan of organization, included such constructive ideas as "equality between different courses of study. In this," he said, "I especially developed ideas which had occurred to me as far back as my observations after graduation at Yale, where the classical students belonging to the 'college proper' were given a sort of supremacy, and scientific students relegated to a separate institution at considerable distance, and therefore deprived of much general, and even special, culture which would have greatly benefited them." [2] As a result of this service, White adds: "During my life, which is now extending beyond the allotted span of threescore and ten, I have been engaged, after the manner of my countrymen, in many sorts of work, have become interested in many conditions of men, have joined in many efforts which I hope have been of use; but, most of all, I have been interested in the founding and maintaining of Cornell University, and by the part I have taken in that, more than by any other work of my life, I hope to be judged." [3]

[2] *Ibid.*, p. 341.   [3] *Ibid.*, p. 443.

The seventh decade of the last century was a time
favorable to the enlargement and enrichment of university and college education. The Civil War had
come to its close. War should be for a nation, either
in its victory or in its defeat,—if the defeat be not
too disastrous,—a period of intellectual renaissance.
To a people fighting for what they are pleased to regard as a moral or religious principle, war is often
a new baptism of force. One cause of the unique and
splendid efflorescence of the age of Pericles lay in the
triumph of Greece over Persia. One never forgets
that the foundation of the University of Leyden represents not simply the endowment of the University
by William of Orange, but also the interest of the
people in education while they were still suffering
from the horrors of war. Neither can one fail to
recall the founding of the University of Berlin at a
time when it was doubtful whether there would be a
Prussia at all to support a higher national school.

The period of the American Civil War was a period
when the dominance of the classical type of education
was vanishing. The discoveries made in the sciences
of biology, of chemistry, and of physics, were opening
new fields of education. As knowledge enlarges,
education is to possess itself of new forces and new
materials. Great college presidencies were coming
to a close or were beginning. Eliot, in the year 1869,
following five brief presidencies at Harvard, covering
twenty-four years, was beginning his fruitful service
of forty years. Yale was closing the classical period

of Theodore Dwight Woolsey. Princeton was soon
to feel the quickening power of the virile McCosh.
The University of Pennsylvania, it may be confessed,
was still sleeping the sleep which Provost Pepper
once said to me it had slept since its foundation by
Benjamin Franklin, a sleep which, he added, continued till he came. The times were ripe, therefore,
for a new university of a new type, of broader ideals,
of larger comprehensiveness, and of a more quickening spirit.

To the service of founding and the subsequent building of Cornell University, White brought chiefly himself. He was an orienting personality. His principal
work, as he says, was to set people at thinking: "The
first and best thing to do is to *set people at thinking,*
and to let them discover, or think that they discover,
the truth for themselves." [4]   Again, writing of his
teaching in the University of Michigan, he says:

"It was not difficult to point out many things in
the past that had an important bearing upon the
present, and my main work in this line was done in
my lecture-room. I made no attempts to proselyte
any of my hearers to either political party, my main
aim being then, as it has been through my life, when
dealing with students and the public at large, to set
my audience or my readers at thinking, and to give
them fruitful historical subjects to think upon." [5]

"As regards the popular-lecture pulpit, my main
wish was to set people thinking on various subjects,

[4] *Ibid.*, p. 81.   [5] *Ibid.*, p. 83.

and especially regarding slavery and 'protection' '' [6]

Rich were the opportunities opened to White in political life. But the forum had little attractiveness for his quiet scholarly soul. As he says, "My ambition, whether I have succeeded in it or not, has been to set young men in trains of fruitful thought, to bring mature men into the line of right reason, and to aid in devising and urging needed reforms, in developing and supporting wise policies, and in building up institutions which shall strengthen what is best in American life." [7]   He embodied what one of his great sons has called "democracy of the intellect." This democracy was a quickening power for the individual and for the whole community.

White's methods of effecting his purpose among the students of Cornell and of Michigan were diverse. He was a teacher of history, even while he served as a president. This teaching, begun at Michigan, continued to the close. He was also a lover of art. Yale asked him, in 1866, to become the head of a new School of Art. At Cornell he founded a School of Architecture. His home was in a true sense an art museum, as also it was a library, (one of the largest of all private libraries, numbering no less than forty thousand volumes. Lord Acton's great library contained fifty thousand). By precept and by example, he sought to make thinkers, and never to impose his ideas on other minds. On his eightieth birthday, he wrote a letter "To each and all of the Students of

[6] *Ibid.*, p. 269.   [7] *Ibid.*, p. 224.

Cornell University.'' In the letter he gave his boys and his girls no less than a dozen specific counsels. These counsels cannot have too wide a reading or practice. First, he indicated his belief in exercise in the gymnasium. Such exercise he emphasized. Secondly, he urged the importance of military exercise. Third, he indicated the value of vocal exercise, intimating that a strong pleasing voice is one of the best factors of success, both in and after college. Fourth, he urged that Sunday should be a day of rest from one's ordinary work, a day of reading and of thinking, of a type unlike the ordinary, and also should be a day of worship in the church. Fifth, he intimated the importance of general lectures and reading, such as are embodied indeed in a theme so broad as ''The History of Civilization.'' Sixth, he pointed out the value of good literature for reading and for memorizing. Seventh, he affirmed the importance of intellectual concentration. Eight, he warned of the peril of indecision, indicating that the will may sometimes suffer a temporary paralysis. Ninth, he presented the wisdom and the unwisdom of the fraternity and the club. Tenth, he further warned against the crude superstition that memory is the chief tool of education. The three great ends, he says, are ''Knowledge, Discipline and Culture.'' Eleventh, he gave emphasis to the value of the power of will as an element in individual success. Twelfth, he summed up all the indispensable results of a university career in the word *''Character.''*

The counsel which, at the age of eighty, he gave to the students of Cornell, one may add, he had largely followed from his own youth.

Though White was thus an executive and a teacher, one does not forget the diversity of his commanding interests. Early were heavy responsibilities of a fortune placed upon him by the death of his father, responsibilities which he bore with comparative ease. For, he was a master of circumstances. He was one of the few college presidents possessed of riches, a condition which one could wish belonged to all. Early was he elected to the senate of his native state. The opportunity thus opened to him for a great political career was unique. But such a career did not prove at all to be a temptation. The diversity of his service while still a president, and following his resignation, is full of meaning. He was minister, or ambassador, to Germany in two periods, covering no less than seven years, and to Russia for two years. He was member of the Peace Commission at the Hague in 1899, and president of the American delegation. He was presidential elector, and also, from time to time, a member of manifold commissions. Each of these opportunities called out the best that lay in him. Near the close of his life, however, he says, "I feel certain that, were I to begin life again with my present experience, that [journalism] would be the career for which I would endeavor to fit myself." [8]

Of all White's service given beyond Cornell, the

[8] *Ibid.*, p. 254.

most outstanding was the diplomatic. Many are the college presidents who have served in diplomatic posts. Illustrations of the earlier and of the later period are not lacking. Among the presidents who entered into the great service are Everett of Harvard, Angell of Michigan, Hill of Bucknell and Rochester, Collier of George Washington, and Droppers of South Dakota. The most recent is the transfer of President Schurman from Peking to Berlin. It may also be said that two college presidents have declined the most important diplomatic post. Noah Porter, of Yale, was offered, by President Hayes, the place of minister to Great Britain, and declined it. Informally, President Wilson offered the same post, made an ambassadorship, to President Eliot. President Eliot declined to consider the offer with any degree of favor. It may also be noted that, in his early life, Gilman, who became president of John Hopkins, was once appointed attaché to the American minister at St. Petersburg. In diplomacy, White has a place among the highest. He was appointed by President Hayes minister to Germany, where he served from 1879 to 1881. By President Harrison, he was made minister to Russia, in 1892, where he also served for two years. He was again asked to accept the post in Berlin, by President McKinley, in 1897. There he again served, and for five years.

In the nine years of his foreign service, and in all the diversity of his many interests at home, White met many men of many minds who were to him quickening spirits. The ablest in the home country, and the ablest in Germany, in Russia, and in England, were for years among his personal friends. For a half-century the commanding men in American politics, in American education, in American literature, were his associates. In England, Lecky, Froude, Lord Lytton, and of course Bryce; in France, de Lesseps and Pasteur; in Germany, university professors, foreign ministers, and the Kaiser; in Russia, Tolstoy, were among his friends. All these offerings of friendship and of experience, he held not for himself, but for the enrichment of the life of his beloved university. His world-life as a diplomatist he gave to his presidency.

The fact is that the qualities which make a great diplomatist are the qualities which are trained in a college presidency. The diplomatist is to possess an intellectual appreciation of the duties and rights of the nation which he represents. He is also to be equally well acquainted with the fundamental principles and methods of the government to which he is accredited. In this understanding of both nations, the analytical habit of mind is of primary worth. To this quality is to be added the quality of patience, both intellectual and moral. Of course, it is not necessary to say that he is to be a gentleman of cosmopolitan tastes. In this understanding, he is also to appreciate what I may call the intellectual gradations, or proportions, of principles, of duties, of rights. It is not necessary to add that these great qualities of the diplomatist are the qualities required in a great college president, and are the qualities also which the great office nourishes and disciplines. White's diplomatic experience added to his worth as a college executive, and his academic administration made more effective his service at the great governmental capitals.

President White, be it also said, was deeply religious. It is more important to make this remark, because in the early years of his public career an opposite impression prevailed among the people. His desire to free Cornell from the fetters of a sectarian theology and his proposing to elevate and to broaden the teaching of science, were causes of the belief that he was an agnostic or even an aetheist. In the introduction of his great book on the "Warfare of Science with Theology," he says:

"Our purpose was to establish in the State of New York an institution for advanced instruction and research, in which science, pure and applied, should have an equal place with literature; in which the study of literature, ancient and modern, should be emancipated as much as possible from pedantry; and which should be free from various useless trammels and vicious methods which at that period hampered many, if not most, of the American universities and colleges.

"We had especially determined that the institution should be under the control of no political party and of no single religious sect, and with Mr. Cornell's approval I embodied stringent provisions to this effect in the charter.

"It had certainly never entered into the mind of either of us that in all this we were doing anything irreligious or unchristian. Mr. Cornell was reared a member of the Society of Friends; he had from his fortune liberally aided every form of Christian effort which he found going on about him, and among the permanent trustees of the public library which he had already founded, he had named all the clergymen of the town—Catholic and Protestant. As for myself, I had been bred a churchman, had recently been elected a trustee of one church college, and a professor in another; those nearest and dearest to me were devoutly religious; and, if I may be allowed to speak of a matter so personal to myself, my most cherished friendships were among deeply religious men and women, and my greatest sources of enjoyment were ecclesiastical architecture, religious music, and the more devout forms of poetry. So far from wishing to injure Christianity, we both hoped to promote it; but we did not confound religion with sectarianism, and we saw in the sectarian character of American colleges and universities, as a whole, a reason for the poverty of the advanced instruction then given in so many of them."[9]

The purity of the motives of Mr. Cornell and of President White did not, however, prevent opposi-

[9] "A History of the Warfare of Science with Theology in Christendom." Introduction, Vol. I, p. VI.

tion, bitter, prolonged, and at times apparently vicious. From such antagonism both the university, White himself, and his memory, have long passed. His own religious beliefs he has been so free as to intimate in various parts of his revealing auto-biography. He says:

"It may now be asked what is the summing up of my relation to religion, as looked upon in the last years of a long life, during which I have had many suggestions to thought upon it, many opportunities to hear eminent religionists of almost every creed dis-cuss it, and many chances to observe its workings in the multitude of systems prevalent in various coun-tries.

"As a beginning, I would answer that, having for many years supplemented my earlier observations and studies by special researches into the relations be-tween science and religion, my conviction has been strengthened that religion in its true sense—namely, the bringing of humanity into normal relations with that Power, not ourselves, in the universe, which makes for righteousness—is now, as it always has been, a need absolute, pressing, and increasing.

"As to the character of such normal relations, I feel that they involve a sense of need for worship: for praise and prayer, public and private." [10]

In the midst of these several interpretations of the great services and rich worths still stands White him-self, the man. To the eye he seemed to lack physical

[10] "Autobiography." Vol. II, p. 568.

vigor and capacity of aggressiveness. No one of the university presidents of his time had a body apparently less fitted to create and to maintain the forcefulness required in a university executive. His was the student's mood, and his the thinker's robe. He bore the manner and manners of the large-minded scholar and of the gracious-hearted gentleman. Early began his association with the best which the world offers, and the association continued to the end. He united the bearing of the gentleman of the world with the simplicity, genuineness, heartiness of the simple American citizen of Central New York State. One cannot think of any society,—the dining room of the Bismarcks, a common room in Oxford, a bank directors' meeting in Syracuse, a faculty conference in Ithaca,—in which he would not have been thoroughly at home, both giving and receiving the best. In early life, Moses Coit Tyler called him "a glorious fellow." Late in life, he called Tyler, "My dear old boy."

Beneath this personal manner, characteristic of the man, ever seems to abide a virile reasonableness or a rational appreciation of all values. His was a mind, —like that of John Morley, or of Matthew Arnold,— of noble interpretativeness. His understanding, however, was not purely intellectual. His was not simply the dry light of truth, a light which is liable to be, if used alone, drying up to the one using it. It was indeed this, but more. It was united with the love of beauty and with real affection for individuals. This reasonableness is only another name for sound judgment, freed from narrowness, untouched by prejudice, resulting in wisdom, and bathed in personal tactfulness.

President White lived to see the great ideals, first beheld by him in a dream, achieved. He lived to receive and to recognize the gratitude of a world which had, at times, given to him depreciation and beset him with antagonisms. As one, who has a better right to speak of him than any other associate, Professor George Lincoln Burr, said, on his eightieth anniversary:

"A grateful world has set its crown upon his noble life. That life it is that speaks to us in his person— that life so busy, yet so full of leisure for chat and conference, for music and travel, for private helpfulness and public service—that life which in all its eighty years has had no time to kill, no need of other sport than exercise, other conviviality than conversation, other amusement than the play of kindly humor and the ennobling joys of art. Dared I attempt its summary in a single phrase, it should be the phrase he loved to quote us from the Spanish writers who describe Columbus: *tenia gusto en cosas grandes*, 'he had a taste for great things.' "[11]

Also another, an outstanding college president, whose work remains and whose testimony weighs, one of his boys, David Starr Jordan, says:

"To him who saw the end from the beginning,

[11] "Cornell's Debt to President White." By George Lincoln Burr. *The Cornell Era.* Vol. 45, 1912, No. 2, p. 95.

to the first president of Cornell University, the creator of the 'Cornell Spirit,' our nation owes a debt as great as it has owed to any one man in all its history.''[12]

Andrew D. White is among the greatest of the great. His place is secure.

[12]''The Leadership of President White.'' By David Starr Jordan, '72. *Ibid.*, Foreword.

V

CYRUS NORTHROP

CYRUS NORTHROP was born in Ridgefield, Connecticut, September 30, 1834; died April 3, 1922. A.B., Yale, 1857; LL.B., 1859; admitted to Connecticut Bar, 1860; clerk of Connecticut House of Representatives, 1861; Senate, 1862; editor, New Haven Palladium, 1863; professor of rhetoric and English literature, Yale, 1863-84; president of the University of Minnesota, 1884-1911; president emeritus, 1911-1922. Published weighty volume of Addresses: Educational and Patriotic, in 1910.

CYRUS NORTHROP

It has been said that the history of the two centuries of Yale College and University is marked by four characteristics: democracy, faith, conservatism, constructiveness. These four elements seem to me to characterize the life and career of one of her most beloved and distinguished sons, Cyrus Northrop.[1]

For, Northrop was a democrat. A better word for him than democrat is humanist, not in the cultural, but in the human, sense. For he believed in man, in MAN. He himself seemed to incarnate the tremendous monosyllable. He recognized rights, fundamental, broad, and high. But he also never forgot duties equally fundamental, broad, and high. The visible token of the man well intimated the invisible character. The big manly head, well poised on a strong neck, found a fitting support in a massive, vigorous body. The manners were direct, simple, plain without bareness, informal without familiarity, hearty without any sign of boisterousness, with a talk punc-

---

[1] Parts of this sketch, as well as parts of following chapters, have been published in *The Congregationalist*, of Boston.

tuated by happy allusion and jest, and bearing illustrations that quickened smile and laughter.

A great companion he was, of either the hour or of the day. A great citizen he was, too; the greatest of his time in his adopted State. He belonged to all the people of his noble metropolis and of his noble commonwealth. A great co-worker he was, too, sparing not himself, leading—but leading far less by formal commission or compulsion than by the essential qualities of his own great manhood. A great administrator he was, rather by force of character than by formal direction or deed. No one of the college presidents of his generation was more akin, in his simple democracy, to the democrat of all democrats, Abraham Lincoln. Northrop has himself described a call which he once made on the great President. Interesting in itself, it also is a token of his whole genuine humanity:

"I went to him, once, and sat with him in the White House. I went down there as the messenger of Governor Buckingham, of Connecticut, to plead with him for a change of policy in a certain particular affecting our ability to carry on the war. He received me just as I suppose he received every one else, with a courtesy that could not be surpassed. He threw his leg over the arm of his chair and he sat there and talked with me as familiarly as if I had been Governor Buckingham himself instead of his messenger. And I saw then, and I have never forgotten, why it was that Abraham Lincoln in that long struggle in the years that followed, kept the great body of the Northern people so in touch with himself, when statesmen of no mean reputation and generals of great popular favor and editors of papers that had voiced the sentiment of his party, deserted him; it was because he never forgot that he came of the people, that he was of them, that by them he had been raised to power, and that for them the services of his life were to be rendered."[2]

A man of faith, Northrop also was. By faith I mean his acceptance of and his following of the Christian teaching and revelation. This faith was manifest in many ways. Among these ways was membership in the Congregational Church. He was given the most distinguished honor of that Church —the Moderatorship of its National Council. He loved and worked in the individual church, and was a tower of strength to the successive ministers of an historic pastorate. He served as an officer of the American Bible Society. For the higher life of the commonwealth, such outstanding, definite, religious loyalty had impressive meanings. In his inaugural address, he declared principles which it was ever his satisfaction, and the satisfaction of the great State, to recognize and to follow:

"A sense of honor, a regard for truth, the practice of virtue, the recognition and observance of all those obligations which rest upon us as individuals and as social beings, not omitting the highest of all obliga-

[2] "Lincoln, Statesman and Orator." "Addresses: Educational and Patriotic." pp. 451-452.

tions, those which we owe to God,—certainly the value of all these can not be overlooked by wise educators anywhere; and it will not be overlooked here. We can not, as we cultivate the minds of the young, be indifferent to the moral purposes which shall control them, and shall determine the uses to which increased mental power and knowledge will be put. Education is far from being in itself a panacea for human ills. It is alike a power for evil and for good. It renders much greater the possibilities of both. If devoted to evil, it becomes a curse both to its possessor and to mankind; but if consecrated to the service of mankind, and thus to the glory of God, its value is beyond calculation. This University is not and can not be sectarian. It is not and can not be partisan. But it is, it can be, and it shall be faithful to truth. I am not an agnostic, and I do not propose to become an instrument for making agnostics of others. I think that life is worth living, but I should very much doubt it if I did not believe that there were for every human being possibilities of glory and honor and immortality hereafter, revealed in the Gospel of Jesus Christ. Cherishing this belief as in some measure the inspiration of life, I must be permitted to act in all my relations, public and private, as befits a man who does cherish such a belief; and I know that far greater evil will come to those entrusted to my care should I be faithless to my belief, than will ever come from the strictest fidelity thereto.'' [3]

[3] Inaugural Address. *Ibid.*, p. 134.

A quarter of a century later, speaking at Whitman College, in 1908, he re-affirmed the same sentiments:

"We of the state universities heartily rejoice in every influence which tends to strengthen Christianity, to keep alive, in young people, the love of God and the love of neighbor, and to make the teachings of Jesus the directing principles of their lives." [4]

Yale College has been distinguished also by its conservatism, as Harvard has been by its progressiveness. Northrop was a worthy son of Yale. Also there was in him a certain progressiveness more akin to the Massachusetts than to the Connecticut foundation. One is tempted to call him western, western in his vision, his forth-putting powerfulness, his disregard of conventions, his desire for achievement. Yet, he was conservative in his respect for the past, in his knowledge that to-day is the child of yesterday, and that to the parent the child looks for enrichment and for guidance. Truthfully does he say in his inaugural address:

"The course of study in this university seems to me to be characterized by a wise conservatism, which is reverent towards all that is good in the education of former times, and by a wide-awake spirit of progress, which appreciates the learning of the present." [5]

As an educator and as a man, he kept to the middle of the road, and it was a very wide middle in which he walked. He recognized that every bird flies with

[4] "Greater Whitman College." *Ibid.*, p. 360.
[5] Inaugural Address. *Ibid.*, p. 135.

two wings. The attempt to fly with only one is fore-
doomed to crookedness and to disaster.

His sense of both conservatism and of progressiveness is manifest in the element of constructiveness in
his work as a university president. In the forty years
and more which have passed since he began his
presidency, the state universities have experienced
a tremendous development. The history of the development of one is significant of the history of the development of each. The more general and cordial
acceptance of the principle of the higher education as
a function of the commonwealth, the larger grants
made by special appropriation or through the general
law of a fixed percentage of the public income, the
additions to the richer endowment of professional
schools, the greater attention paid to agriculture both
as an art and as a science, the more inspiring affiliation of the university with other forms of public
education, the more cordial relations of the state
university to other universities and colleges of the
commonwealth, the enlargement of university functions, and the multiplication of university buildings,
the increase of the teaching staff by the hundreds, and
of students by the thousands—these and other elements characterize the history of the American state
university in the last two score years—years which
unite the inauguration of Northrop, in 1884, with the
day of his death in 1922. To Minnesota came a just
proportion of these rich results. Many causes contributed and many conditions gave favoring in-

fluences. But in Minnesota, in and through and by these forces and circumstances, was seen the great citizenship, the big-heartedness, the abounding optimism, the inspiring leadership, of Northrop.

In these larger elements of character and of achievement was also found, moreover, an interest in persons as persons. In serving man, he did not forget to serve men. In his noble inaugural, he makes mention of the element of personal affection between teacher and student:

"It is a delightful experience for a teacher to quicken the intellect of a scholar. It is a no less delightful experience for a teacher to quicken the moral faculties of a student, and make him strong to resist temptations to evil. To win the confidence and regard of his pupils, while holding them fast to courses of discipline and inspiring them to seek the highest things in knowledge, so that he may be to them not merely 'guide or philosopher,' but 'friend,' to whom in any emergency, in any moment of special trial, they would come with a full assurance of sympathy and help, as they might to their own father in the distant home, this, it seems to me, must be the crowning joy of the wise educator; for he knows that so long as his pupils are bound to him by the ties of personal affection, his power both to stimulate them in intellectual work, and to restrain them from everything hurtful will be almost complete." [6]

This characteristic, which he so beautifully inter-

[6] *Ibid.*, pp. 138-139.

prets, was embodied in his own relationships. It was
seen in his professorship at Yale. It continued in his
presidency in Minnesota. My dear friend, the late
Professor Bernadotte Perrin, told me that once, in
walking along a street in New Haven, Northrop
overtook him, laid his hand on his shoulder, and
commended him for a certain piece of work. Perrin
never forgot it. A distinguished member of the Minnesota faculty tells of the call which Northrop made
on him in his editorial office in New York. The
editor had neither notion nor wish to migrate, or to
settle on the western bank of the Mississippi. But
Northrop persisted in his request, to become a member of the University's teaching staff. It was finally
the affectionate personality of Northrop which per-
suaded an acceptance,—an acceptance which has
brought forth good and lasting fruit for a score of
years. The present noble president of the University
of Illinois has lately said that he was a freshman
student of Northrop at Yale, more than forty years
ago. Once he called on Northrop at his house in Min-
neapolis. The door was opened by Northrop himself.
Each looked at the other for a moment without speaking. After a time, Northrop said: "Your hair is not
so red as it was once! Come in!" Northrop saw in
the gray head of the distinguished college president,
the red-haired Scottish boy of the long ago. This tender personal feeling is well voiced in verses of his
students, verses which prove that the feeling belonged
to both president and student, one of which I quote:

"In Prexy's face
Are many stories—some of them are glad—
  Told in a smile for youthful joy and mirth;
  And some of them are tender, having birth
In tears of sympathy when hearts are sad.
Power, strength, and comfort, all are there
  And even a dim soft shadow, sorrow's trace,
With these the hand of Time has set Love's seal
  In Prexy's face." [7]

In any interpretation of Northrop, one cannot but think of his wit and of his humor. The gift—and it was a gift—was genuine, and overflowing. The wit flashed like a keen-edged sword. The humor bubbled and tumbled over itself like a waterfall. It would be hardly fair to say that it spared none. But it is fair to say that, as tradition tells, on one historic occasion it did not spare, but rather mastered, one of the greatest of American humorists. Each friend will recall instances. I content myself with referring to two or three which are found lodged in his great oration given at the Bicentennial of Yale:

"Dr. Bacon was a free-trader, but he always voted the Whig or Republican ticket. He said he had been wanting for years to get a chance to vote the Democratic ticket, and so emphasize his views on the tariff; but the Democrats always did some foolish thing or other just before election that compelled him to vote against them." [8]

[7] From the Students' Journal of the University of Minnesota.
[8] "Yale in Its Relation to the Development of the Country."
The Yale Bicentennial Celebration, 1901. p. 298.

He also says:

"That the undergraduates have always known just how great the faculty was, individually and collectively, every graduate of the College is perfectly aware." [9] And again: "Indeed, any college that has not conferred the doctorate on Gilman is *ipso facto* not really respectable." [10]

Not a few, in thinking of Northrop, will think of him as the master of eloquent speech. We college presidents, as a class, are not masters of eloquent speech. In fact, we are rather dull and stupid. Of course, one is glad to add, there are exceptions. There was Eliot, commander of utterance, lucid, progressive, interpretative, argumentative, the finest type of conversational oratory. There is Butler, massive, comprehensive, affluent in thinking, vigorous, whose thought sweeps on in political or educational interpretations, broadening as a river in its swift flowing. There is Alderman, the most gifted of all in that divine afflatus that quiets or thrills, as the speech of that vibrant voice moves forward in noble periods. With them, and with other men of like eloquence, belonged Northrop. His soul went into his public, as into his private, speech. It trembled in deepest feelings and meanings. It quickened the hearer in its appeals. It strengthened the will unto great choices, and it gave to one strongest girding for tackling tough tasks and for achieving highest ideals.

His biographer says of his public speaking: "They

Ibid., pp. 301-302.   [10] *Ibid.*, p. 312.

[his speeches] began early; they lasted to the end; and the tax which old age—even extreme old age—levied upon his oratorical power was very slight. He came to himself upon the platform; his instrument was the assembled people. Power in a cabinet, though it had been power over an empire, would not have sufficed; he would have found his joy in that also, but what he needed most was the relation at once personal and public, at once civic and intimate, which was furnished by the platform. He loved the individual; he loved the commonwealth; and an audience was a middle term, at the same time a fact and a symbol, which both multiplied the individual and typified the commonwealth. Facing a mixed crowd or a select assembly, in the expansion of brotherhood which comes to men of his type through the act and fact of leadership, he was proud and glad to feel that, in reaching the private heart, he might promote the welfare of a nation." [11]

There were found in Northrop five other qualities which are either lacking in college presidents, or which, if found, are not so elemental or constructive as they ought to be.

The first which I name is just the opposite of the quality of eloquence of which I have written: Northrop was a good listener. To listen is not a quality with which college presidents, as a class, are gifted. A great teacher tells me of his frequently going to

[11] "Cyrus Northrop: A Memoir." By Oscar W. Firkins. p. 473.

call on his President, also distinguished and able: "I call in order to ask a question. The President greets me with a story, passes on to a second tale, and, after talking for ten minutes, I go away having had no chance to ask my question." Such was not the mood of Northrop. Rather, as Firkins says: "The President listened. He had the gift—not always granted to the golden-mouthed—of listening. You might be a mere mote in his cosmos; you might rise out of nowhere into his world and pass almost instantly into nothingness; but, while he gave himself to you, he gave himself to you completely. His whole mind was at your disposal, and you felt perhaps a little like a man who should have for a moment an amphitheatre to himself. When you had stated your case, there was often a silence—brief enough perhaps if measured by seconds, but having compass and area for all that, and the President, who had weighed the applicant, weighed the proposition.

"When the answer came, it often took the form of a question. He asked *you* if *you* did not think in this or that way about the matter. This was one of his happiest arts. He lifted the topic to a superior region in which your own judgment could take an unclouded view of your own interest or your own prejudice. He invoked—one might without too much exaggeration affirm that he evoked—the judge in you." [12]

A second element, and of a large degree of

[12] *Ibid.*, p. 371.

uniqueness, was found in his relation to his faculty. The relation of a college president to his faculty may take on any one of several types: first, intimacy with individual mmbers; second, indifference or remoteness; third, antagonism. With Northrop, intimacy was the prevailing mood. His colleague and interpreter says:

"There were publicities doubtless in which he showed himself more triumphant, and there were intimacies in which he showed himself more lovable; but the composite, semi-public, semi-private faculty meeting brought out in the happiest fashion the playful royalty and sovereign ease which gave him mastery and fascination. He loved his students best —of that there can be no question; but he loved his faculty with a very personal and special love. His way of pronouncing the very word 'faculty' was peculiar to himself; as the word came from his lips, it seemed to expand like a domain; it was pronounced with a stately and considered homage, and yet an undernote of wardership, a suggestion of a chastening or cautioning finger, was audible or sensible beneath it all. For him and for them the meetings were enjoyable, and his enjoyment sunned itself in theirs.

"As presiding officer no one was ever more efficient; yet the supply of force so far exceeded the demand that ample margins, as it were, were left on either side for repose or for diversion. The work was done with a finish that suggested art and an unconcern that mimicked play. He did not say so very much; in fact he rather distinctly left the bulk of the explanations to others. But his very silence *presided.*" [13]

It has just been said that Northrop loved his students. But, also, he loved them most of all. Such love, every college president should feel and show. In manifold ways, Northrop gave his heart to his girls and boys. His office door was always and easily open to their coming. It was reported that he once said, in the chapel service, "If you are homesick come into my office and let me try to cheer you up." [14] Their individual joys, sorrows, disappointments, victories were his. Their collective exultations moved his soul: "His love for them was no convention, no urbane form, no point of strategy; it was not even the incidental conduit of a sincere but vague and general benevolence. It was inbred; it was part of his life; it was a thing in which and upon which the man lived. Public in its form, it was intimate in its reality; it peopled his solitude; it consoled his privacy. A feeling like this could not escape the notice of its objects, and its effect was heightened by its association with a gratitude that in its touching, simple way was almost meek. . . . In his relation with the individual student he was always the master, the counselor, the 'liberal and princely giver'; but in his view of the students as a body he felt something of that deference which all men of receeding years

[13] *Ibid.,* p. 392.   [14] *Ibid.,* p. 388.

and powers must feel for the superb phalanx of advancing youth."[15]

"He saw, not merely the student, but the boy or girl, and he spoke to the real boy or girl, not to an academic expectation or hypothesis which it pleased a self-deluding faculty to identify with the object in skirts or trousers that faced it in the college class-room. It is difficult to believe that any teacher in the Anglo-Saxon world, that Arnold of Rugby or Hopkins of Williams, has been more trustfully and reverently loved. The feeling was common to boy and girl; it included all the colleges, the most distant and the least susceptible; it met the entering fresh-man at the threshold of the University, and the de-parting senior carried into the chill outside world the comfort of its unabated warmth."[16]

There was a fourth element in Northrop's ad-ministration which deserves special notice. He em-phasized the value of the daily chapel service. He regarded this service as of great worth in promoting the unity of the students, in giving an opportunity for presenting subjects in which students were con-cerned, as individuals or as a body, and also as afford-ing a means for moral instruction and for religious worship. In too many colleges, the chapel service is formal and ritualistic. It, therefore, is to most a cause, or condition, of either indifference or an-tagonism. In too many colleges, also, the service is made an oral bulletin board for the reading of notices.

[15] *Ibid.*, p. 377.　　　　　[16] *Ibid.*, pp. 372-3.

In yet others, it is used as a chance to give addresses of "uplifting," which, good in themselves, become wearisome as a constant academic irritant, or method of approach, to the undergraduate mind and heart and will and conscience. To Northrop, the few minutes, flung into the middle of the forenoon, was an opportunity of richest value of which he made the utmost use. His biographer says of the service:

"He was right in viewing 'chapel' as central and typical in his University work. His best and strongest selves—the counselor, the moralist, the patriot, the humorist, the good fellow, everything indeed except the man of the roof-tree and the hearth—came out in these encounters with his students." [17]

He himself says:

"I valued this daily assembly most highly not merely on account of its possible religious influence, but as the best means for my meeting the students, for their meeting and knowing me, even if I did not know them individually as after a time when students multiplied it became impossible for me to know them. It was a splendid opportunity every day to test the spirit of the students, to ascertain the trend of their inclinations, to set before them true and high ideals of life and to inspire in them longings for the best things. I used this opportunity to a reasonable extent; but I was careful to avoid overdoing the exhortation and preaching business. When it needed that a word should be spoken, it was spoken. When there

[17] *Ibid.*, p. 390.

was no special reason for saying anything, I usually
did not say anything. I did not give any 'course of
lectures' at these services. When I spoke it was
spontaneously, without written preparation, and
often without any special preparation, the occasion
for speaking arising unexpectedly. From the testimony of many students as shown in letters written
to me and to others, I conclude that in no way did
I make a greater impression on the students or do
them more permanent good than I did by these extemporaneous off-hand talks in chapel." [18]

But, above all elements and qualities, and indeed
comprehending and uniting all elements and qualities,
Northrop was a great personality. In particular,
Firkins writes of two characteristics:

"There was in the man a strength—let us rather
say a might—which commanded an immediate and
ample homage. Here was a power that could elec-
trify anything—even a platitude. If there were those
who thought his *ethics* feminine—the biographer is
not included in their number—his *virtue* was unquestionably male. If his ideals vouched for his character with the sympathetic majority, his character
vouched for his ideals with the unruly few. Ideals
which might have seemed feebly amiable in the
mouths or minds of men who made them an asylum
for their weakness took on the guise of strength in a
nature strong enough to have profited by their renunciation. Men found admirable in him the doc-

[18] *Ibid.*, pp. 373-4.

trines of love and service and reverence which they
might have ignored or despised in a woman or a
child or a minister, just as a man who is normally indifferent to flowers might note with joy a flower
that grew upon a rampart.

"In the second place he had in eminent degree
the qualities that hold the imagination of the young.
Over and above his moral and mental power, he was
rich even in the worldly glamors; he had the arrest-
ing qualities—eloquence and wit and presence and
dexterity and tact, and he was in a position where
they could all be frequently—not to say continuously
—tested and displayed." [19]

But, be it also said that his personality was embodied, to the physical eye and ear, in his simple
presence. It was indeed a great presence, commanding without being autocratic; genial and, at times,
quite jolly, without softness or being guilty of lack of
dignity; sympathetic and altruistic, without loss of
individuality; intellectual in impression and impressiveness, without coldness or remoteness. His very
presence conquered respect and commanded loyalty.
This presence served to make fresh and vivid his
thinking on things old and well-worn. This presence
gave unity to his separate principles, or interpretations, as heard in public speech. This presence animated and quickened the general presentation of great
causes.

In these five respects, as a listener, as embodying

[19] *Ibid.*, p. 376.

princely love for his colleagues and for his students, as emphasizing the worth of the daily chapel service, and of being a great personality, Northrop takes a high place in a group, lamentably small, of great American college presidents.

Twenty years ago, Northrop gave an address in memory of his dear friend and co-worker, a noble pioneer of the Northwest, John S. Pillsbury. With a change of only two or three words, which I venture to make, the paragraph fitly interprets dear Northrop, and the feeling of some of us for him:

"His greatest monument is the University of Minnesota, which was so dear to his heart, and for which he gave so generously of his time and strength and means, and his memory as a noble benefactor and friend will be cherished, outside of his family circle, longest by the students and graduates and faculty of the University, which owes its . . . prosperity in large measure to him. . . . Dear President Northrop, kind-hearted, great-souled father of the University, farewell!" [20]

[20] John Sargent Pillsbury. "Addresses: Educational and Patriotic." p. 474.

VI

MARK HOPKINS

Mark Hopkins was born in Stockbridge, Massachusetts, February 2, 1802; died June 17, 1887. Entered sophomore class, Williams College, 1821; B.A., 1824; tutor, 1825; graduated from Berkshire Medical School, 1829; professor of Moral Philosophy and Rhetoric, Williams, 1830-87; licensed to preach 1833; president of Williams College, 1836-72; urged to accept presidency of the University of Michigan, 1852; president of the American Board of Commissioners for Foreign Missions, 1857-87; Lowell Lecturer, 1860-61, 1867-68, 1871-1872.

Author: Lectures on Moral Science; Christian Ethics; An Outline of Study of Man; and Teachings and Counsels, and many magazine articles.

VI

MARK HOPKINS

MARK HOPKINS belongs to those far-off years when
the college president was first a teacher, and secondly a president. He does not belong to the decades
of Gilman, of the elder Angell, of Eliot, and of
Harper,—decades which, alas! in the passing of the
years, become less vivid. He does belong to the years
of Woolsey of Yale, of Wayland of Brown, of Woods
of Bowdoin, of Felton, and of Walker, of Harvard.
He is a part of the age, not of the president as an
administrator, but of the president of teaching and
of personal relationships. For Mark Hopkins dealt
in that process and product of the college which we
call ideas, a process and a product needing constant
nourishing and fertilizing.

For the college might be defined as that force which
is concerned with ideas. Ideas form its origin, constitute its field, and create its results. Ideas are its
capital, and interest on this capital represents new
ideas. Ideas, too, are its workmen, and they are
workmen who, in turn, quicken other ideas. The

campus stands for a field where ideas are sown,
nourished, harvested. The typical college laboratory
is an idea laboratory. The typical college lecture
room is a place where ideas are expressed, understood,
criticized, rejected, accepted. The study of history,
of philosophy, of English, of science, of sociology,
gets its chief worth from the creative process of ideas.
The personal association of teacher and student, of
student and student, is made most precious by reason
of the birth, the re-birth, and the nourishment, of
ideas. It is sometimes said that one goes to college
to form friendships; and the formation of friendships, of course, has much value. It is also declared
that one goes to college to gain certain civilities; and
be it said that good manners are never to be minim-
ized. It is rather frequently affirmed that one goes
to college in order to become a better citizen, or to
pursue a vocation with greater efficiency, and these
purposes are, of course, most worthy. But, above all,
comprehending every purpose, underlying and over-
lying every academic condition, is the interpretation
that ideas—to create them, to fertilize them, to make
them of greater worth, stronger force, richer content,
wider relationship—is the essence of the academic life.
Ideas are the citizenship of the college world. However important, however broad, however high or deep,
are other interpretations of the worth of a college
education, it is yet true that ideas represent the whole
cubical content. If one may make a new application
of the title of Newman's great book, one might be

allowed to say that "The Idea of a University is the IDEA."

Mark Hopkins used ideas in classroom, pulpit, parlor, library. But his method of using ideas was perhaps more significant than the ideas themselves, however significant may have been the ideas. The constant and broadest opportunity for using ideas was found in the classroom. For, during no less than fifty-six years, he taught philosophy, (in a large interpretation of the word) in Williams College, a term equaled in length of teaching by few. As student and teacher, he was associated with the college for no less than sixty-one years. The teacher's desk was his throne, and royal and regal he made the mastery which he thus and thence wielded. From it he influenced no less than two thousand students. The method was Socratic. The questions which Socrates asked, as reported by Plato, often seem trivial, as for instance, in the opening of Gorgias, "And are we late for the feast?" But the replies made to the questions Socrates uses for further research and for arousing the intellectual interest of the witness. The questions which Dr. Hopkins asked of his students may or may not have been important in themselves, but the replies offered a basis of further questioning and of remarks which aroused the mind. In an address, given in the fiftieth year after his election to the presidency, in June, 1886, he said: "The ideal is, of an institution, where a young man, during the critical period of transition from boyhood to manhood, and even later, may have an opportunity to do for himself the best that he can do; and also one that shall do for every such young man the best that can be done for him.'' The college, indeed, should give the student, through its liberal education, three things—a body, sound; a mind, disciplined; and a right character. This trinity represents a cubical manhood of infinite relationships.

In respect to the place he gave to teaching in the college curriculum, we have two interpretations, one made in his inaugural address of 1836, and one made about two score years after. In the first address, the new president said:

'' 'It is far easier for a teacher to generalize a class and give it a lesson to get by rote, and hear it said, and let it pass, than it is to watch the progress of individual mind, and awaken interest, and answer objections, and explore tendencies, and, beginning with the elements, construct together with his pupils, so that they shall feel that they aid in it, the fair fabric of a science with which they shall be familiar from the foundation to the top stone.' The laboratory method, so popular now, was his conception from the beginning.

'' 'He who carries the torch-light into the recesses of science, and shows the gems that are sparkling there, must not be a mere hired conductor, who is to bow in one company and bow out another, and show what is to be seen with a heartless indifference; but must have an ever-living fountain of emotion, that will flow afresh, as he contemplates anew the works of God and the great principles of truth and duty.' " [1]

In the year 1877, he wrote to a friend, saying:

"You inquire . . . whether I find the same interest as formerly in teaching. I think so, and account for it partly from the fact that I teach this system, which expands upon me, as I study it more, and evidently becomes a power in moulding the whole mental life of the class, and often giving bent to their moral and religious life. It commends itself most to the best minds, and they often express their satisfaction in the clearness of insight they gain. I account for it also partly from the manner of my teaching. Nothing pleases me more than to have the class ask questions, and so it sometimes happens that we spend the hour in what is really conversation, making no progress in the book, and the result of that is often most satisfactory. I do not find that impertinent or captious questions are asked. This, of course, causes the recitations to be different every year, according to the minds to be dealt with, and gives nearly as much variety as there would be if it were a new thing." [2]

These two interpretations represent the more essential elements of teaching: first, the vitality of the student and the adjustment of teaching to his special intellectual needs; second, the freshness of the application of truth to each new body of students. The truth itself may be new or may be old, presented for the first time, or for the last of many times. But the

[1] "Mark Hopkins." By Franklin Carter. p. 62.
[2] *Ibid.*, pp. 292-293.

truth has a special vividness by reason of its application to a mind which never before had perceived that truth. Third, the value of truth as an agency of intellectual discipline; fourth, the value of the intellectual agency and facility in the promotion of moral and religious character.

In respect to the method of Dr. Hopkins and its effect, his colleague, John Bascom, one of the most notable of many notable colleagues, and also one of the most effective of all college teachers, has said:

"His chief merit as a teacher was that he went, at once, to the substance of his topic, with an animated and interesting play of thought. He was quite sure to awaken the mind of the pupil, and put it 'in act and use.' He was formidable in the recitation room, but not in the least dogmatic. . . . Few have equalled him as a teacher in a lively, gracious interchange of ideas with those under his direction, and to many, therefore, he became the first vigorous, intellectual presence they had encountered, and went with them, in this delightful relation, through all their lives."[3]

The primary result of such teaching over the minds of Williams graduates was the result of learning to think. The acuteness of the mind of the teacher created acuteness in the mind of the student. The thinking became more than the thought, the method more precious than the end, the causative process of higher worth than the resulting product. The Scot-

[3] "Things Learned by Living." By John Bascom. pp. 105-106.

tish philosophy was the type of his philosophy. But, whether it was true or false, the intellectual training secured in its understanding was of primary worth in and of itself, and became ultimately of primary worth in all of life's reasonings and relations. His chief interest was lodged in the student, and not in the system of ethics or of metaphysics. His purpose was not so much to convey the system to the mind of the student and to cause its adoption as to set the student himself intellectually on fire.

"To learn to inquire, to learn to postulate, to learn to discriminate, and to learn to conclude at least a little, was the task perpetually laid before these young men." [4]

The system he expounded in book as well as in classroom. But the exposition he used to enlarge the mind, to quicken the conscience, to strengthen the will of the student. Ideas opened a pathway to a practical idealism. Truth led either to worship or to duty, and both duty and worship resulted in service.

Washington Gladden, a student of Hopkins in the very fullness of the teacher's power, said of him:

"It was in the senior year that the students came in touch with Dr. Hopkins; a large share of the work of that year was in his hands; the seniors met him every day and sometimes twice; in philosophy and ethics, in logic and theology, he was their only teacher. The tradition of his masterful instruction was always

[4] "Williamstown and Williams College." By Arthur Latham Perry. p. 784.

descending; the freshmen heard of it from all above them; it was the expectation of every student that, however unsatisfactory other parts of the course might turn out to be, there would be something worth while in the senior year. The expectation was not disappointed. There was nothing sensational in Dr. Hopkins's teaching; his method was quiet and familiar; his bearing was modest and dignified; but he was a past-master in the art of questioning; he knew how by adroit suggestion to kindle the interest of his pupils in the subject under discussion, and by humor and anecdote he made dry topics vital and deep waters clear. What his best students got from him was not so much conclusions or results of investigation, as a habit of mind, a method of philosophical approach, a breadth and balance of thought, which might serve them in future study. What Garfield said (and I heard him say it, at a Williams banquet at Delmonico's in New York) expressed the feeling of many another graduate of the Berkshire college: 'A pine bench, with Mark Hopkins at one end of it and me at the other, is a good enough college for me!' " [5]

The remark of the most distinguished graduate of Williams, regarding the worth of Dr. Hopkins' teaching, is confirmed by the remarks more philosophic than the traditional interpretation of the "log." While a student at Williams, in the winter of 1856, Garfield wrote, saying: "We are now gathering the

[5] "Recollections." By Washington Gladden. p. 72.

ripest fruit of the college course and our beloved and powerful President Hopkins is leading us with a strong hand along paths of thought which my feet have never before trodden. I hope to save some of the treasures he is giving us, to use in coming life." [6]

The biographer, Professor Theodore Clarke Smith, also gives his interpretation in saying: "For the rest [of his studies] all was concentrated upon philosophical subjects under a man, who, unlike any teacher Garfield had ever encountered, not only tried to see whether he had learned what the textbook said, but endeavored to make him think about the subject studied." [7] But Garfield found that Mark Hopkins possessed other elements besides a keen, interrogative intellect. For, he writes of an evening's reception, saying: "Our President, good noble soul that he is, was all around among us with a kind and familiar word for every body and so he adds to our admiration for his greatness a strong deep love for his good kind heart." [8]

I may be allowed to add that a son of Garfield, himself a successor of Mark Hopkins in the presidential office, has confirmed to me, in personal talk, that the worth of the teaching of Dr. Hopkins to him was, first, the intellectual discipline, and, second, his bearing forth into his life a remembrance of specific remarks which have proved to be of great help as touch-

[6] "The Life and Letters of James Abram Garfield." By Theodore Clark Smith. Vol. I, p. 97.
[7] *Ibid.*, p. 96.   [8] *Ibid.*, p. 100.

stones of character and guideposts in conduct. To my specific question, "Did Dr. Hopkins love the individual student?" was made the reply, "Yes, as a son of God."

President Hopkins would be among the first to say that he was not learned in his great subject. He was rather a thinker than a scholar. The sphere of German metaphysics was not opened to, or by, him as was the hemisphere of the Scottish philosophy. Kant is seldom named in his books and no one of the three great Critiques had a place among his texts. President G. Stanley Hall, one of his most distinguished students, says:

"I had many confidential talks with Dr. Hopkins. . . . In one of these talks he asked me what I thought of Kant and said that he had never tried to read him except in Bohn's Translation and in that was never able to get beyond the first paragraph of the *Critique of Pure Reason,* which he could not understand. His range of thought and reading included, I think, almost nothing of either the German or the Greek thinkers in this field and his mind was not historic." [9]

The philosophy of the absolute, beginning with Fichte, continuing through Schelling, Hegel, Schopenhauer, and ending with von Hartmann, made on him little impression. In this time, James Marsh was president of the University of Vermont, and was

[9] "Life and Confessions of a Psychologist." By. G. Stanley Hall. p. 169.

using translations from the great Germans. But in this unique movement, Dr. Hopkins did not share. At Harvard, Francis Bowen was teaching German philosophy, and was for a decade reading Schopenhauer and von Hartmann with his students. But Edinburgh, Aberdeen, and St. Andrews had more influence in Williams, than Berlin, Heidelberg, or Jena. His colleague, Professor Leverett Wilson Spring, says of him:

"For Dr. Hopkins, whatever his inclinations and aptitudes may have been, the life of a scholar was impossible. During the first twenty years of his administration, in addition to the inevitable executive work, he 'taught all the studies of the Senior class, corrected all their literary exercises, and preached every Sunday'—an exacting routine leaving little time or strength for scholastic investigation. The majority of teachers that get attention in the educational world secure it by research rather than by the independent action of their intellectual powers. Mark Hopkins belongs to the class of great men who are relatively independent of books and reading." [10]

Mark Hopkins was the teacher, not simply in his classroom, but also in and through the daily chapel, and the Sunday service. One advantage of the president as a clergyman is the opportunity given in the chapel prayers of each morning and in the preaching of each Sunday. The advantage far outweighs the

[10] "A History of Williams College." By Leverett Wilson Spring. p. 219.

advantage of a layman's freedom and fellowship. Of such opportunities Dr. Hopkins availed himself constantly, and to the edification of all students. His successor and biographer, Carter, says:

"His preaching in the college chapel was uniformly extemporaneous, and was often strikingly effective from the combination of close logical thought and apt illustration. Some of the students, when I was in college, took notes of his sermons, which were then quite uniformly doctrinal, and wrote them out fully. Doctrinal preaching for undergraduates seems now less suitable than formerly, and it was certainly an evidence of great power that Sunday after Sunday Dr. Hopkins, when president, preached a solid, logical sermon, and kept the attention of the students. Those sermons were an education to some of the maturer boys, and now and then an impression was made that was never forgotten. The critical and skeptical books of the time were often touched upon, not always by name, but always with a keenness that excited discussion among those who understood the allusions." [11]

The daily chapel service is in peril of being used by the students as an opportunity for a brief period of preparation for the forthcoming recitation or lecture. Students attending have usually come from, or are to go to, a recitation room. Their interests are not primarily devotional, or even intellectual. The most effective method of making the service a

[11] "Mark Hopkins." By Franklin Carter. p. 183.

means of both quieting and of quickening is the intellectual method. If the address or talk of the preacher be keen, incisive, apt, timely, the service is useful. If it lack these elements of arousing and holding attention, its chief value is as a roll-call. Such a value, however, is untimely, anomalous, unfitting. In his conduct of the service, Dr. Hopkins gave vision, created thinking and thoughtfulness, and thus helped to give to character a permanent direction and setting. He and Northrop alike used this service unto richest results.

But the public address was by no means confined, of either the week-day or of Sunday, to the chapel walls. The baccalaureate sermon has come to occupy a rich and unique place in the life of the college community. It is the last address of the president to the student after four years of companionship, and before his departure through the historic gateways. It presents a noble opportunity for reviewing brief, personal history, for stimulating reflection, for creating inspiration, moral and intellectual, and for a prophetic vision of the long future. The president usually finds this opportunity rich, inspiring to himself, and wholly beautiful. There are exceptions, one of the exceptions being found in the learned Woods, of Bowdoin. In the use of such an opportunity, Dr. Hopkins excelled. The topics considered indicate the sweep of his vision, the timeliness of his counsel, and the power of his thinking. Dr. Carter says that the themes of his discourses "were always lofty, and the

hearer was never allowed to lose sight of the lofti-
ness of the theme."[12]   In the last baccalaureate
sermon he ever preached, in the year 1872, he said:

"At this hour, when you are about to step into
active life, and when so many voices are calling you,
the one voice which you are to hear is that of Him
who says, *'Follow me.'* Hear that voice, and then
you will take your places under his banner by the
side of those who are waging with Him the great
battle of all time. It is around Him that the thick
of this battle has always been. Around Him it always
will be. Take, then, your places. You are needed.
The veterans are falling. Who shall take their place?
The strong men are fainting. Who shall succor them?
Go ye, and the earth shall be the better and the
happier for your having lived in it."[13]

The association of Williams College with the most
outstanding of all foreign missionary societies began
early, and has continued intimately. Dr. Hopkins
was president of the American Board of Commissioners for Foreign Missions for thirty years, 1857-
1887. The most moving event of its annual meetings was the Thursday evening address by the
president, and the address was one of the most outstanding events of his own public life. Without the
rhetorical brilliancy or massive eloquence of Storrs,
his successor in the great office, his addresses held
the vast audiences by the clearness of their statement
of Christian principles, by their interpretation of the

[12] *Ibid.*, p. 190.   [13] *Ibid.*, pp. 195-196.

unity of the Divine Kingdom, and by their commandingness of the duty of the church to educate and to
evangelize the nations who still sit in darkness. In
such a universal appeal and application one seemed
to see and to feel Dr. Hopkins as standing in front
of the Haystack Monument (not far from which he
himself lies buried) and speaking with the undying
passion of Mills and his comrades whose names are
cut into its stone, declaring that the field is the world.

Taken all in all, Mark Hopkins remains, and I believe will remain, as one of the richest and most useful ministers to the higher life of the nations of his
generation. The men whom he influenced and the
men whom they in turn influenced, and still influence,
are his testament and his witnesses. The list of the
great ones whom he loved and helped to become great
is most impressive. They and their comrades are
more significant than a commanding institution which
many college presidents seek to build. Among his
sons are Field of the Supreme Court, and his broth-
ers, Wells, the economist, Canfield, the teacher, president, and librarian—a man of unique and diverse
powers, and most impressive personality—Henry M.
Alden, the mystic, who became a great editor, Horace
E. Scudder, the editor and the writer, Hamilton
Wright Mabie, William Keith Brooks, the biologist,
William Dwight Whitney, the philologist, Samuel
Chapman Armstrong of Hampton, Washington Glad-
den, the preacher, Stanley Hall, the psychologist, and
President Garfield himself. His books represent the

highest excellence of the ethical treatises of their
time, and they are still vital and moving. Through
them Mark Hopkins has taught in the mission schools
and colleges of Bombay and Rangoon, of Peking and
Canton, of Kobe and of Tokio. But through his boys,
as well as through his books, he is a teacher in all
parts of the world. To him, as well as to his boys
the field has been and still is indeed the world.

Such abounding usefulness sprang, as ever it must
spring, from personality. This personality began in
a body, large, massive, vigorous, crowned with a
broad dome and forehead, bearing a face of keen
eyes, a Roman nose, and supported by a chin fine
and firm. The whole aspect was of impressive in-
tellectuality, insight and acuteness. His manner
and manners indicated power, bathed in an atmosphere of courtesy and of grace. He moved like a
Homeric hero. Dignity and benignity sat upon him
as a well-fitting robe. His presence commanded attention and recalled Burke's words about the elder
Pitt. Stanley Hall says he was "of commanding
stature and with an unusually impressive face,
stately, with old-fashioned manners, venerable with
age, wise and experienced in policies." [14]

A peril of a teacher, strong in character, beloved,
and intellectually acute, is the peril of the loss of
the individuality of the student himself. He is in
danger of becoming a poor and feeble imitation of

[14] "Life and Confessions of a Psychologist." By G. Stanley Hall. p. 166.

the master. The graduates of Williams College were not set in this peril. No one of them was in danger of becoming a Hopkinsian. Garfield apparently felt this peril, but from it he escaped. His reverence for Mark Hopkins did not carry along with itself imitation for, in the year 1859, he wrote to Hinsdale, saying:

"It is every man's duty to preserve his own individuality, though this is not incompatible with his being influenced and guided in his development by others. But there are some schools where one mind or one set of ideas exercise a tyrannic control in moulding & directing the views and sentiments of students. As marked instances of this I would mention Oberlin among literary institutions and Andover among Theological Seminaries. Now this kind of influence I deprecate as wholly evil in its tendencies."[15]

His was indeed a unique character and a unique life. It was a character which we miss in the college president of the present time. It was "unique," as a successor, Carter, says, "in its lengthened continuance of unabated powers, wonderful in the normal beauty of the family relations, unique in the grandeur of its endowments, unique in the extent and intensity of its personal influence,—so that he, like Abraham, by heroic sainthood became, as it were, the intellectual and spiritual leader of a great race;—unique in

[15] "The Life and Letters of James Abram Garfield." By Theodore Clarke Smith. Vol. I, p. 117.

the openness and receptivity of his mind, unique in
the cordial love that came to him from every side." [16]

Among the most moving of all of Matthew Arnold's poems is "Rugby Chapel," in which he seeks
to interpret his great father. Perhaps also one of
the most moving interpretations of Mark Hopkins
is the poem which one of his students, Washington
Gladden, read at the Commencement of 1887, only
twelve days after his death.

> We see thee standing there,
> The tall form gravely bent:
> The thin and silvery hair
> O'er the lordly dome besprent;
> The keen uplifted glance:
> The long arm's curving sweep:
> The serious countenance
> Where the merry twinkles sleep:
>
> We hear thee speaking now,
> Each weighty word well weighed—
> Simple and clear and slow—
> Not rattling fanfaronade
> Of words, but a master's thought,
> Untainted by sneers or gibes,
> Like His who the people taught
> With authority, not as the scribes. [17]

[16] "Mark Hopkins." By Franklin Carter. p. 364.
[17] *Ibid.*, p. 110.

VII

WILLIAM TORREY HARRIS

WILLIAM TORREY HARRIS, born in Killingly, Connecticut, September 10, 1835; died November 5, 1909. Fitted for college, Phillips Academy, Andover; spent two and one-half years with class of 1858, Yale, but did not graduate. Teacher, principal, and assistant superintendent, 1857-67, and superintendent, 1867-80, St. Louis public schools; obliged to resign by reason of poor health; went to Concord, Massachusetts, becoming associated with its School of Philosophy; United States Commissioner of Education, 1889-1906. Received honorary title of "Officier de l'Academie," Paris Exposition, 1878; represented United States Bureau of Education, International Congress of Educators, Brussels, 1880; and at Paris Exposition, 1889 (received from French Government, in 1889, title of "Officier de l'Instruction Publique"); established, and conducted till his death, Journal of Speculative Philosophy, 1867-1909; chief editor, Appleton's School Readers; edited Appleton's Educational series; edited department of Philosophy in Johnson's Cyclopædia, writing many important articles; editor-in-chief of International Dictionary, 1900-1909.

Author: Introduction to the Study of Philosophy; The Spiritual Sense of Dante's Divina Commedia; Hegel's Logic; A Book on the Genesis of the Categories of the Mind; Psychologic Foundation of Education.

VII

WILLIAM TORREY HARRIS

THE METAPHYSICIAN WHO WAS ALSO AN EDUCATIONAL ADMINISTRATOR

WILLIAM TORREY HARRIS touched life, and life touched him, on many sides and through many and diverse forces. To each he gave, and from each he received, much. He was a great educational executive, serving as head of the public schools of St. Louis for thirteen years (1867-1880), and as United States Commissioner of Education for seventeen (1889-1906). He was a philosopher who published a journal of the most erudite type of metaphysics, and was an unflagging student of German metaphysical thought. He was an author and editor, his volumes being many and of diverse method and subject, running from small pamphlets to the revision of Webster's great dictionary. He was also, and above all else, a friend—a friend whose friends were numberless and a friend whose heart was very big. That helper of thousands of American teachers, Dr. Albert E. Winship, has said of him in a personal note: "No other American educator combined as did Dr. Harris the qualities which won affection, compelled admira-

tion and developed worship. The personal element
was always in evidence, whether it met response in
affection, in admiration or adoration.''

The records of Dr. Harris' life are, like the records
of most great lives, simple, yet profound and significant. A Connecticut country boy, he studied in the
district and other schools. After experiences in several academies, he completed his preparation for
Yale, at Phillips, Andover, and entered Yale in 1854.
Becoming dissatisfied with the course when about
half completed, he went to St. Louis, becoming a
teacher in 1858, and, nine years later, was chosen
Superintendent of its Public Schools. The next
thirteen years brought to him, through his administration and writing, a reputation national, and
covering the world. Resigning the office in 1880, he
went to Concord. With the Concord essayists and
philosophers, he presently took a large and proper
place. As one piece of work, he helped to found and
to carry on the Concord Summer School. Nine years
were devoted to writing and to lecturing on philosophy, education, and art. In 1889, President Harrison appointed him the United States Commissioner
of Education. In this position he continued for
seventeen years. To this educational throne he added
grace to dignity. In 1909 he died.

Such a record, of which only the barest outline is
given, so diverse, so pregnant in great influences,
so profound in its principles, was never before made
by any American educator. It is doubtful if, under

all the changes of educational and literary conditions, another is even possible.

In and through all these, and other facts, I find certain characteristics which have worth for my special purpose.

Harris, like Emerson, illustrates the value of a large, inherited and personal, intellectual deposit. He himself says: "As my ancestry on my mother's side included clergymen in its two chief branches, and as my great grandfather on my father's side was a metaphysician as well as a physician and surgeon, I suppose it possible that I had some inherited aptitude for abstract studies, which accounts for my great delight in grammar while a youth, and for a still keener relish for philosophic studies in later life. I seemed to find an intellectual food in these things which perfectly satisfied a gnawing hunger." [1] The "gnawing hunger," if satisfied from time to time, still continued to gnaw. For the hunger began at the age of four and did not cease so long as life in the body lasted. Of all my friends, too, he is one whom I would select as most eager for truth in the life of the mind beyond and outside the body.

Writing of his life at Phillips Academy, Andover, he says of the great teacher, Dr. Samuel H. Taylor, to whom a chapter of this book is given:

"I had never before met a disciplinary force that swept me completely off my feet and overcame my

[1] "How I Was Educated." *The Forum*, Vol. I, August, 1886. p. 556.

capricious will. My intellectual work had been all haphazard, a matter of mere inclination. I now began to hear a great deal about mental discipline and to see manly industry. I took myself to studying in earnest, and tried to see how many hours of persistent industry I could accomplish each day. In my short stay at Andover I gained more than at any other school, and have always highly revered its discipline and instruction."[2]

Entering Yale in the autumn of 1854, he continued for about two and a half years. At Yale, he gained much and yearned for more. While there, however, he says he achieved that important art in learning to perform a large task in a brief time. "There was a written examination at the close of each term, for which preparation must be made by private reviews. To be able to go over one's entire work for the term in two or three days of study, brought into discipline a new power, usually called the power to 'cram.' Of all my school disciplines I have found this one of the most useful. The ability to throw one's self upon a difficulty with several times one's ordinary working power is required again and again in practical life on meeting any considerable obstacles."[3] He found, however, that many of the studies, especially mathematics, of the college, he had previously pursued, and he fell, he himself confessed, into lax habits of study, at least in one or

[2] *Ibid.*, p. 559.
[3] *Ibid.*, p. 560.

two subjects. At Andover, he had read Humboldt's "Cosmos," and he became especially interested in natural science. "I began to disparage the study of Latin and Greek as dead languages. Language itself was 'only an artificial product of the human mind.' I wished to know nature. This thought came to possess me more and more, until it finally overmastered me. About the middle of the junior year I withdrew from my connection with the college, full of dissatisfaction with its course of study, and impatient for the three 'moderns'—modern science, modern literature and modern history."[4]

But he himself further adds in the autobiographical article from which I quote, that he soon "discovered that my slender knowledge of Latin and Greek was my chief instrument in the acquirement of new ideas. I found that the words in the English language which are used in the expression and communication of general ideas are derived almost entirely from the classic languages. Knowing the literal meaning of the roots, I was able to get the full force of the English vocabulary used for science and real thought. Some years afterward, too, I came upon a more important insight. I saw that our entire modern civilization is derivative, resting on the Greek for its æsthetic and scientific forms, and on the Roman for the forms of its political and legal life."[5]

The intellectual hunger continued and deepened.

[4] *Ibid.,* p. 500.   [5] *Ibid.,* pp. 560-561.

It was simply insatiable. In an autobiographical article on the books that had helped him, he refers to what might be called an intellectual conversion, or step, in or toward his intellectual sanctification. The author of this change was Kant, and the volume which opened his eyes, as it has opened the eyes of unnumbered other thinkers, was the "Critique of Pure Reason." Harris himself says:

"I was gradually training my feeble thinking powers, and soon after I had devoted a year to the 'Critique' I broke through its shell and began to reach its kernel. It formed a real epoch in my life. It seemed to me that I had just begun to find life worth living. The year seemed so eventful to me that I was accustomed to say, 'I have made an intellectual step this year as great as the whole step from birth up to the time I began to study Kant.'" [6]

From Kant to Hegel was a proper development, and of Hegel he became the great American expositor. "This work ('Logic') of Hegel's comes nearer to being a genuine theodicy, a justification of Providence in human history, than any other work I know. 'The world-history,' says he, 'is the onward progress of man into consciousness of freedom.'" [7]

From Hegel to Emerson was also a proper progress. "Although I began to read Emerson's 'Essays' directly after I read the 'Hero Worship,' it was long before his serene insight became visible to

[6] "Books That Have Helped Me." *Ibid.*, April, 1887. p. 147.   [7] *Ibid.*, p. 149.

me. His brilliant epigrams dazzled me, but I missed any connection between them. There was no sequence. It was first in studying his essay on 'Experience,' years afterward, that I discovered a unity. I found the same unity in the book on 'Nature,' and afterwards, in other ways, the poems came to have new meaning. I have no greater favorites than the poems entitled 'The Lords of Life' and 'Spiritual Laws.' " [8]

But it was not simply books through which the spiritual hunger was at once satisfied and intensified. He declares that the "Last Judgment" of Michael Angelo, after two years of study in an outline engraving, began to have a permanent meaning for him. "I saw that the picture presented symbolically the present condition of the saints and sinners, not as they seem to themselves and others, but as they are in very truth. It placed them under the form of eternity." [9]

The intellectual avariciousness of Harris was continued and yet further emphasized, however, in the variety of the tasks to which he set himself. Throughout his life he was a tremendous worker, and a worker upon a vast variety of things and of themes. His printed books and papers run, as I have said, from a few pages to his revision of "Webster's New International Dictionary," embracing no less than four

[8] *Ibid.*, p. 150.
[9] "The Spiritual Sense of Dante's Divina Commedia." p. vi.

hundred and seventy-nine titles. The variety of themes, moreover, covers a diversity surpassing ordinary comprehension. They represent subjects as diverse as the "Last Judgment" of Michael Angelo, "The Value of Latin and Greek in Modern Education," "Individualism," "Indian Schools," "The Soul's Immortality," "Calculus" and "Calisthenics," "Orientalism" and "Orthography," "Pessimism in Relation to Educational Reform," "Psychological Observation in the School-room," "Simplified Spelling," "Single Tax" and "Sin," "Freedom of the Will" and "Consideration of the Charges against the Public Schools of Washington." This great variety of themes, however, does not represent superficiality in thinking or in writing. For, to the consideration of any subject, however trifling, he brought the thoroughness of a well-trained mind and comprehensive intellectual principle. He bore to each detail of a complex problem the force and light of systematic thinking. By a proper method, therefore, his conclusions were reached, and in justice and wisdom.

Dr. Harris was among the greatest of all humanists, a humanist not in the mediæval sense, but a humanist in what I may call a modern sense, of being human, as one who lived with and by and of and through humanity. He was indeed an individualist in and for and by and through himself, and, because he was an individualist, he, in his emptying himself, became great as a humanist. He had something worthy to give, and he was also large enough in height, breadth, and depth, to receive, and to accept gratefully, what humanity had to offer to him. This double state, or condition, he has well expressed in his great little book on "The Spiritual Sense of Dante's Divina Commedia":

"Man's ideal spiritual state is one of participation with his fellow-men. He does something for them, and they do something for him. He pursues some special vocation, and gaining great skill by limiting himself to one kind of work, he is able to produce much more than he would do were he to undertake all things. But this division of labor renders necessary a complete system of interdependence. Each one depends upon the rest for what he does not produce himself; that is to say, for all articles of food, clothing, and shelter, except the limited item that he produces. . . .

"With the mutual interchange of material productions in social union, there goes on the far more important interchange of intellectual and moral experience. Each person has something unique in his own experience, something that he has seen or felt that no one else has. And yet all the feelings and thoughts, all the life-experiences of each individual, are possibilities of all other individuals. The total revelation of humanity—humanity in all its possibilities—can only be made through the entire race. Each individual's life-experience is only a fragment of this revelation of human nature. How infinitely important it is, therefore, that each person shall behold the spectacle of this revelation of humanity in others. What lies in him potentially, and what would take millions of years to realize, he may see all realized in his fellow-men around him.

". . . A man enjoys the fruits of experience vicariously. He lives through the lives of others. All that they have seen is treasured and reported to him, all that they have reflected is also given to him. The collisions which they have made against the moral law, the collisions against the state, the family, and the church, all these collisions and their results on themselves, and on society, are described and communicated one to another, and by low aggregations make up the experience of the race. And this experience is the inheritance of all who receive the training and culture of civilization." [10]

The great human "fundamentalism" of Harris was manifested in many forms, and under a vast variety of conditions. He emphasized the importance of the course of study as set in the various schools. This importance is based on the fact that its content relates the student to civilization. Its different studies touch different sides of the great human polygon. These studies may be thus outlined:

"These different phases, or coördinate groups, called the five windows of the soul, are (1) mathematics; (2) geography and biology; (3) art and literature; (4) grammar and the technical and scientific study of language leading to logic and psychology, etc.; and (5) history. The whole elementary

[10] pp. 187-188.

course may be considered as the mastering of the art of reading and the application of the art to special fields—for example, literature, arithmetic, grammar, and history."[11]

The course of study not only relates the student to civilization, but also affords an important instrument and means of culture. The culture represents cultures. For, each group touches and enriches at least one part of the student's mind. All groups touch and enrich all parts of that mind. The course should be free from the gusts of educational passion. Its frills should be eliminated, and its fads not at all suffered. It should be solid, stable, regular, consistent. It should also be symmetrical, representing proper combination of studies, relative to both man and to nature, inclusive of both the fundamental, the derived, and the auxiliary. The course should make an appeal, not only to the intellectual, but also to the ethical and emotional, and æsthetic faculties,—faculties in which, of course, the intellectual is involved.

These working interpretations, derived from the great human fundamentals, are also summed up in three elementary considerations to which Dr. Harris was, in both intellect and heart and will, devoted. An intimate and wise friend says that the fundamental principles which he applied to every problem, the fundamental answers which he gave to every question, arose from or ended in "the personality of God, the freedom of the human will and the im-

[11] "William Torrey Harris." By John S. Roberts. p. 109.

mortality of the soul! Insight into the demonstrable truth of these three doctrines became the basis of all his educational work, that by which, doubtless, he is best known to the general public. They were the touchstones for all educational theories. Any theory inconsistent with them he knew to be defective, and ultimately untenable, and he was as certain of his conclusions as is the well-trained inventor that the circle will never be squared, and that no machine will ever be invented that will generate force and furnish perpetual motion, no matter how hard and long men may strive to accomplish it. Philosophy became to Dr. Harris and his associates the most practical of all species of knowledge. They used it to solve not only all problems of school-teaching and school-management, but the 'dialectic' of politics and political parties, and they applied it to the interpretation of literature and of art in its every phase. Dr. Harris saw that the highest form of philosophical thinking is the only form which is consistent with a true theory of education; therefore, it was to the test of this highest form of thinking that he subjected every educational question. Seeing the world explained by the principle of 'absolute person,' he found the world of institutions—the family, society, the state, the church—a world in harmony with such a principle."[12]

[12] "William Torrey Harris." An interpretation, by C. H. Ames. *The Journal of Philosophy, Psychology and Scientific Methods.* Vol. VI, No. 26, 1909. p. 701.

The general critical remark to be made upon the educational principles of Dr. Harris, both fundamental and derived, is that his interpretation fails to give a sufficiently large place to the teacher. For, in education, as in most concerns, it is the person who is more influential than the proposition, be the proposition never so truthful or comprehensive. A small subject, taught by a great teacher, is more formative of intellect and of every part of character, than the great subject, taught by the small teacher. Conclusive are the evidences for such propositions. Of course, the maximum worth is had when both the great subject and the great teacher are joined, and the minimum, alas! is touched when the small subject and the small teacher are united.

But, for the present purpose, it is to Doctor Harris as a man and as a friend that one brings a special offering of happy interpretation. In him the apparent contradictories were reconciled. He was among the ablest of all men I have known, yet was also among the humblest. The humility which filled his heart, and covered him in his bearing with the robe of modesty, was yet in no sense a garment of humiliation. He knew that, compared with ordinary men, he was able. But he did not so compare himself, but rather with the unmeasured pillars, and therefore he recognized how small he was. I have never known a man who could so naturally talk about himself as a third person. He was egoistic without being egotistic, and self-ward without a tinge of selfishness. He lived

at once in this world of ours and above it. The vision
of his being and the reach of his power were in and
toward the infinite. Yet his service belonged to the
here and the now. He once said to me, in laughter,
that one of his chief duties as United States Commissioner of Education was to propagate and to protect herds of reindeer in Alaska. This duty was accepted as important, and it was well performed. In
him were joined together a mind keen, alert, inquisi-
tive, comprehensive, with a heart of tenderness, love,
and appreciation. Between such a mind and such a
heart, and perhaps uniting them, was a conscience—
the conscience of a Puritan New Englander—and,
above all and in all, was felt the faith of a devout
and devoted Christian. In him were found incarnated two elements of his theory of education: Education was concerned with the fittingness of the
individual to his own age, a certain "subsumption"
(as he put it) to his species and environment. Education was also concerned with the emancipation of
the individual unto the infinities and the eternities.
In dear Doctor Harris we ever find the union of the
citizenship of his own age and the freedom of the
whole human race joined to that liberty which belongs to the sons of God. Death seemed to have no
more power over him than it had over his great friend
and teacher, Kant. For age was his youth. At a
dinner given to him on his seventy-fifth birthday, he
remarked that he was just becoming able to apply his heart unto wisdom. I still think of Doctor

Harris going on and still applying that heart, which means also a mind and a soul, unto a wisdom which belong to the circumference of the world of omniscience.

VIII

WILLIAM RAINEY HARPER

WILLIAM RAINEY HARPER, born in New Concord, Ohio,
July 26, 1856; died January 6, 1906. Graduate of
Muskingum College, 1870; member, Masonic College, Macon, Tennessee, 1875-76; tutor, 1876-79;
principal, preparatory department, Denison University, Granville, Ohio, 1879-80; professor of Hebrew, Baptist Union Theological Seminary, Chicago,
1879-86; professor of Semitic Languages, Yale,
1886-91; professor of Biblical Literature, 1889-
91; principal of Chautauqua College of Liberal
Arts, 1885-91; head professor of Semitic Languages
and Literature, and president of the University of
Chicago, 1891-1906. Member of the Chicago Board
of Education, 1896-98; director, Haskell Oriental
Museum.

Author: Constructive Studies in the Priestly Ele-
ment in the Old Testament; Religion and the Higher
Life; The Structure of the Text of the Book of
Amos; The Structure of the Text of the Book of
Moses; The Trend of the Higher Education; Amos
and Hosea (International Critical Commentary);
and books on Hebrew, Latin, and Greek, texts.
Editor, The Biblical World, The American Journal
of Theology, and The American Journal of Semitic
Languages and Literature.

VIII

WILLIAM RAINEY HARPER

OF a summer night, many years ago, I found my-self traveling with Harper from Charleston, South Carolina, to Washington. At an early hour, I saw him lying in his berth wearing his big spectacles. I expressed a bit of curious surprise. "Oh, yes," he replied, "I always wear my glasses at night. I can see, if anything happens, and am ready for any-thing." The little incident illustrates three char-acteristics of Harper—vision, prevision, energy. For Harper had vision without visionariness, and his vision was prophetic. Following the sight and the prophetic foresight, the sense of achievement went forth from his understanding.

The same three elements are dominant likewise in the character of his friend and co-worker, Mr. John D. Rockefeller. Uniting Mr. Rockefeller's qualities with the same qualities in Harper, the movement of this double trinity of great forces to an identical end could not fail in creating a uniquely rich result. The result was and is the University of Chicago.

163

Harper was primarily a student, a scholar, a teacher. Early did he use his power as a student. Many men are obliged to be content with being just students. (One might add that they ought to be very happy if they are even students!) But Harper, the student, soon became Harper, the scholar, without, of course, ceasing to be a student, indeed because he was a student. And Harper, the student and the scholar, soon became Harper, the teacher; and Harper, student, scholar, teacher, became an administrator, and so continued, till a relentless disease put its fatal hand upon his body.

In these three intellectual relations he used and showed the qualities and elements of the educational executive—an educational executive who became a university president, and, as a university president, his public recognition early and firmly became fixed, and will, I believe, remain a rich memory and heritage.

An institution, known as Chicago University, was founded in the year 1857. Its founders and chief supporters were members of the Baptist Church. After twenty-nine years of service, it surrendered its charter in 1886. Near that time, the leading members of the Baptist churches in the United States, especially the officers of its Education Society, became interested in establishing an institution of the higher learning and teaching as an offering of their church to the highest forces of the world. At one period it seemed not improbable that the University

of Rochester, enlarged and enriched, might be selected
as the institution for making so noteworthy an offering. Chicago was, however, finally chosen. Mr.
Rockefeller became, or was already, interested. He
made a large contribution to the resulting new University of Chicago, a contribution which, followed by
many others, finally came to aggregate, as reported
to me by the auditor of the university, $34,708,375.28.
This vast sum is, I think, the largest sum ever given,
during his life-time, by one man to a single institution of learning. Contrast this vast sum with the
$50,000, which in 1847 Abbott Lawrence gave to
Harvard University to found the Scientific School
which bore his name. At that time this sum was said
to be the largest sum given at one time to a college
by an individual during his life-time.

To the headship of the re-founded institution, William Rainey Harper was called. At the time, Harper
was professor of the Semitic Languages at Yale. For
the following sixteen years, and for the sixteen years
only, did he live and labor.

"Here thou art fallen in thy joyful days,
Life quench'd within thy breast, light in thy eyes." [1]

The period, however, was long enough to introduce
and to fix certain definite policies which have become
general values and forces for the higher education.
Among them are, first, the establishment of the fun-

[1] "The North Shore Watch." Canto I. By George E.
Woodberry.

damental elements of what subsequently became
known as the junior college; second, the division of
the academic year into four terms of three months
each—a division which is coming in fuller measure,
to be a form or function of the university; third,
the general spread of education by correspondence,
and by university extension. To the establishment
of these forces and to the promotion of the more
normal functions of a university, Harper brought an
original and originating mind, a forceful will, and
a controlling, persuasive, and pervasive personality.

In all these years he continued to teach. Though
Harper will be known as the first president of the
University of Chicago, he would prefer, I am sure, to
be remembered as a teacher. He once said to me,
"There are only three happy college presidents in
this country. One is Eliot, one is Northrop (the
third must now be nameless)." "You are happy,
aren't you?" I asked. "No, I am not," he replied.
"I am going to resign this presidency just as soon
as I can. I am not so happy as I should be as a
teacher only."

Many, diverse, and rich were Harper's gifts. The
richest and the most embracing of them all was his
energy. Harper had energy tremendous. He had
initiative, power, a unique forth-puttingness. His
energy was shown not only in his presidency, but also
before its years. He was the head of the great popular movement known as Chautauqua, in certain important relations. He was, while an academic pro-

fessor of Hebrew, making the world learn Hebrew, and making the world learn Hebrew by letter-writing. I have seen, heard, and felt him teaching the language to a class of beginners. The hour was the hour before breakfast. He not only had the three o'clock courage, but he also had the half-past-five morning hour of study and labor. He was in his daily appointments earlier than Harnack, to whose classroom in Berlin I have gone at seven o'clock of the morning. For many years he went to bed at midnight and got up at five. To a theological student, depressed because he could arrange no hour to meet the teacher for advanced work, Harper said, "Are you free at five-thirty in the morning?" "Yes!" "Then come every day at that hour." He was a member of the Chicago Board of Education, and served as chairman of its most important committee. His successor, Harry Pratt Judson, who gave a noble realization to Harper's policies, soon after Harper's death, wrote of him:

"He was a great teacher. The history of colleges in this country records not a few men among college presidents who were in the truest sense teachers— Mark Hopkins, Wayland, Nott, Anderson. Dr. Harper was marvelously different from any one in this list. He had, however, first of all, the teacher's enthusiasm. It was his delight to impart instruction, to invigorate the ambitions of young men, to draw out their strong qualities, to surround his subject with living interest. He had the teacher's faculty

of winning young minds. He never ceased to be in
thorough sympathy with the thought and ideals of
youth. He could therefore fully understand how
the mind of the young man worked, how it made its
approaches toward grasping a new knowledge, how
it grew and developed in many ways. He had the
rare faculty of organizing his material in a lucid and
rational way. He was always an inspiration in the
classroom, and further he had also this very peculiar
faculty of the true teacher, that the classroom was
always an inspiration to him."[2] For he "had high
ideals of what a university professor should be. He
must be a teacher indeed, but first and foremost he
must be a scholar, in love with learning, with a passion for research, an investigator who would search
new fields of knowledge and who would give the results of his studies to the world."[3]

A former student, now a distinguished clergyman,
has said to me that the greatest of several great influences which Harper had over him lay in his power
to "quicken my will to work. Why, I would work
for him day and night. The end of every lecture at
once sent me to the library where I toiled unceasingly
and with all enthusiasm. Of my other teachers, one
gave me a method of study, a method which I still
follow; another gave me thoughts as seeds which are

[2] "William Rainey Harper." By Harry Pratt Judson.
National Education Association: Fiftieth Anniversary Volume,
1857-1906, p. 294.

[3] "Ernest De Witt Burton: A Biographical Sketch." By
Thomas Wakefield Goodspeed. pp. 29-30.

still sprouting; yet another pronounced in his class-room an oration which was so perfect that, at its close, the class sat spell-bound. But Harper made me work and with a will which still remains.'' Each of these methods has value, though the oratorical the least. But the other three have worths greatest. The second named was used by Harper's successor by one remove, Burton, of brief, yet constructive, term, ended by death.

The books which Harper wrote are an illustration and give proof of his abounding forcefulness. They are numerous, covering more than a dozen titles, and on themes as diverse as the Book of Amos, the religion of the Old Testament priests, the prospects of the small college, and the trend of the higher education.

The president of a college and its chief benefactor, or benefactors, do, or should, represent relations of complete understanding and of warm friendship. Such a relation existed between Mr. Rockefeller and Harper. It is worth while to quote at length what Mr. Rockefeller says in his ''Random Reminiscences of Men and Events,'' a volume published in 1909. This interpretation comes to take on a more impor-tant meaning by reason of having the approval of so great a co-worker, with both Mr. Rockefeller and President Harper, as Dr. Wallace Buttrick, whose death—so recent—emphasizes his essential greatness. Mr. Rockefeller says:

''The mention of this promising young institution [The University of Chicago] always brings to my mind the figure of Dr. William R. Harper, whose enthusiasm for its work was so great that no vision of its future seemed too large. My first meeting with Dr. Harper was at Vassar College, where one of my daughters was a student. He used to come, as the guest of Dr. James M. Taylor, the president, to lecture on Sundays; and as I frequently spent week-ends there, I saw and talked much with the young professor, then of Yale, and caught in some degree the contagion of his enthusiasm.

"When the university had been founded, and he had taken the presidency, our great ambition was to secure the best instructors and to organize the new institution, unhampered by traditions, according to the most modern ideals. He raised millions of dol-lars among the people of Chicago and the Middle West, and won the personal interest of their leading citizens. Here lay his great strength, for he secured not only their money, but their loyal support and strong personal interest—the best kind of help and coöperation. He built even better than he knew. His lofty ideals, embodied in the university, awakened a deeper interest in higher education throughout the Central West, and stirred individuals, denominations and legislatures to effective action. The world will probably never realize how largely the present splen-did university system of the Central Western States is due indirectly to the genius of this man.

"With all his extraordinary power of work and his executive and organizing ability, Dr. Harper was a man of exquisite personal charm. We count it among the rich and delightful experiences of our home-life that Dr. and Mrs. Harper could occasionally spend days together with us for a brief respite from the exacting cares and responsibilities of the university work. As a friend and companion, in daily intercourse, no one could be more delightful than he.

"It has been my good fortune to contribute at various times to the University of Chicago, of which Dr. Harper was president, and the newspapers not unnaturally supposed at such times that he used the occasions of our personal association to secure these contributions. The cartoonists used to find this a fruitful theme. They would picture Dr. Harper as a hypnotist weaving his magic spell, or would represent him forcing his way into my inner office where I was pictured as busy cutting coupons and from which delightful employment I incontinently fled out of the window at sight of him; or they would represent me as fleeing across rivers on cakes of floating ice, with Dr. Harper in hot pursuit; or perhaps he would be following close on my trail, like the wolf in the Russian story, in inaccessible country retreats, while I escaped only by means of the slight delays I occasioned him by now and then dropping a million-dollar bill, which he would be obliged to stop and pick up.

"These cartoons were intended to be very amusing, and some of them certainly did have a flavour of humour, but they were never humourous to Dr. Har-

per. They were in fact a source of deep humiliation
to him, and I am sure he would, were he living, be
glad to have me say, as I now do, that during the
entire period of his presidency of the University of
Chicago, he never once either wrote me a letter or
asked me personally for a dollar of money for the
University of Chicago. In the most intimate daily
intercourse . . . the finances of the University . . .
were never canvassed or discussed.

"The method of procedure in this case has been
substantially the same as with all other contributions. The presentation of the needs of the university has been made in writing by the officers of the
university, whose special duty it is to prepare its
budgets and superintend its finances. A committee
of the trustees, with the president, have annually
conferred, at a fixed time, with our Department of
Benevolence, as to its needs. Their conclusions have
generally been entirely unanimous, and I have found
no occasion hitherto seriously to depart from their
recommendations. There have been no personal interviews and no personal solicitations. It has been
a pleasure to me to make these contributions, but that
pleasure has arisen out of the fact that the university
is located in a great center of empire; that it has
rooted itself in the affections and interest of the people among whom it is located; that it is doing a great
and needed work—in fine, that it has been able to attract and to justify the contributions of its patrons,
East and West. It is not personal interviews and

impassioned appeals, but sound and justifying worth, that should attract and secure the fund of philanthropy." [4]

I make this quotation at so great length for two reasons: first, the passage reveals Mr. Rockefeller's aims and methods in the use of large sums of money for educational purposes; and, secondly, it intimates an ideal relation which should ever exist between college benefactors and college executives.

I wish I were able to make an etching, physical, intellectual, moral, religious, personal, of Harper. A full face and a round head, crowning a chubby form, with features well adjusted to each other, with intimations of a smile of light and of radiance breaking forth from the whole countenance, with an intellectual and emotional alertness manifest in eye and moving face—such in bare and brief outline was the dear and great man. The exterior was the clothing of a mind philosophic, linguistic and literary, but more linguistic than philosophic. Lord Bryce has said of Henry Sidgwick, that his "was a mind of singular subtlety, fertility, and ingenuity, which applied to every topic an extremely minute and patient analysis." [5] Harper's mind was rather of the broad, generalizing type, giving visions and intimations, more concerned with tides than with the individual waves of scholarly movements. His was essentially

[4] pp. 177-182.
[5] "Studies in Contemporary Biography." By James Bryce. p. 332.

a rationalizing mind, seeing things in proportion, and reasoning by well-balanced processes unto wise and just conclusions.

Without impulsiveness, Harper had tremendous power of inspiration. His laboriousness and enthusiasm were contagious. He was cordial, companionable, democratic. Without the gift of free, extempore public speech, he talked to personal friends freely, frankly, with a constant sense of intellectual and emotional quickening. He could talk of his own work and of himself with a full sense of humility and of modesty; for he was an idealist, although given to practical and immediate concerns and duties. He sought to see, to feel, and to use all in the light of the highest relations. He had a genius for friendship, quite as much as for teaching, loving individuals more than classes. He was informal, genuine, tolerant, laying hold of realities beneath appearances. Though the president of a university, about two-thirds of whose trustees, by the original foundation, were required to be members of the Baptist Church, he was, of course, far more of a Christian than he was a denominationalist. In the recent elimination of certain sectarian elements in the formal instruments of the university, his spirit cannot but rejoice. He lived and worked, seeing the invisible. He knew that the material form, even of a university, is temporal and must pass. But he knew, also, that the true and the good and the beautiful, in character and in human institutions, are to endure.

The last year of his life confirmed the real greatness of his character. It was a year of suffering and of pain, the end of which he and all recognized as inevitable. Of that year, his associate, the late Bishop Vincent, has a right to be a special interpreter, an interpreter who was also a great co-worker:

"The apostle of culture, the aggressive promoter of colossal educational schemes had one more testimony to give, one more appeal to make to an eagerly attentive constituency. But that testimony needed an ordeal of limitation and pain, of agony inexpressible. And God led him—our noble and heroic Harper—down into the darkness, and a path of suffering few men are required to tread. And the ordeal was accepted. From the lips of the resolute leader, the brilliant organizer, the self-reliant and scholarly teacher, came the words of prayer and witness in the valley of pain: 'God help! . . . God will help! He always helps!' Thus to his splendid lesson of enterprise, resolve, persistency and energy he added the supreme lesson of personal confidence in and surrender to the God of Israel." [6] To him may well be applied the verses which Tennyson gives to his young friend, Hallam, likewise fallen in his youth:

> "And thou art worthy; full of power;
> As gentle; liberal-minded, great,
> Consistent; wearing all that weight
> Of learning lightly like a flower."

[6] "Dr. Harper and Chautauqua." By. John H. Vincent. *The Chautauquan.* Vol. XLIII, March, 1906. p. 64.

"And, doubtless, unto thee is given
A life that bears immortal fruit
In such great offices as suit
The full-grown energies of heaven."

IX

JAMES HARRIS FAIRCHILD

JAMES HARRIS FAIRCHILD, born in Stockbridge, Massachusetts, November 17, 1817; died March 19, 1902; graduated from Oberlin College, 1838; ordained to ministry, 1841. Tutor, 1838-42, professor of Languages, 1842-47, professor of Mathematics, 1847-58, professor of Moral Philosophy and Theology, 1858, president, Oberlin College, 1866-89 (resigned); Finney professor from 1889, afterwards professor emeritus, Oberlin Theological Seminary. Author: Moral Philosophy; Needed Phases of Christianity; Oberlin: the Colony and the College; Elements of Theology; Woman's Right to the Ballot.

JAMES HARRIS FAIRCHILD

WESTWARD the star of the higher education has taken its way, keeping time with peoples moving over the mountain and crossing the prairie in the covered wagon. The movement has on the whole been along the northern parallels. The Southern States have not been as deeply concerned, although Virginia's influence was felt in the foundation of the colleges of Kentucky. It was also a movement contemporary with the increasing anti-slavery agitation from 1825 to 1861.

The academic flight was moreover guided and quickened by wise and daring leaders. The record is a new calendar of great men:

Chase, the first Bishop of Ohio and of Illinois, the founder of two colleges, Kenyon and Jubilee, a constructive pioneer whose first episcopal palace was a log hut, and whose students had, as their dormitories, blockhouses, whose prophecy of the future was made good in the centennial year of Kenyon;

Sturtevant, enthusiastic, independent, heroic, persistent, laborious, who lived to see the tireless labors of his early and mature years firmly established in Illinois College;

Storrs, of the great family, first president of Western Reserve College, of whose passion for the freedom of the slaves Whittier sang:

> "Glory to God forever!
>   Beyond the despot's will
> The soul of Freedom liveth
>   Imperishable still.
> The words which thou hast uttered
>   Are of that soul a part,
> And the good seed thou hast scattered
>   Is springing from the heart.
>
> In the evil days before us,
>   And the trials yet to come,—
> In the shadow of the prison,
>   Or the cruel martyrdom,—
> We will think of thee, O brother!
>   And thy sainted name shall be
> In the blessing of the captive,
>   And the anthem of the free."[1]

William Greenleaf Eliot, the first Unitarian preacher west of the Mississippi, first president of the board of directors, and chancellor, of Washington University, St. Louis, consecrated to a great vision, eager to know, and to do, his duty, rejoicing in self-sacrifice, a veritable John Harvard of the Central West;

[1] "To the Memory of Charles B. Storrs." By John Greenleaf Whittier.

Magoun, forceful in mind, eager, expectant, enthusiastic, an optimist, a theologian, compelled at home to be an executive, and abroad a solicitor of funds, who laid great foundations for the noble college at Grinnell;

Chapin, a gracious personality, who won his way by kindness, considerateness, a man of far-searching vision, the father of Beloit;

Butterfield, with the manners of a prince and the heart of a king, and with more than the typical king's mind, laboring to make a little college at Olivet true to its name;

Strong, a gentleman at home in any society, a wise counselor of considerate friendliness, beloved, sacrificing, and willing to sacrifice, all for his beloved Carleton;

Brooks of Tabor, vigorous of body to match a quenchless spirit, enduring all to establish his little college in Iowa;

Merriman, the philosopher in the pulpit and executive chair, who united the zeal of the old-time prophet with the fighting quality of the new theologian;

Ward, of the late time, the man of faith, of tender heart, and of the long, long thought, who founded at Yankton, the first college in the boundlessness of the Upper Missouri Valley.

Oh, it is a glorious company of prophets, apostles, martyrs, and saints. They take their places with the best that this earth has given and has received. They, and scores of others whom I might name, who preceded and followed them, formed constituent forces and factors in the civilization of the nineteenth century. They had the faith in God with which the Mayflower Pilgrims were inspired. They were possessed by a belief in the power of the Gospel which sent the Jesuit fathers into and through the Canadian forests. They had that confidence in learning and in the Gospel which quickened and sustained the Puritans who founded Harvard. They were the worthy successors, companions, and forerunners of generations who have followed the westward star of the Christian empire for four centuries.

Among all these heroes of the academic faith, however, uniting the earlier and the later decades, none is more commanding than Fairchild—Fairchild, be it added, of Oberlin. For the two names deserve to be joined. Fairchild was a member of its first freshman class of 1834, and his connection with the college ended only with his death in 1902, a length of association longer by six years than the association of Mark Hopkins with Williams.

Oberlin, beginning in 1833, preceding by only a year Fairchild's entrance, was also the forerunner of other great beginnings, and for at least a generation, too, Oberlin continued to be a condition and an agency of reforms, as well as of origins. It was indeed historically sympathetic with its own early and envisaging period. For that fourth decade of the nineteenth century was an age of wonder and of wonders, as Mr. Lowell has described in some moving paragraphs; and among all these wonders, social, theological, philosophic, stands Oberlin. Contrasts of wonders, too, were not lacking. The freedom given to women in education was matched, and perhaps surpassed, by the liberty given to colored people in social affairs. The theory of perfectionism, of theological teaching and writing, found a counterpart in the manual work of self-supporting students. Its seclusion in the primeval wilderness—a reservoir of power—seemed to give a special impulse to the foreign mission bands which it sent to the corners of the earth. Its "foibles," as its historian has called its conditions and forces, seen in the light of subsequent achievements, have helped to prove that certain apparent foolishnesses may finally become symbols and powers of wisdom. In and of all such forces and conditions and methods, as manifest in Oberlin, Fairchild composed a large part. With him, be it added, men of power and of place were associated at different periods. Of them, Finney was chief, and following him, Mahan, Morgan, Cowles, and Dascomb.

To all who knew James Harris Fairchild intimately, and for the generations, as well as to me who knew him imperfectly and for a few years only, he has ever seemed to be the incarnation of impartial judgment and justice. I heard President Eliot say, in the great response which he made to the demonstration given for him on his ninetieth birthday, that, of all the testimonials offered, that one which commended his fairness was most pleasant. Fairchild embodied a like quality. He was, as was Eliot himself, a good listener. He was unlike too many college presidents to whom professors come to ask a question, and who so overcome the petitioner by their own talk that the professor departs without having had an opportunity to state his problem. Fairchild wished, before giving answer, to hear all sides of the question proposed. His commanding head ever seemed to me to be typical of his mind, well-proportioned, spherical. A friend speaks of "the fine balance of [his] powerful faculties," and of his having "a genius for sanity."[2] Another friend says that he was "not a genuis but an example and a monument of universal completeness won by scholarly work; an ideal example to every college student—calm, sagacious, scrupulously just."[3] A dean of women of his college, Mrs. Adelia A. F. Johnston, says of his judicial mind: "Always calm and seemingly unmoved himself he presided over the most exciting discussion in such a judicial manner that not a man felt for a moment that he had escaped from control."[4]

This judicialness showed itself in executive act and procedure as well as in decision. In the year 1855, when the struggle to make Kansas a free state was in its crisis, many Oberlin students decided to go to Kansas to give aid. Certain members of the faculty favored the emigrating movement. In the midst of the excitement, conducting the chapel service, Fair-

[2] "James Harris Fairchild." By Albert Temple Swing. p. 199.   [3] *Ibid.*, p. 200.   [4] *Ibid.*, p. 357.

child prayed, says a student, that the young men might not run before they were sent. He made clear, in a way judicial, calm, persuasive, conclusive, that the young students could better serve their country by pursuing their studies in quietness. His judicialness in executive act, as well as in judgment, was a primary element in his character, and a primary element in his service. As his associate and biographer, Swing, says:

"He welcomed every deep revelation of truth, but he held in rigid restraint every wild and radical tendency. Standing out in the forefront of one of the most free and aggressively evangelical communities in all the Puritan land, and facing squarely and hopefully towards the future, President Fairchild was one of the noblest conservatives which our American Puritanism has yet produced. By his clear and comprehensive grasp of the fundamentals of Nature and Revelation, by his wise and frank agnosticism in the presence of unrevealed mysteries, by his calm and trustful cheer extended to the inquiring doubter, he was a bulwark of strength for a transitional age. And to James H. Fairchild more than to any other one man is due the fact that conservatism and progressiveness came into a new harmony, and an era of good understanding dawned in our new world."[5]

With this judicialness what may be called his simplicity—personal, intellectual, moral—was closely linked. Simplicity may be bare, barren, forbidding.

[5] *Ibid.*, p. 210.

Or it may be rich, enriching, complete, deep, comprehensive. Fairchild's simplicity was of the type which Emerson commends, of the "grand" form, or of a form so grand that it helped to constitute—as Emerson also intimates it may be—greatness. The simplicity began as far back as the outer experiences of his childhood. Of these experiences he himself has said:

"The experience of children brought up in the simplicity of the new country can scarcely be repeated at the present day. The advantages of civilized society, talked of by parents but never seen by the children, made a powerful impression. The steepled church back in the eastern home wrought upon the imagination of the child, as it could not if an object of daily sight. The thought of the college, to one who had only seen the log schoolhouse, was material for castle building by day and for dreams at night. From mountain summit, and towering monument and capitol dome, in later years, my eyes have rested on many a goodly scene of nature and of art but the thrill of surprise and satisfaction which I experienced on my first view of the village of Elyria, from my father's ox wagon, has never been equaled. The village at that time consisted of perhaps twenty buildings. No such surprise awaits the children of the present day."[6]

This simplicity, thus originating in the exterior condition, continued throughout life. He seemed to

[6] *Ibid.*, p. 40.

embody what Tennyson interprets the Duke of Wellington as possessing:

> "Rich in saving common sense,
> And, as the greatest only are,
> In his simplicity sublime." [7]

The environment of the first years, continued for all the decades, was fitting to his intellectual development. Writing, in the year 1841, to the woman who afterward became his wife, he says:

"Do not think now that I have had any striking revelation made to my mind. No, it is only an apprehension of these simple truths which lie on the surface of things. God is good. I am bound to love Him. His creatures are wretched. I am under obligation to direct them to 'the Lamb of God who taketh away the sin of the world.' " [8]

To his theology and to his preaching, as well as to his character, belonged such simplicity. It has an illustration in the headings of a sermon which, it is said, made a deep impression upon its hearers. The chief propositions of the sermon were:

"A sinner is one who lives for some other purpose than to do good. . . . The proper end and aim of life is to do good and attain good. . . . In this life [of religion] so just and right and good no sinner has a share. . . . Thus the mischief of sin reaches to God. It cannot pluck Him from His throne, or dim His

[7] *Ibid.*, p. 390.   [8] *Ibid.*, p. 115.

glory, or thwart the good purpose of His goodness; but the ingratitude of sin must pain Him. . . . But God's substantial blessedness is beyond the sinner's reach. . . . The sinner sometimes tries to find comfort in the idea that he does not *intend* mischief and that he has no wish to do *harm*. . . . But it is upon the sinner's own good that sin works with the surest and most fatal effect." [9] Such orderliness of logical reasoning from proposition to proposition, such simplicity, or even simplicities, and such evident judicialness resulted in, and were in turn the result of, a democratic spirit, and a point of view also democratic. Fairchild was as remote from the autocrat as from the aristocrat. His was a character grown out of the early soil of the Lake Region of Ohio. President Eliot, who has sometimes been interpreted as embodying autocratic power, and in most respects falsely, has said:

"The president of a university should never exercise an autocratic or one-man power. He should be often an inventing and animating force, and often a leader; but not a ruler or autocrat. His success will be due more to powers of exposition and persuasion combined with persistent industry, than to any force of will or habit of command. Indeed, one-man power is always objectionable in a university, whether lodged in president, secretary of the trustees, dean, or head of department. In order to make progress of

[9] *Ibid.*, pp. 178-183.

a durable sort, the president will have to possess his soul in patience." [10]

Such was Fairchild, as a man and as a president. No more impressive illustration of his social democracy could be desired than what he says in a notable paragraph in his inaugural address, given in 1866, regarding the negro:

"Our work has brought us into connection with the world without, and has contributed to give direction to our efforts. I refer to the attitude of the college towards the colored people of the land. . . . It has been a privilege to the colored student to be admitted here. It has been an equal blessing to his white brother to be so educated as to take naturally a right position on the great question of our country and our time. Our educational work would have been greatly marred if this work had been omitted. But it is not a fact of the past alone; it reaches into the future. The work of the education and enfranchisement of the colored people is before us for another generation. The war has not completed but merely introduced it. A share in this work is laid upon us, in the providence of God, by our constitution and our history." [11]

As president, too, Fairchild represented the very opposite of the despotic element which certain inter-

[10] "University Administration." By Charles W. Eliot. p. 238.
[11] "James Harris Fairchild." By Albert Temple Swing. p. 233.

preters associate with the great office. A colleague, Judson Smith, says of him:

"He shared with his professors all the honor and repute and glory that came to the college during his administration. We were made to feel that the college was *ours* as truly as it was *his,* that its success depended on *us* as much as on *him,* that we were equal partners in a great enterprise into which it was our duty and our joy to throw all our enthusiasm and gifts and powers and to devote to it our lives themselves. We all knew that *he* was the *great* man among us, that he meant more to the college than any one of us ever could; and it was a privilege to work with him, under his leadership, in a great task to which his presence gave dignity and a priceless worth." [12]

The democratic spirit of equality, liberty, and fraternity, manifest in his relations to his colleagues of the faculty, were no less manifest in his association with another body, constituting the college, the board of trustees. A member of this board for twenty years, General A. B. Nettleton, himself a fine spirit of commanding power, says:

"In matters of routine, about which he would naturally know better than any trustee, he always had a definite program, clearly stated, which commended itself by its reasonableness and which was always confirmed for substance. On questions in-

[12] *Ibid.,* p. 389.

volving new departures or changes of policy, with courtesy and deference he stated the case and invited discussion and thus seemed to evolve a plan from the suggestions and consensus of the board, while in fact a closer scrutiny showed that the conclusion reached usually embodied his own well-matured thought and previous judgment. He was careful to have it understood that in matters affecting the college faculty or their work, they had been fully consulted and had approved the suggestions submitted by him. He was never other than open-minded and hospitable to new suggestions, provided they were reasonable. He was uniformly modest in presenting his own views on a controverted point, yet without timidity. As the presiding officer of a business board he was ever the gentleman in business, never the autocrat nor the dogmatist. I cannot recall an instance in which the president's judgment in matters financial as well as educational did not prove to be sound and far-sighted.'' [13]

Yet though, like Mark Hopkins, and Wayland of Brown, Fairchild embodied the great qualities of the president, he was also, like Hopkins and Wayland, no less great as a teacher. For, a teacher he was before he became an executive, and a teacher he continued to be while serving as president. In a college, such as Oberlin was in the later decades of the last century, the pleasures of the president need not interfere fundamentally with the duties of the professor.

[13] *Ibid.*, pp. 379-380.

Fairchild taught, and taught, like many early professors, many subjects. He was for a time "Professor of Languages," as the old phrase went, teaching Latin, Greek, and Hebrew. English composition and declamation also fell to his lot. The chair of mathematics he filled, and filled to overflowing. But his teaching of moral philosophy and of theology constitute his chief oral contributions, as do his books, on these two fundamental themes, his principal written offerings. The diversity of these subjects reminds one, both by likeness and by contrast, of what Saintsbury tells of himself when a student at Merton. In his early time, he says that, of a single day, he read Heine's poems, The Three Musketeers, Hebrew, and Thucydides.

It was not, however, the aim of scholarly wealth as a religious and ethical content and purpose which dominated and guided Fairchild's teaching unto great ends. His aim was just as practical as it was practicable. That aim was to make "the end of his teaching to develop manhood and to secure Christian service in their wider relationships. . . . His teaching of theology and of ethics was for the purpose of revealing the great fundamental and eternal laws of Being and making them conscious forces in bringing men nearer to each other and to God,— to establish the moral and religious unity of the Universe." [14]

The content of Fairchild's theological teaching was

[14] *Ibid.*, pp. 187-188.

a continuation of Finney's system. It helped to constitute what has become known as the "Oberlin Theology." He presented and developed the principles
and tenets of Finney—at once a theologian and evan-
gelist. But Fairchild represented rather the theological than the fiery evangelistic traditions of Finney. That duty is eternal and imperative,—the general following-out of Kant's principles,—that the
obedience, sufferings, and death of Christ, constituting
his atonement, form the great motive in the repentance of the sinner, that punishment for the unre-
pentant is inevitable, were among the great theological
fundamentals. Fairchild presented them as appealing
to the common sense of man, and as embodying both
intuitive and logical relationships. Such propositions
he laid down, with the force of a judicial reasonableness, and in a mood of quiet reserve and commanding
power.

With this solidity of content in teaching went
along a warm and high conception of the personal
relation of teacher and student. Great teachers embody both a great content and intimate penetration
of mind and of heart with the heart and the mind
of the student. He "considered the teaching function a very important one in education, and he believed that the best teaching quality would be called
out in one who stood near the pupil rather than in a
purely scholastic world at a great distance from
him." [15]

[15] *Ibid.*, p. 146.

To this relation of the teacher and president, as well as to every other relation of life, Fairchild brought the best qualities of a heart, tender and brave. Its tenderness was remote from softness as was its bravery from hardness. He went about doing good in the college and general community, as a citizen and as a friend. His relation was pastoral, both in college and village. There was no sorrow in a home in which he did not sympathize, no gladness in which he did not exult, no thought of baseness against which he was not indignant, and no act of baseness against which he failed to express his scorn.

Since the accession of Finney in 1851, Oberlin has had five presidents. Finney, himself, a great man of his generation—great as a president and as a thinker —whose theological system was bathed in the atmosphere of fiery zeal; Ballantine, the rich and enriching scholar; Barrows, the preacher of eloquence, for the people and for the thoughtful; King, the philosopher and the executive, beloved of all. But no one of the quintet seems to unite the qualities and elements of the teacher and of the president as the spiritually-minded, judicious, and judicial, the pacific, great-hearted, and the high-purposing Fairchild. In his personality, the best Oberlin character and influence flowered forth in moving beauty and radiance. Among all the academic heroes and pioneers, with whose names I began this chapter, no figure is more commanding and no memory more lasting than Fairchild of Oberlin.

X

RICHARD SALTER STORRS

Richard Salter Storrs was born in Braintree, Massachusetts, August 21, 1821; died June 5, 1900. Graduate of Amherst, 1839; teacher in Monson Academy and Williston Seminary; studied law under Rufus Choate, but gave up law because of his deeper interest in theology; graduated, Andover Theological Seminary, 1845; ordained to ministry, 1845; pastor, Harvard Congregational Church, Brookline, Massachusetts, 1845-46; pastor of the Church of the Pilgrims, Brooklyn, New York, 1846-1900; president of American Board of Commissioners for Foreign Missions, 1887-97; an editor of The Independent, 1848-61.

Author: Report on the Revised Edition of the English Version of the Bible; The Constitution of the Human Soul; Conditions of Success in Preaching without Notes; Early American Spirit, and the Genesis of It; Declaration of Independence, and the Effects of It; John Wycliffe and the First English Bible; Manliness in the Scholar; Recognition of the Supernatural; Bernard of Clairvaux; Divine Origin of Christianity; The Prospective Advance of Christian Missions; Forty Years of Pastoral Life.

X

RICHARD SALTER STORRS

PREACHER OF SPLENDID ELOQUENCE

IF the Boston historians, Prescott, Parkman, Motley; if the Concord essayists, Emerson, Thoreau, Alcott; if the Cambridge poets, Lowell and Longfellow, represent definite and historical movements, "the Brooklyn preachers" stand for a distinct age in the American pulpit. Other historians, essayists, poets, there were than those who dwelt on the banks of the Charles or of the Concord River. So also there were other preachers than those of Brooklyn Heights. There were Bushnell, of Hartford, a genuis; Phillips Brooks, of human and more than human vision; Park, of regal power; Phelps, of spiritual unction; A. L. Stone, of both Boston and San Francisco, a quickening spirit; Murray, of Park Street, a brilliant and lurid flame; Thompson, of Broadway Tabernacle, a scholar in the pulpit; John Hall, the sober and wise expositor. But, above them each, at least in the Congregational ministry—a ministry devoted to preaching—stood forth, as towers, Henry Ward Beecher and Richard Salter Storrs.

Storrs was foreordained to the ministry long be-

fore he was ordained to it, by the laying on of hands,
in the year 1845. At least three generations of
clergymen contributed to his professional heritage.
His great-grandfather was a chaplain in the Revolu-
tionary Army; his grandfather was a pastor at Long-
meadow; and his father, whose name he bore, had,
with the exception of half a decade of missionary
service, a lifelong pastorate at Braintree. He himself
likewise, leaving out a brief first year in Brookline,
was the minister of a single parish for more than fifty
years. He came of and contributed to a noble succession. In a great epoch he wrought, and he wrought
worthily of the greatness of the epoch.

Storrs wrote books, but they were books which were,
in a sense, the transcript of his speeches; or one might
say that his speeches were transcripts of his books.
For it was to public speech in address, historical,
memorial, biographical, interpretative, as well as in
sermon, that he gave himself; and it was through public speech, in diverse forms, that he interpreted, and
through which he influenced, his age.

Storrs' speech was of the classical type of eloquence. One scholar might call it Ciceronian. Another scholar would declare it had the content and the
elevation of Burke. It took to itself great themes. It
was like "Paradise Lost" in its sweep and comprehensiveness. It was religious in its content. It concerned the relationships of God to man, of man to
God, and of men to each other. It was based upon
"a serious, devout, intelligent, inspiring conviction

of the Divine origin and authority of the Gospel, and of its transcendent importance to men.''[1]

The very titles of his addresses, given at the annual meetings of the American Board, illustrate this interpretation: ''The Vision of Christ the Inspiration to Foreign Missions''; ''Our Country's Tribute to the World's Civilization''; ''Foundation Truths of American Missions''; ''The Permanent Motive in Missionary Work.'' In the addresses made under these titles, and in the many other addresses, are found highest elements of eloquent speech. What lofty statement of fundamental principles, what splendor of diction, what grandeur of utterance, what nobility of paragraph and of phrase, what richness of single words! His speech was the speech of the Elizabethan age transferred to America in the nineteenth century. The style reminds one, too, of Macaulay's noble, marching utterances, felt in history, essay, and speech in the House of Commons. It has a 'vigorous quick-step which one always wants in speaking to men, with an earnest conviction.''[2] His professional education, beginning with training for the bar in the office of Rufus Choate, fell at a time when great lawyers addressed a great bench and pleaded before Suffolk County juries. ''Mr. Webster was there, in the intervals between the sessions of the Senate, in the maturity and splendor of his majestic intelligence. Mr. Choate was there—under whose

[1] ''Preaching without Notes.'' By Richard Salter Storrs. p. 74.   [2] *Ibid.*, p. 101.

direction I was prosecuting my studies—whose genius seemed an oriental exotic, brilliant, luxuriant, among the common ferns and brake of New England. Mr. Benjamin R. Curtis was there—recently deceased, then in the prime of his force and his career,—whose power of perspicuous and persuasive legal statement surpassed that, I think, of any speaker whom I have since anywhere heard.''[3]

In a long-continued intimacy, many years ago, I once found myself alone with Dr. Storrs, after one of his Thursday evening addresses at the annual meeting of the American Board. With a twinkle in my eye, I asked him how he did it? With a responsive twinkle in his eye, he told me this incident: ''While I was a student in the office of Rufus Choate,'' he said, ''my health began to flag. I was advised to give up study and to go into the country. I decided to go to Andover. I asked Mr. Choate what books I better take with me. His answer was, 'Take Gibbon!' I took Gibbon and I read Gibbon with the utmost thoroughness. If any influence has helped to form my style, it was Gibbon's 'Rise and Fall'!''

If one compares any page of Gibbon with any page of Storrs' addresses, or, to be particular, if one compare the paragraphs in which the historian pictures the sack of Constantinople with the final paragraphs of the address on ''The Incentives to Missionary Work,'' it is easy to infer that Dr. Storrs was right in

[3] *Ibid.*, p. 13.

his interpretation. The ornate and richly laden chapters of the historian are re-created in the heavily embroidered and elaborately wrought paragraphs of the preacher. The best types of Gothic architecture are illustrated in both utterances.

The results represent what we call extempore speech; for Storrs' speech was usually, though not always, without written notes. But behind the speaking was preparation in wide reading and in constant and deep reflection. History was his peculiar field. His was not the scholarship of the sources; it was the scholarship of the printed volume. His knowledge the technical scholar would call superficial; but in this knowledge he caught the significance of an epoch, the tendency of an age, the traditions of a movement. In illustrative proof, one has only to consult the first two chapters of his "Bernard of Clairvaux," bearing the titles "The tenth century: its extreme depression and fear"; "The eleventh century: its reviving life and promise." The full, if not the critical, knowledge of an era, he made his own. The spirit of a period filled his mind. The lasting teachings of the centuries he caught, interpreted, transmitted. To the mind, thus instructed and disciplined, was given the gift of unwritten speech. The gift, however, he has affirmed, was rather an achievement than a gift. It was utterance, splendid, ornate, tropical. It often suggested the golden glories on wall and canvas of the Italian renaissance. I wish I could give some illustrations. One must be content with simple references to his

volumes,—alas! few, too few, even if of many pages.[4]
The lack, too, of a proper biography further proves
our poverty.

It is ever to be borne in mind that Dr. Storrs was
quite as completely a parish priest and minister and
preacher of the individual Congregational church as
he was the public orator. Of the Church of the Pilgrims he was pastor for more than fifty years. In a
long ministry, the character of the minister weighs
the more as its length increases. In the make-up of
the character of such a pastor, the heart fills a part
at least as important as that of the intellect. In Dr.
Storrs, heart and mind were closely united; so closely
united that one hesitates to attempt to analyze the
whole character. In him affection was joined to intellect, strength to tenderness, forcefulness to graciousness, and individuality to deep and broad sympathies.
People had for him both admiration and affection, and
the affection increased, without admiration diminish-
ing, as knowledge of him deepened. Faith,—quite as
much an emotional grace as an intellectual achievement,—hope, and charity were pervasive and controlling. If he was august, he was also gentle; and if
dignity clothed him as a robe—as it did—the texture
of the robe was woven of the threads of kindness and
of love. These elements sprang from and flowered
forth into consummate culture—a culture of reasoned
judgment, united with an appreciation of the beau-

---

[4] "Addresses on Foreign Missions." p. 153. "Bernard of
Clairvaux." pp. 422-423. Have special illustrative value.

tiful in nature and in man. Indeed, I always felt in
his presence a certain cultured massiveness, or intellectual opulence. A giant he was, yet he never used
his strength like a giant. For if he was bold—as he
was—he was also cautious and prudent; a gentleman
without fear and without reproach. Pure in heart, he
communed with his God, and proclaimed the truths
of God as he perceived and felt them. If his heart
was tender and loving—as it was, and as his parish
knew better than all the rest of the world—his emotions never swept him away from his strong and firm
standards. His own judgments and beliefs were well
buttressed in mighty convictions, yet his sympathy
with those who failed to assent to his positions was
appreciative.

In the tempests of the American Board of Foreign
Missions of the ninth and tenth decades of the last
century, he proved himself a great pilot. He kept
his rudder true in the tossing seas. He brought the
ship into the desired haven, not without damage,
but with the great craft staunch from stem to stern,
able to endure many another hard, long, adventurous
voyage. He had the spirit of the Puritan, as his great
oration intimates; but his Puritanism was pervaded
by the graciousness of the Beatitudes. He embodied,
above most men of his time, the Greek conception of
the true, the good, and the beautiful. The truth he
sought to know, and to express, the good was
wrought into his manhood, and applied in righteousness, and the beautiful became the unconscious in-

carnation in himself of his quest of the highest and
the best.

There was in him, also, wit and humor; more wit
than humor. Illustrations of it abound in remembrance and on printed page. I must content myself
with only a single illustration, which has value of
several sorts. "When I was ordained," writes Dr.
Storrs, "I was in somewhat delicate health, not long
recovered from a serious sickness, thinner and paler
than I have since been. The 'Charge' was given to
me by a most excellent man, a friend of my father
for many years, a friend of my own from my boyhood up, to whom I was attached by many tender and
grateful ties, and whom I had every reason to revere.
He was a man of very full and florid habit, who had
not seen his knees, as they say, for twenty years;
and as he stood speaking on the platform, while I
stood listening beneath, the contrast between us was
undoubtedly striking. It was emphasized, perhaps,
to some of the congregation, when, looking at me with
tears in his eyes, he said very earnestly: 'My young
brother, I charge you, Keep under the body!' " [5]

In the middle and last decades of the last century,
America had three great preachers,—Henry Ward
Beecher, Phillips Brooks, Richard Salter Storrs. On
the Sunday after Beecher died, Brooks, in a sermon,
called Beecher "the greatest preacher in America." [6]
James Bryce once said to me that America had had

[5] "Preaching without Notes." pp. 91-92.
[6] "Life of Phillips Brooks." Vol. II, p. 645.

two great preachers—Henry Ward Beecher and Phillips Brooks. Less known, but to some equally great, was Richard Salter Storrs. Storrs, in an address made immediately after his consecration, as bishop, called Brooks "that magnificent Christian man and teacher."

In certain respects, each of the three excelled the others. In Beecher, the insight of truth was more immediate. In Broooks, truth was a human process and product. In Storrs, truth was an achievement to be won. Beecher had more passion; Brooks, more sustained earnestness; Storrs, greater splendor and majesty in thought and expression. Beecher made a more direct appeal to the masses—he was John Bright and Spurgeon; Brooks, to the youth of the college—he was the academic Gladstone; Storrs, to the classes of noble tradition and fine environment— he was Liddon, but with more earnestness than the Dean of St. Paul's. Beecher's pulpit was a platform. Every worthy cause had a hearing. Brooks' pulpit was a pulpit; it stood for religion in broadest and deepest relations. Storrs' was a desk for intellectual teaching, and for moral and Christian quickening. Beecher was the public orator; Brooks, the expositor; Storrs, the inspirer. Beecher was, at times, the more brilliant; Brooks, the more sustained in great thought; and Storrs, the more magnificent in speech. In Beecher, the thought and expression were the more extempore; in Brooks, the more general and apt for the hour and the place; in Storrs, the more solid and substantial. Beecher's sermons read the least well. Brooks', in the reading, throb with the original thought and feeling. Storrs' move in a dignity and splendor which seem remote and cold to those who never heard that vibrant voice. Each was inspired by the oracles of the Bible, and each worshiped the Christ, the Son of God, the Son of Man, as the source and author of power. Each experienced the rapture and reward of the man of eloquence when he becomes more, far more, than himself, when he with his audience loses himself, when intellect and will and conscience are alike submerged in the surging feelings.

Undoubtedly to some, Storrs' addresses were examples of superficial rhetoric. The shivered rainbows of his discourse seemed to them splendid visions; but for me, however, a pot of intellectual gold rested at its base. The gold and the crimson of his varicolored paragraphs were to some simply autumnal splendors soon to vanish; but to many and to more they were illustrative proof of the ripened growth of the intellect and of the beauty of truth.

Beecher, Brooks, Storrs constitute a trinity of preachers and of Christian ministers not unworthy of inclusion with the Boston historians, the Concord essayists, and the Cambridge poets, their contemporaries. They dwelt, it may be said, as Storrs remarked of the preacher, "in intimate communion with the mind of the Most High."

XI

FRANK WAKELY GUNSAULUS

FRANK WAKELY GUNSAULUS, born Chesterville, Ohio, January 1, 1856; died March 19, 1921. A.B., Ohio Wesleyan, 1875; A.M., 1887; ordained Methodist ministry, 1875; entered Congregational ministry, 1879; pastor, Columbus, Ohio, 1879-81; Newtonville, Massachusetts, 1881-85; Baltimore, 1885-87; Plymouth Church, Chicago, 1887-99; Central Church, Chicago, 1899-1919; president of Armour Institute, 1893-1921. Author: Metamorphoses of a Creed; November at Eastwood; Phidias and Other Poems; Loose Leaves of Song; Songs of Night and Day; Monk and Knight; Transfiguration of Christ; Life of William Ewart Gladstone; The Man of Galilee; Paths to Power; Paths to the City of God; Higher Ministries of Recent English Poetry; The Minister and the Spiritual Life.

FRANK WAKELY GUNSAULUS

FRANK WAKELY GUNSAULUS was, of recent years, one of the most eloquent of the speakers of our English tongue. He may be compared with any member of the small circle who use English eloquently, and in it he would hold a place in the first rank. Gunsaulus had not the sweetness of voice of George William Curtis which both charmed and inspired. But he had a religious force which was not native to the disciple of Brook Farm, or to the occupant of the Editor's Easy Chair of *Harper's Magazine.* He had not the sharpness of eloquent thrust and the insidiousness of wit of Wendell Phillips. But he had a sincerity and moral earnestness which were foreign to the interpreter of "the lost arts" and which were as great as the pleader for the freedom of the slave possessed. He had not the massive fullness of thought of Phillips Brooks, who still remains regnant. But he had a variety of voice and a diversity of manner which to Brooks were foreign. He lacked the splendor of utterance and of verbal diction of Richard Salter Storrs. But he possessed a warmth

of manner which Storrs never intimated in his Gib-
bon-like periods. He had not the versatility of Henry
Ward Beecher, versatile as he himself was. But he
had a certain commandingness and dignity which
Beecher sometimes lacked. He had not the evangel-
ism of Spurgeon, a preacher for whom the agnostic,
John Morley, expressed a liking and whose sermons
Nicoll of the *British Weekly* advised ministers to
read. But he had a range of richness and fullness of
thought far larger and deeper than the man of the
great Tabernacle possessed or used. He had not the
exegetical wisdom and power of Whyte of Free St.
George's. But he had a compellingness in eloquence
which was seldom felt in the Edinburgh preacher and
leader.

All these masters of assemblies have I heard. But
to two others I wish to refer,—whom, of course, I was
not privileged to hear,—Liddon and Newman. If
Gunsaulus lacked the solidity in content, and the
rigor in logic, of the Dean of St. Paul's and the author
of the Bampton Lectures, on the Divinity of our
Lord—as, of course, he did—and if he lacked also the
incomparable music of style of the preacher of St.
Mary's, and the disciple and apostle of the Birming-
ham oratory—as also, of course, he did—he was possessed by a conquering passion in speech and an
oceanic movement in utterance which were unknown
to both the Dean and the Cardinal.

The eloquence of Gunsaulus gave itself to both platform and to pulpit, but to the pulpit more. The

eloquence, too, devoted itself to great themes, as biographical,—Savonarola, and Gladstone,—but, more and most, to religious subjects, and to the Apostles and to the Founder of the faith. He belonged primarily to the order of preachers. Had he lived in the Middle Ages, he would have been made the chief of an order of preaching monks, whose fame would have filled Christendom. His sermons lifted and enlarged thought, quickened and stirred emotion, like a great orchestra. They gave altitude and amplitude, and created vision. They had affluence, intellectual and emotional. They bore one swiftly and strongly, as a mighty river, toward some far-off point of understanding, of sympathy, and of duty.

Gunsaulus was great in other elements besides preaching, as I shall presently intimate. But the throne on which he sat the highest was the throne of the preacher. Bishop Bristol, of the Methodist Church, has repeated the remark which Gunsaulus once made to him: "Frank Bristol, you know that above all else in this world I have wished to be known and I now wish to be remembered as a minister of the Gospel."[1]

And whence came this power? It was the gift of the gods. It was a part of the constitution with which nature endowed him. The angels must have sung the greatest truths in halleluiahs to his mother while she carried him in her bosom. He was born so. The be-

[1] "Dr. Gunsaulus, The Minister." By Bishop Frank M. Bristol. Frank Wakely Gunsaulus: *In Memoriam.* p. 44.

loved Professor Williams, of the Greek Department
in Ohio Wesleyan University, where Gunsaulus graduated, once said, "In the days of Chapel orations, we
always had a full attendance on Chapel exercises when
it was known that Frank Gunsaulus was to give the
oration." [2] Of course, culture, training, discipline,
education contributed their share, but the original
endowment was nature's gift. If the culture was
human, divine was the seed. If the application was
below, the impulse was above, the sky.

The cause and the content of his preaching lay in
nothing less broad, deep, high, rich, than religion.
A great result demands a correspondingly creative
and compelling force. When Columbus first saw the
great rush of waters, now known as the Orinoco, he
reasoned that there was a mighty mountain range
somewhere behind the swelling flood of the resound-
ing shore. With Gunsaulus that creative force was
the Christian faith. A kinsman said of him: "Thinking, then, of the things that were determinative and
formative in the character and service of Dr. Gunsaulus, let me say at once that among all the varied
interests of his many-sided life and its wide-reaching
activities, his major interest was religion. That gave
significance to all his other interests and essential
unity to his diversified activities. He never used the
pupit as a lecture platform; but, on the other hand,
he very often turned the lecture platform into a pulpit. His supreme interest was in religion, and it was

[2] *Ibid.*, p. 46.

more than an intellectual or historical or homiletical interest.'' [3]

In his understanding and presentation of religion, the doctrine of God was supreme: "No prophet or Puritan of old believed more profoundly in the sovereignty of God than he. Preachments like those of Mr. Wells concerning a finite God, heroically struggling on toward perfection, seemed to him sheer nonsense. He believed not only in the companionable God, but in the cosmic, transcendent God, infinite in power and in wisdom. He believed in God over all, transcending all other powers in heaven and in earth, before Whose judgment seat all human authorities must give an account—all kings and councils, all rulers and governments, all autocracies and all democracies.'' [4] Professor Park once said in the classroom that the times demand the teaching and the preaching of the doctrine of God. Early in his public life Gunsaulus wrote: "The Trinity is a truth not to be held upon one's tongue. We can write about it—no one can write it. In life, it presents no contradiction, but is the grand fact focalizing all the rays of eternity. So of the Atonement; so of the doctrine of Providence; so of all great and highest truth. Human nature lives them, but does not explain them.'' [5]

Religion, as the foundation of the temple of his preaching, was supported, and made impressive and

[3] ''Memorial Address.'' By Clarence T. Brown, at the Ohio Wesleyan University. *Ibid.*, p. 91. [4] *Ibid.*, p. 93.
[5] ''The Metamorphoses of a Creed.'' p. 376.

quickening, by a power which is usually found in men of eloquence. It is the appreciation of the beautiful. He worshipped at the altar of the grand and of the sublime. He loved beautiful things painted on canvas, spread on frescoes of the wall, molded in clay, chiseled in marble, cast into the enduring bronze. The Art Institute of Chicago gives abounding evidence of his aesthetic taste and of his judgment. His creative love for the beautiful was most manifest in poetry. He wrote many poems and on many themes, gathered together in no less than three volumes. However precious the verses, I am now chiefly interested in them as the evidence of a poetic soul which found its complete utterance in the eloquence of the pulpit. Rufus Choate still stands as one of the most commanding figures in the legal history of New England and of the whole country. I have just been reading many speeches which Choate made, and on many occasions. One prevailing element in them all is their lyrical quality. That quality moves, also, and even at times in meter, through the majestic periods of Gunsaulus.

If his preaching was based on religion and was clothed in beautiful garments, it was also a very human preaching. If the content was of divinity, it was preached by a man and to men. It was aimed, and aimed directly, at the human soul. It was not the disquisition of a learned professor of theology, important and useful as the disquisition may be, and great as is the place of the teacher of theology. It was not a series of propositions, like Calvin's Institutes, embodiments of intellectual analyses. It was not a course of sermons, like the elder President Dwight's, designed to expound and to establish a system of theology, valuable as such a system may be. It concerned humanity, man, men, here, now. It was preaching winged with the wish and the will to help men, to strengthen men in their struggle, to cheer men in their loneliness, to reinforce men in their fight for righteousness, to comfort men in their sorrows, to guide men in their wandering, to save men from, and in, their perils. It was a preaching founded, somewhat on emotional sentiments, but more on intellectual convictions. It was therefore convincing. It was not bathed in technicalities, in words and phrases of vocal rhetoric; it was voiced in fine, firm, dignified, classical speech. It was not an unrelated collection of thoughts on a hastily formulated, minor topic, but it was an orderly presentation of arguments and of interpretations of great fundamental themes. At times it was a preaching which seemed to be inspired, and it was always inspiring. It ever possessed a certain massiveness which moved the hearer. It was picturesque. Imaginative in idea and phrase, it always bore thought, and therefore created thoughtfulness in the devout and devoted hearer. It quickened one for service. As said the Athenians after hearing Demosthenes, "Let us go and fight Philip!," so said the American auditor, "What can I do to make this a better world?"

The human and humanized purpose resulted in
Gunsaulus becoming the president of a technical
school—an office which, on general grounds, it would
be said, was most foreign to him. Well known is "the
story of that famous sermon preached in Plymouth
Church nearly thirty years ago on the needs of the
children in the growing city, at the close of which
Philip D. Armour came up and said to the young
preacher,—then only thirty-seven years old,—'Young
man, do you really believe what you have said?' 'Of
course I do,' was the answer. 'Then, if you will give
five years of your life, I will give the money, and we
will do it together.' "[6] Of this service, to the giving
of which he was thus called, he had a just understanding, a just understanding of its opportunity, value
and power. In the undertaking he was moved by two
great purposes, as said Dean Monin of the Armour
Institute,—"the one to develop personality, and the
other to prepare for performance. Personality means
self-development. Performance means service and
self-restraint. Personality needs inspiration and
power; performance needs instruction and discipline,
and these two streams of influence he gathered up in
his comprehensive conception of what an engineering
college should do, and . . . of what every educational
institution should procure."[7]

[6] Address by Rev. Charles W. Gilkey. Frank Wakely Gunsaulus: *In Memoriam.* p. 17.
[7] "Doctor Gunsaulus, the Educator." Address by Louis C.
Monin, Dean of Armour Institute of Technology. *Ibid.*, pp.
56-57.

These two great works, as a preacher and minister of Jesus Christ and as the president of Armour Institute of Technology,—each greater than any man should bear,—he carried forward together. He might say that man has two shoulders, two feet, two arms, and a double-barreled brain. Perhaps each function or force should aid the other. The work of the president of a scientific school helped to give substance to the sermon. The sermon, in turn, stirred the imagination for the daily duty and the common task. Each service was of life, by life, in life, and for life. Each service created and bore an elixir of youth, the perpetual over-flowing of quenchless human and divine forces. Both the ministry and the administration were, moreover, for the present, yet more for the future, of men. Therefore, youth was to him the great opportunity in which, and through which, and for which, he wrought.

Of course, Gunsaulus was not a critical scholar. Men of eloquence seldom are scholars. For, scholarship is not a form of the emotions, and emotion is a source and form of eloquence. College presidents should be scholars, or at least scholarly, or they should, at the very least, have deep appreciation of scholarship, and a hearty sympathy with scholars. Gunsaulus could indeed be called, by a general reference, scholarly. His knowledge was broad, if not deep. He did have thorough appreciation of scholarship and hearty sympathy with scholars. Scholarship, it is to be remembered, in these years, represents expert knowledge. Gunsaulus was not an expert. He preferred breadth to depth, wideness to narrowness. His relationships were many, diverse, absorbing, and consuming.

Such, they seem to me, were the two fundamental and prevailing elements and forces of the full life of this great and dear man; and yet religion and its eloquent interpretation were more and most fundamental and prevailing. Still, in them, one does not forget the friendships, numberless, with all sorts and conditions of men, found in all lands and beside all seas. In these friendships, how he rejoiced, and how intense was his loyalty to them! Joined in these friendships, as both cause and result, was his talk. For he was one of the best of talkers known to me,— and I have known many of the best,—touching on great themes, but not too heavily, punctured with fitting allusion, illustrated by story and anecdote, radiant with wit, and environed with humor. The talk had raillery, properly confined, and mimicry that left no sting, only showers of laughter, bathed in atmospheres of happiness and of enthusiasm. For he was an optimist who believed in yesterday, much, in to-day, more, in to-morrow, most. His hours and experiences always seemed white-crested, moving toward blessed consummations. As I have intimated, he was a hard worker in many relationships, but seldom was he seen to be at work. "When do you prepare your sermons?" he was asked. "All the time," was the answer. He read much and of many kinds of literature, and he wrote much and of many kinds, too. His books remain: *litera scripta manet*. They are a rescript of himself. As books, they seem at times to give intimations of declamation. They remind one of Macaulay's marching essays. But heard or read, they are sincere and real understandings. In them are found not only poems, but also biographies and novels, as well as sermons.

With all these services, of the preacher, of the administrator, of the author, and of blessed companionship, he was also a great citizen. The most representative American city never had a nobler citizen, one whose voice spoke her thought so well, one whose ideals so completely united her aspirations, one whose character so fully embodied the best that was in her. Above all, I think of my friend, whom I call "Gun," as standing for a fullness of life of which Tennyson sang, a poet whom he loved, for a fullness of life of which the Christ, whom he worshipped as Savior, was the incarnation.

XII

HENRY ADAMS

HENRY ADAMS, born in Boston, February 16, 1838; died March 28, 1918. A.B., Harvard, 1858. Private secretary to his father, (American minister at London), 1861-66; assistant professor of history, Harvard, 1870-77; editor, North American Review, 1870-76; removed to Washington, 1877. Author: Essays in Anglo-Saxon Law; Documents Relating to New England Federalism, 1800-15; Life and Writings of Albert Gallatin; John Randolph; History of the United States (Jefferson's and Madison's Administrations); Historical Essays; Mont Saint Michel and Chartres; Letter to American Teachers of History; Life of George Cabot Lodge; Education of Henry Adams; Democracy, Esther, (novels), etc.

XII

HENRY ADAMS

TEACHER, HISTORIAN, SUPERFICIAL PESSIMIST, PROFOUND
OPTIMIST

"No! I shall never write my biography and have
forbidden —— to do it after my death. It is usually
a rather dishonest sort of writing, and there is little
in my life which the next generation would care to
read about. Only such kind fanatics as yourself can
think otherwise."

This paragraph was written by a great man, a dear
friend, in answer to my request that he should write
his autobiography. No such charge, however, of essential deception on the side of self-laudation can be
made about the "Education of Henry Adams." It
is possible that a charge of deception on the ground
of self-depreciation could be made against the great
book itself, as well as against the great man. For,
a copy of the original folio edition, privately
printed and bearing date of 1907, lies before
me. It was sent to me by the man himself and
with this inscription, made in his own beautiful,
copperplate writing: "Take your old book! it's a
rotten one anyway!" There also lies before me a

note-book of his course in what was known at Harvard College as "Medieval Institutions" or "History 3," of a time fifty years ago. In this course, it was my privilege to be a student, a privilege among the richest of all the many advantages given me by Harvard College.

"The Education of Henry Adams" has usually been taken as a sober-minded, sincere interpretation by and of a man who was judged to be a confirmed pessimist. On its face, it is such a book. Having both the misfortune, and fortune, of being born into a great historic family, the misfortune of Adams was continued by conditions of fateful circumstances and by the limitation of his own inabilities. The bright spots in his life bear the names of John Hay and of Clarence King. They make what he regarded as the surrounding darkness of inanities and of unavailing effort the more visible and impressive. Failure, as declares the book, was written on the tomb-stone of the life of Henry Adams long before it was erected. The failure of Henry Adams was simply part and parcel of the failure of humanity. His brother, Brooks, writes of him: "He was not a failure, for he succeeded, and succeeded brilliantly, in whatever he undertook, where success was possible; and he was not disappointed, for the world gave him everything he would take." [1] The brother adds that Henry Adams knew well he was not a failure. I once re-

[1] "The Degradation of the Democratic Dogma, by Henry Adams. Introduction by Brooks Adams. p. 6.

marked to him that I wished he might continue his history. His reply was that the American people had never shown that appreciation of his history which would warrant him in further writing. No desolation could be more desolate than that which marked his progress through life, and no defeat more absolute than that which, while he slept, brought his career to its close.

Such interpretations, although genuine and sincere and painfully current, have long seemed to me to be false. "The Education of Henry Adams" is not a book to be taken in seriousness. It is not, and was not designed by him to be, a full interpretation of his life. It is rather a conversational jest, or gesture, which he was so often inclined to give, and which, offered in talk, no one would or could take seriously. For a book, the jesting is carried too far. The book is an expression of sheer intellectual exuberance and defiance. For, Henry Adams was, upon one side of his nature, given to raillery, to scoffing, to reviling, which, measured by words and monologues, seemed bitter; but which, to those who knew his heart, was not of gall. The volume is indeed somewhat of a pose, assumed in part at least as amusement to himself. As he said of Clarence King, Adams loved paradoxes. His brother, Brooks, says: "Nor was I ever myself quite sure how much he believed in his own paradoxes." [2] "He [King] started them like rabbits, and cared for them no longer, when caught or

[2] *Ibid.,* p. 4.

lost." But the paradoxes "delighted" Adams. "For," as he adds, "they helped, among other things, to persuade him that history was more amusing than science. The only question left open to doubt was their relative money value."[3]

Going into his library one day, although I had been announced, he looked up in his alert way, and seeing me, he said, "The devil, Thwing! Is this you?" The remark was the interpretation of the method of the man. It was a pleasant raillery and guileless scoffing. Again and again in conversation, he would put forth extreme interpretations of humanity and of humanity's life and history, yet concluding his diatribe with the remark, "What do you think of that, Thwing?" Of course Thwing had few or no ideas to offer. But Adams just wished to see what the effect of his literary onslaughts was upon the auditor.

The evidences which I might offer of the truth of my interpretation of him as an optimistic pessimist, or, better, as a pessimistic optimist, are manifold. They are found in letters of the great man himself, as well as in various paragraphs of the "Education," and other books. In his famous and somewhat obscure Letter to American Teachers of History, written in 1910, he says: "In reality pessimists and optimists have united on a system of science which makes pessimism the logical foundation of opti-

[3] "The Education of Henry Adams." Folio Edition. pp. 272-273.

mism." [4] They also are embodied in many conversa-
tions. The evidences of the letters rest not only in
letters which Adams wrote himself, but also in letters
which John Hay, for instance, wrote to him. As early
as the year 1862, writing from London to his brother,
Charles Francis, Adams said that he had no encouragement to write further, as his letters had neither
been answered nor acknowledged, although he had
written every fortnight! In the following year, also
writing to his brother, Charles Francis, he said in
seriousness that he believed "the laws which govern
animated beings will be ultimately found to be at
bottom the same with those which rule inanimate
nature." But he concludes the paragraph by adding:
"The devil of it is, supposing there comes a time
when the rebs suddenly cave in, how am I to explain
that! This little example of my unpractical experi-
mento—philosophico—historico—progressiveness will
be enough." [5] Later, he says: "The world grows
just like a cabbage; or, if the simile is vulgar, we'll
say, like an oak." [6] A little later still, in '64, he
writes: "I shall think the devil himself has got hold
of us, and shall resign my soul to the inevitable. . . .
My present impression is that we are in considerable
danger of all going to Hell together. You can tell
me if I am right." [7] In the next-to-the-last day of
the year 1864, he also writes to his brother, saying:

[4] "The Degradation of the Democratic Dogma." pp. 257-
258.

[5] "A Cycle of Adams Letters." Vol. II, p. 90.
[6] *Ibid.*, p. 96.　　　　　[7] *Ibid.*, p. 211.

"There will be nothing left for us in a foreign war except to make the moon a basis, and to march our armies overland to conquer Europe."[8]

The later pages of "Education," however, have paragraphs that are still more valuable, in forming the conclusion of pessimistic-optimistic raillery. Visiting Antwerp on one of the last days of the year 1858, he says: "He never dreamed of trying to educate himself to the Descent from the Cross. He was only too happy to feel himself kneeling at the foot of the Cross; he learned only to loathe the sordid necessity of getting up again, and going about his stupid business."[9] Writing in the same period of his experiences at Rome, he says: "As long as he could argue that his opponents were wicked, he could join in robbing and killing them without a qualm; but it might happen that the good were robbed. Education insisted on finding a moral foundation for robbery. He could hope to begin life in the character of no animal more moral than a monkey unless he could satisfy himself when and why robbery and murder were a virtue and duty. Education founded on mere self-interest was merely Guelf and Ghibelline over again—Machiavelli translated into American."[10]

In the chapter on "Failure," writing of King and of himself, he says: "Adams could never tell a story, chiefly because he always forgot it; and he was

[8] *Ibid.*, p. 238.
[9] "The Education of Henry Adams." Folio Edition. p. 62.
[10] *Ibid.*, p. 71.

never guilty of a witticism, unless by accident. King
and the Fortieth Parallel influenced him in a way
far more vital." [11] (By the way, both Adams and
Hay have said to me, that Clarence King was the most
brilliant man they ever knew.) Adams also wrote
of King, saying, "He remained the best companion
in the world to the end." [12]

Adams and Hay wrote novels, and not far from the
same time, in the late '70's and the early '80's.
The novels grew out from their rather individual
experiences. Hay's, "The Bread Winners," was concerned with his life in Cleveland; Adams' "Democracy" with his life in Washington. Each author
never acknowledged his authorship. But the volumes
are now bearing the great names. Many pages of
the "Democracy" give evidence of the raillery which,
as I am now interpreting it, ruled Henry Adams.
Let me quote at length, therefore, a description of a
ball at the British minister's house in Washington:

"He asked not only the President and his Cabinet,
and the judges, and the army, and the navy, and all
the residents of Washington who had any claim to
consideration, but also all the senators, all the representatives in Congress, all the governors of States
with their staffs, if they had any, all the eminent
citizens and their families throughout the Union and
Canada, and finally every private individual, from
the North Pole to the Isthmus of Panama, who had

[11] *Ibid.*, pp. 271-272.
[12] "Clarence King Memoirs." p. 185.

ever shown him a civility or was able to control
interest enough to ask for a card. The result was
that Baltimore promised to come in a body, and
Philadelphia was equally well-disposed; New York
provided several scores of guests, and Boston
sent the governor and a delegation; even the
well-known millionaire who represented California
in the United States Senate was irritated because, his
invitation having been timed to arrive just one day
too late, he was prevented from bringing his family
across the continent with a choice party in a director's car, to enjoy the smiles of royalty in the halls
of the British lion. It is astonishing what efforts
freemen will make in a just cause . . .

" 'All young and beautiful women,' said he to Sybil,
'are to send me flowers. I prefer Jacqueminot roses,
but will accept any handsome variety, provided they
are not wired. It is diplomatic etiquette that each lady
who sends me flowers shall reserve at least one dance
for me. You will please inscribe this at once upon your
tablets, Miss Ross.' " [13] "Esther," too, offers personal
interpretations not unlike those of "Democracy."

Enough has been said, I think, to prove that there
was in Henry Adams a great element of scoffing and
of what William Roscoe Thayer calls "Voltairean
raillery." [14] To accept his "Education" as an interpretation of himself and of life, in sincerity and
honesty, and in the straight-forwardness of simple

[13] "Democracy." pp. 281-283.
[14] "The Life of John Hay." Vol. II, p. 59.

prose, is a moral and literary mistake, incongruity, misinterpretation.

I wish also to seek to interpret Henry Adams' ideas of what the education of the American youth in the American college, should be made. Adams' idea of education was that education is a training in the weighing of evidence. I recall that once he leaned back, as was his custom, in his chair in a lecture room in University Hall, Cambridge, and said in his Adamsesque voice: "I am a professor of history in Harvard College. But I rejoice that I never remember a date." This enigma he proceeded to explain to us youngsters. The explanation of the remark, which of course was rather surprising to us, was that he remembered events, not in relation to time, but in relation to each other, as cause and effect. To him, education was reflecting, thinking, relating fact to fact, and truth to truth. It was a discipline in relationships. In such an interpretation he writes in one of the first paragraphs of the chapter on "Failure:"

"He knew enough to be ignorant. His course had led him through oceans of ignorance; he had tumbled from one ocean into another till he had learned to swim; but even to him education was a serious thing. A parent gives life, but as parent, gives no more. A murderer takes life, but his deed stops there. A teacher affects eternity; he can never tell where his influence stops. A teacher is expected to teach truth, and may perhaps flatter himself that he does so,

if he stops with the alphabet or the multiplication
table, as a mother teaches truth by making her child
eat with a spoon; but morals are quite another truth
and philosophy is more complex still." [15]

In even a rather personal interpretation, it would
not be fitting to pass over that achievement for
which lasting fame can more justly be claimed for
Adams, leaving out possibly his "Education," than
for any other of his works. I refer to his "History
of the United States," a history indeed covering
only seventeen years. But they were the first seventeen years of the nineteenth century, and they were
concerned with the two administrations of Jefferson,
and the two of Madison. The nine volumes remain,
therefore, in a sense, a family history, dealing with
the personal and public life of his grandfather and
great grandfather. Yet they are distinguished by
their family detachments. They form the most important interpretation made of those creative years
of the American commonwealth. The sweep, the
comprehensiveness, and the details, are intimated in
the bare statement that the index occupies no less
than one hundred and twenty-three pages, of double
columns of fine printing. The history will live, however, not because of its content only, but also, and
possibly more, by reason of its style. That style is
of the most brilliant and the most commanding type.
It has not, of course, the declamation of the most

[15] "The Education of Henry Adams." Folio Edition.
pp. 261-262.

popular historian; yet it is pervaded with Macaulay's forcefulness. Without the picturesqueness of the writing of his friend, Parkman, it also has the beauty of Parkman's sympathetic interpretations of nature, and the evident faithfulness of his brave studies of dim manuscripts. Without the rather bombastic fullness of Bancroft, it has detail without pettiness, and nobility of narration without grandiloquence. It is succinct without being turgid. As an example of such writing, I might easily cite any one of two thousand pages. Let me, however, be content with quoting the concluding paragraph of the concluding volume:

"With the establishment of these conclusions, a new episode in American history began in 1815. New subjects demanded new treatment, no longer dramatic but steadily tending to become scientific. The traits of American character were fixed; the rate of physical and economical growth was established; and history, certain that at a given distance of time the Union would contain so many millions of people, with wealth valued at so many millions of dollars, became thenceforward chiefly concerned to know what kind of people these millions were to be. They were intelligent, but what paths would their intelligence select? They were quick, but what solution of insoluble problems would quickness hurry? They were scientific, and what control would their science exercise over their destiny? They were mild, but what corruptions would their relaxations bring?

They were peaceful, but by what machinery were their corruptions to be purged? What interests were to vivify a society so vast and uniform? What ideals were to ennoble it? What object, besides physical content, must a democratic continent aspire to attain? For the treatment of such questions, history required another century of experience." [16]

But there was wholly another side to the character of Henry Adams which has also suffered neglect. He would be the last to say that I am right, however. In fact, if he were reading what I am writing, he would break out, "Thwing, you are utterly wrong!" But I do affirm that Henry Adams was essentially a religious man. The evidence for such an interpretation is also not lacking. It is found in letters, and in paragraphs of the "Education," as well as in the intimations of many a conversation. Study his "Mont St. Michel and Chartres." He did indeed, as I already have quoted, dream of himself as kneeling at the foot of the cross. Also he ever did think of himself as in the presence of the infinities, the eternities and the immeasurable majesties of existence. Religion to him was not a matter to be spoken of. His interpretation is well set forth in the meaning of the inexpressibly beautiful monument in Rock Creek Cemetery. John Hay, in 1891, wrote to Henry Adams of this monument, saying: "The work is indescribably noble and imposing. It is, to my mind, St. Gaudens's masterpiece. It is full of poetry and

[16] Vol. IX, pp. 241-242.

suggestion. Infinite wisdom; a past without beginning and a future without end; a repose, after limit-
less experience; a peace, to which nothing matters—
all embodied in this austere and beautiful face and
form."[17] The mystery, the Buddha-like resignation
and strength, the vision of the unseen, of the stone,
were incarnated in the faith of Henry Adams. Perhaps the most weighty and definite evidence of the
essential religiousness of Adams is found in his
"Prayer to the Virgin of Chartres." These verses
were "found after his death in a little wallet of
special papers. These verses were apparently written
just after the 'Chartres' book, and while he was con-
templating the 'Education,' and were shown by him
to only one friend, a 'sister in the twelfth century.'
One can understand that he did not care to publish
them during his lifetime, for he never wished to lift
the veil. In this 'Prayer' Henry Adams makes an
act of faith in the Son's divinity. He ends by saying
in his own words what Saint John said twenty centuries before: 'In him was life; and the life was the
light of men. And the light shineth in darkness, and
the darkness comprehended it not.' Henry Adams
felt the failure of the world to receive the light, but
he leaves no shadow of doubt that he himself perceived 'That was the true Light.'"[18] The concluding verses of the "Prayer" are:

[17] "The Life of John Hay." By William Roscoe Thayer.
Vol. II, pp. 60-61.
[18] "Letters to a Niece, and Prayer to the Virgin of
Chartres." pp. 26-27.

"Help me to see! not with my mimic sight—
    With yours! which carried radiance, like the sun,
Giving the rays you saw with—light in light—
    Tying all suns and stars and worlds in one.

"Help me to know! not with my mocking art—
    With you, who knew yourself unbound by laws;
Gave God your strength, your life, your sight, your
        heart,
        And took from him the Thought that Is—the
        Cause.

"Help me to feel! not with my insect sense,—
    With yours that felt all life alive in you;
Infinite heart beating at your expense;
    Infinite passion breathing the breath you drew!

"Help me to bear! not my own baby load,
    But yours; who bore the failure of the light,
The strength, the knowledge and the thought of
        God,—
    The futile folly of the Infinite!" [19]

I am unwilling to say that faith was the background
of his character. Rather I would say that faith, such
as this prayer breathes, was the substance of his life,
penetrating and interpenetrating its thinking and
feeling. I would not say it was to him what blood
is to the body; rather would I say that it was to
him what life is to the body and to the spirit.

    [19] *Ibid.*, pp. 133-134.

XIII

JAMES BRYCE

JAMES BRYCE, first Viscount, created 1914, of Dechmont, Lanarks. Born May 10th, 1838, in Belfast; died January 22, 1922. University of Glasgow; Trinity College, Oxford; B.A., 1862; Fellow, Oriel College, 1862; at Heidelberg University, 1863; barrister at Lincoln's Inn, 1867; practiced till 1882; Regius Professor of Civil Law, 1870-1893 (resigned); M.P. for Tower Hamlets, 1880; Under Secretary of State for Foreign Affairs, 1886; Chancellor, Duchy of Lancaster (with seat in cabinet), 1892; president, the Board of Trade, 1894; chairman, the Royal Commission on Secondary Education, 1894; member, Senate of London Society, 1893; corresponding member, the Institute of France, 1891 (foreign member, 1904). Received numerous honorary degrees, from universities in the United States and many other foreign countries. Chief Secretary for Ireland, 1905-07; Member of Parliament, Aberdeen, South, 1885-1907; Ambassador at Washington, 1907-13; honorary member, the Faculty of the Law University of Santiago; president, the British Academy; and trustee, National Portrait Gallery; Honorary Fellow, the Royal Geographical Society; one of the British Representatives at the Hague Court.

Author: The Flora on the Island of Arran: The Holy Roman Empire; Report on the Condition of Education in Lancashire, 1867; The Trade Marks Registration Act, with introduction and notes on Trade Mark Law, 1877; Transcaucasia and Ararat; The American Commonwealth; Impressions of South Africa; Studies in History and Jurisprudence; Studies in Contemporary Biography; The Hindrances to Good Citizenship; South America: Observations and Impressions; Modern Democracies, etc.

XIII

JAMES BRYCE

WORLD-CITIZEN, FRIEND OF AMERICA

It is now fifty years since, as an under-graduate,
I first read a book by James Bryce. It was, of course,
the essay, which some still consider his best work,
"The Holy Roman Empire." I have just finished
reading the two noble volumes, "Modern Democracies." In the half century and more which divides
the writing of the earlier from the later volumes, my
little life has been touched and influenced by reading
other volumes of his making. To this influence has
been added the quickening of a personal acquaintance. The personal acquaintance became, through
the years—it is I think not too much to say—a
friendship. Of course I could do no more for him
than to try to answer his many and searching questions. But he did much, very much, for me. The
reading and the personal relations have joined themselves together, year by year, on this side of the sea
and on the other, unto my grateful happiness and
constant enrichment.

For many years before his death, James Bryce had
come to be the best known and most beloved, of all

men not in official place, of the whole world. In
South America he was recognized as a wise interpreter
of her complex racial life and of her equally complex
political problems. In South Africa his travels of
many years ago, the source of a noble volume, were,
and are still, gratefully remembered. In Australia
and New Zealand his name is spoken by the best
people with affection. Iceland, too, was among his
conquests—a country whose people he told me he
believed to be the most interesting of all peoples. In
India, China, and Japan, his volumes on "Jurisprudence" and "The American Commonwealth," are
studied by tens of thousands of students as wise ex-
positions of profound questions of modern life. In
America his face was as easily recognized, his voice as
familiar, and his books are as largely read, as in the
British Isles. James Bryce was everywhere known,
and therefore, being what he was, was everywhere
loved.

Many and moving are the characteristics of the
great man. I select a few, such as seem to me to be
the more outstanding for the present purpose.

Perhaps the more obvious of all the qualities of
James Bryce was his intellectual avariciousness.
His intellectual avariciousness resulted in intellectual
inquisitiveness, and his intellectual inquisitiveness
showed itself in his intellectual acquisitiveness. He
knew. He knew *multum*, and he knew *multa*. The
diversity of his knowledges seemed to be strangely
consistent with the thoroughness of his knowledge.

Just to name his volumes is sufficient evidence of the breadth and depth of his learning. I need not name them, but I do venture to select from the volume entitled "Studies in History and Jurisprudence," the titles of a few of the essays: "The Extension of Roman and English Law throughout the World," "The Action of Centripetal and Centrifugal Forces on Political Constitutions," "The Law of Nature," and "The Relations of Law and Religion." These and other titles represent a knowledge and knowledges approaching the learning of Lord Acton.

Bryce's avariciousness showed itself, as is intimated, in his inquisitiveness. He was the typical questioner. In his probing of persons and of problems, he was a Socrates. Every one whom he met was a source of knowledge. I recall that, at a dinner in Washington, he asked me the reason of the bribery of voters in Adams County, Ohio. At another dinner, at Mrs. John Hay's home—in which Henry Adams was also a guest—the talk fell upon the origin and meaning of the "Cake Walk." No theme that belonged to man was too humble for his inquiry, no subject too great or complex for his analysis and thinking. For his knowledge, though immense and diverse, deep and broad, did not congest his thinking. He analyzed, arranged, codified. He saw the relations of facts and of truths. His mind was reflective, reasoning. It was philosophic as well as historical, both interpretative and descriptive, practical and scientific, judicial and picturesque.

His intellectual force and equipment were fortified by a sense and a source of physical vitality. His body was slight, of not more than the average height, and the impression which it gave was of lightness. But with the lightness and the slightness was united apparent litheness. He was, like Leslie Stephen, a great walker and a proud climber of mountains—one of the few who had ascended Ararat—an explorer of volcanic craters. At a luncheon at his house in Buckingham Gate, a few months before his death, he told me of his narrow escape from death. Alone he was walking over the field covered by Kilauea in Hawaii. Suddenly he fell into a small crater. "I was," he said, "calm and cool as I am now. Above, on the side of the crater, there grew a small tree or shrub; a branch bent over. It was within my reach. The question to me was whether that tree would hold my weight." "If it had not held his weight," Lady Bryce added, "there would have been no 'Modern Democracies.'" He nursed well his strength. His body he kept as a first-rate tool for his executive work as a member of the House of Commons or of the House of Lords. It was a necessary and effective force in the making of his books, or in the giving of his lectures. It provided staying power for all the endurances and endeavors that were his.

This physical vitality was at once both cause and result of vitality, intellectual and emotional. How alive was that mind, how warm that heart! The intellectual pulse-beats were strong and full, as they were regular and uniform. Truth to him became truthfulness: it took on personal meanings without losing its objective relationships. Faith and belief were incarnated. He saw life sanely, and saw it whole. But the vision, wise and comprehensive, was a seeing with his own eyes. This vitality is felt in his written style, as well as in his personality. Any one of thousands of pages could I quote as illustration and proof. Let me be content with a passage from each of his three great books. From "The Holy Roman Empire" I draw forth the following:

"In its essence the Empire rested on the feeling of the unity of mankind; it was the perpetuation of the Roman dominion by which the old nationalities had been destroyed, with the addition of the Christian element which had created a new nationality that was also universal. By the extension of her citizenship to all her subjects heathen Rome had become the common home, and, figuratively, even the local dwelling-place of the civilized races of man. By the theology of the time Christian Rome had been made the mystical type of humanity, the one flock of the faithful scattered over the whole earth, the holy city whither, as to the temple on Moriah, all the Israel of God should come up to worship." [1]

From his last great book, "Modern Democracies," I extract the following as proof of the vitality of the interpreter:

"No government demands so much from the citi-

[1] p. 297.

zen as Democracy, and none gives so much back. Any free people that has responded to the call of duty and come out of a terrible ordeal unshaken in courage, undimmed in vision, with its vital force still fresh and strong, need not fear to face the future.

"The statesmen and philosophers of antiquity did not dream of a government in which all men of every grade should bear a part: democracy was for them a superstructure erected upon a sub-structure of slavery. Modern reformers, bolder and more sanguine, called the multitude to power with the hope and in the faith that the gift of freedom and responsibility would kindle the spirit self-government requires. For them, as for Christian theologians, Hope was one of the Cardinal Virtues." [2]

From his most popular book, "The American Commonwealth," I take the following in further illustration:

"They do not, like their forefathers, expect to attain their ideals either easily or soon; but they say that they will continue to strive towards them, and they say it with a note of confidence in the voice which rings in the ear of the European visitor, and fills him with something of their own hopefulness. America has still a long vista of years stretching before her in which she will enjoy conditions far more auspicious than England can count upon. And that America marks the highest level, not only of material well-being, but of intelligence and happi-

[2] Vol. II, pp. 608-609.

ness, which the race has yet attained, will be the judgment of those who look not at the favoured few for whose benefit the world seems hitherto to have framed its institutions, but at the whole body of the people." [3]

I might continue these extracts, page after page, but sufficient, and more than sufficient, have been adduced to prove what I have intimated concerning the warmth of his heart, the breadth of his intellect, the vitality of the great man himself.

This vitality, even though thus conditioned, helped to make possible his industry. This industry was constant, unflagging, devoted to diverse duties. All his friends recognized the tirelessness of his manifold services. He spared not himself. He wrote largely with his own hand. Every sheet of the manuscript of the eleven hundred large pages of "Modern Democracies" came from the point of his own pen. Many are the letters I have received from him, and each of them is autographic. His tirelessness was as great at Williamstown, in his last summer, as in the years of his Regius Professorship of Civil Law at Oxford. It showed itself under conditions as diverse as the Atlantic liner and the jerking New Zealand railroad train. It was seen in his country house and in his Buckingham Gate residence.

In the interpretation of the great man, there are those who do not first think of his scholarly equipment or of the political and civil achievements, but rather

[3] Vol. II, p. 718.

of his friendliness. For he was a great friend. The virtue was in his soul, the grace on his lips and in his manner. He was remote from remoteness. He gave personal warmth and he was repaid with interest. No bare or barren formalities restrained, neither did feeling invite familiarity. A gentleman, he gave more, and better, than a gentleman sometimes gives: he gave affection, and the affection was followed by service and practical helpfulness. Hundreds of persons in all parts can testify to being his grateful pensioners. His friendliness was given to nations, and to communities, as well as to individuals, and in one unique instance given to both. He was asked a long time ago how he came to write the "American Commonwealth." "Mr. Gladstone," he replied, "once said to me that he had been unable to find any satisfactory book on America." The intimation thus given resulted in "The American Commonwealth." When, a few years ago, I was leaving for Australia and New Zealand, he gave me a dozen letters, addressed to the great men, prime ministers, Supreme Court justices, governor generals, of the Commonwealth and of the Dominion. In one of the concluding parts of his Valedictory Lecture, on resigning his professorship at Oxford in 1893, he says:

"Vividly there come back to me as I stand by the open gate, the kindly wisdom of the late President of Corpus Christi, most lovable of men; the luminous and fertile intellect of Sir Henry Maine; the masculine force and high sense of public duty of

Thomas Green; the penetration and learning, not more wide than exact, of Mark Pattison; the fine taste and golden lips of Henry Liddon; the warm heart and vehement discourse and noble love of truth of Edward Freeman; the fire, the courage, the eagerness, the zeal in all good causes of one whose university lectures and sermons were so powerful a stimulus to many of us in our undergraduate days, Arthur Stanley. These men had some sharp contests in their lives, but they are all alike enshrined in our memory as men of whom the Oxford of those days may well be proud." [4] Such friends came from the abounding friendliness of Bryce's great and tender heart.

This quartet of qualities,—intellectual avariciousness, vitality, industry and friendliness,—were incarnated in a character that was distinguished by humility and by a bearing that was marked by the gentleness and modesty of the gentleman. He thought not of himself more highly than he ought to think. He thought soberly. For he measured himself, if he measured himself at all, against the great and high pillars of the race that outlast the single generations, and not against the narrow and low standards of the day. Rufus Choate once said that Shakespeare, Bacon, Milton, Burke, constitute the great four. Bryce would be among the last to say that in such association he belonged. But, consciously or unconsciously, he thought on themes and matters

[4] "Studies in History and Jurisprudence." P. 906.

as diverse as those on which Shakespeare and Bacon discoursed, Milton sang, or Burke spoke and wrote. He would also be the last to say that any of his volumes should stand by the side of the volumes of the first of English political philosophers. Humility, however, was not so much a quality, or characteristic, as it was an atmosphere in which the other great elements of his nature moved and breathed and had their being. In thinking and writing of him, "James Bryce" is the common phrase, and not "Viscount Bryce."

The devoutness of his character was also quite as constructive, or constitutional, as his humility of spirit. His interpretation of life was based on Christian theism. He was a worshiper at the Christian altar. He incarnated the Christian virtues and illustrated the Christian graces. One of the last times I ever spoke with him in London was at a service in the Temple Church of the Inns of Court, at which Dean Inge was the preacher. At the close, he said to me, "You have heard the best preacher in London." To him the church was both a means of ethical and Christian upbuilding, and an opportunity of devout worship. James Bryce was a fellow of Oriel College. A predecessor in this great type of academic honor and opportunity was John Henry Newman. I recently found beneath a drawing of Newman, made in the year 1841, this legend:

"Of immense talent and most extensive reading; his learning equaled only by his temper and judgment, of wit without parallel, regulated by his self-command of a Christian which makes him the most delightful instead of the most disagreeable of mortals.'' The words which are thus used to describe Newman almost a hundred years ago can indeed be well transferred in their profoundest meaning to James Bryce himself.

A single inference, among many which I should like to draw, springs to my pen. It is the inference of the advantage to humanity of a long life in the person of its great men. Had Bryce's friend and political chief, Gladstone, died in middle life, what a loss to the English race! He became Prime Minister for the first time in his sixtieth year. Had Tennyson died at the age of Arthur Hallam, or even double that age, what would English poesy have suffered! Had Eliot, or Angell, or Gilman, or White,—studies of whom form the first four chapters of this book,— died at the age of forty, how grave would have been the tragedy, how lamentable the loss to the cause of the higher education in America! Had Bryce died at the age of forty, the whole world would have been a world less united, less reverent, less thoughtful, less intent upon achieving highest ideals. He lived unto fourscore years and more, and all his years were years of labor, but not of heaviness or of sorrow. They were years of a great life, of rich and enduring achievement.[5]

[5] The following is a copy of the inscription found on the grave-stone, in Edinburgh:

JAMES VISCOUNT BRYCE

of

DECHMONT

P.C., O.M., C.C.V.O., D.C.L., F.R.S.
Son of James Bryce and Margaret Young.

Scholar and honorary fellow of Trinity College
Fellow of Oriel College, and
Regius Professor of Civil Law in the University of Oxford
Bencher of Lincoln's Inn
President of the British Academy
Member of the Institute of France
President of the Alpine Club

Member of Parliament
For the Tower Hamlets 1880-1885
and for South Aberdeen 1885-1907

Under Secretary of State for Foreign Affairs 1886
Chancellor of the Duchy of Lancaster 1892-1894
President of the Board of Trade 1894-1895
Chief Secretary to the Lord Lieutenant of Ireland 1905-1907
Ambassador to the United States of America 1907-1913

Author of
The Holy Roman Empire 1864
Transcaucasia and Ararat 1877
The American Commonwealth 1883
South America 1912
Modern Democracies 1921

BORN AT BELFAST 10th May 1838
DIED AT SIDMOUTH 22nd January 1922

XIV

JOHN MORLEY

JOHN MORLEY, first Viscount, created 1908, of Blackburn. Born at Blackburn, December 24, 1838; died September 23, 1923. Educated at Cheltenham College; Lincoln College, Oxford. Honorary Fellow of All Souls, Oxford; Chancellor of Victoria University, 1908-25; barrister in Lincoln's Inn, 1878; member of Parliament, Newcastle-on-Tyne, 1883-90; twice Chief Secretary for Ireland, with seat in cabinet, 1886, and 1892-95; bencher of Lincoln's Inn, 1891; trustee of British Museum, 1894; member of Parliament, Montrose Burghs, 1896-98; Secretary of State for India, 1905-10; Lord President of the Council, 1910-14.

Author: Edmund Burke, 1867; Critical Miscellanies; Voltaire; Rousseau; The Struggle for National Education; On Compromise; Diderot and the Encyclopædists; Burke, 1879; The Life of Richard Cobden; Studies in Literature; Oliver Cromwell; Life of Gladstone; Recollections, etc.

XIV

JOHN MORLEY

STATESMAN, BIOGRAPHER

On a day in the late summer of 1909, in a Scottish home known as Skibo, John Morley said to me: "Fifty years ago I came up to London from Oxford to make my way." Of course the reply made to him, who was then Secretary for India, was obvious. In fact Mark Pattison, the rector of his college (Lincoln), said that no one of his pupils had "developed so much after leaving College."[1]

It may be remembered that, as early as the year 1867, John Stuart Mill gave a letter to John Morley, introducing him to Emerson, and describing him as "of great capacity and promise and one of our best and most rising periodical writers on serious subjects." Yes, he had made his way. He had made his way in a half-century which was replete with great men, and men whose names are sufficient to dissipate or dispel our current cynicism about the commonplace personalities, the confining proprieties, and meaningless properties and prosperities of the

[1] See "Memories of Men and Books." By A. J. Church. p. 57.

253

Victorian Age. For it was the age of Palmerston,
Cobden, Brougham, Disraeli, Gladstone, John Henry
Newman, Grote, Ruskin, George Eliot, Florence
Nightingale, Browning, Tennyson, Matthew Arnold,
Darwin, Huxley, Spencer, Kelvin, and John Stuart
Mill.

Among these and other men and women, Morley
had great friendships. Of them he suggested some
interpretations which are to me still fresh. Concerning Gladstone he spoke more freely than of any
other. To an opinion expressed that it was the
many-sidedness of Gladstone's mind that caused the
current opinion of his duplicity, he gave assent.
For most men, it was agreed, are able to possess only
one mind or a single interest. When a leader emerges
who has several interests, political, literary, theological, scholastic, the inference is almost inevitable
that he is guilty of a sort of intellectual or moral
legerdemain. Morley's loyalty to his political chief
was evident. But it was also evident that the old and
long association had brought weariness to his soul
from which the decade since Mr. Gladstone's death
had not given full relief. Of an evening, the phonograph was grinding out its songs and speeches. The
head of the house, Mr. Carnegie, remarked, "Would
it not be good if we had had the phonograph in the
days of Mr. Gladstone and could have preserved his
voice for our present hearing?" John Morley replied, with a wearisome sigh, "I heard Mr. Gladstone's voice all I wanted to!" He once said to me

that Mr. Gladstone left no fewer than three hundred thousand distinct pieces of paper, some of large, some of small, content, some of great significance, some of no meaning. "But I had to examine each one, and," he added, "it almost killed me!"

With George Eliot his relations were close. Once she made a remark concerning the improvement in his "mental disposition." Of her he also spoke freely. He said, "Some of us thought that Mr. Lewes was a counterpart of Tito in 'Romola'!'" "It isn't possible," I replied, "for George Eliot is always praising Mr. Lewes as the inspiration of her writing and the comfort of her life,—and Tito was a nasty wretch!" His only reply was, "They were all a strange gang."

On an occasion I ventured a remark that we in America had always wondered why his friend Goldwin Smith came over to America. For the friendship began early, and in the Oxford days Smith was, as he afterwards said, " a shining light to all of us young Liberals." His answer was, "We in England, too, have always questioned." The question has, of course, been somewhat answered by the biographic or autobiographic notes and letters published in these last years.

But his judgment concerning his feeling of friendship for his master in philosophy was perhaps deeper than for any other friend. In the philosophic field, Mill meant to Morley what Gladstone meant in the political field. His friendship is indicated in many parts of his writing. I now content myself with a single quotation. In the Essay on Mill, written in 1906, he says:

"In the later years, when he had travelled over the smooth places of a man's life and the rough places, his younger friends never heard a word fall from him that did not encourage and direct; and nobody that ever lived enjoyed more of that highest of pleasures, the pointing the right path for new wayfarers, urging them to walk in it. 'Montesquieu must die,' exclaimed old Bentham, in a rare mood of rhapsody; 'he must die as his great countryman, Descartes, had died before him: he must wither as the blade withers when the corn is ripe; he must die, but let tears of gratitude and admiration bedew his grave.' So the pilgrim may feel today, as he stands by that mournful grave at windy Avignon, city of sombre history and forlorn memories, where Mill's remains were laid a generation ago this month [May, 1873]. Measure the permanence of his contribution to thought or social action as we will, he will long deserve to be commemorated as the personification of some of the noblest and most fruitful qualities within the reach and compass of mankind." [2]

As he associated with friends, his bearing was distinguished by quietness and repose in manner. He had little of the vivacity of Bryce. His conversation teemed less with allusions to men, measures, things,

[2] "John Stuart Mill: Critical Miscellanies." By John Morley, Vol. IV, pp. 169-170.

and experiences, than Bryce's. Ht had not traveled into many parts, as had the interpreter of "Modern Democracies," as remote as Iceland and Southern South America. His words had less sparkle, but possibly more weight, than Bryce's speech. They lacked the swiftness that belonged to Dicey. The relative fewness of his words added to their impressiveness. Utterly free from ostentation, he gave a certain impression of great reserve, both in manner and in talk. For some years before his death, Mr. Carnegie was engaged in writing sketches of his friends. "I can understand S— and M—," he once remarked, "but I don't know what to say about Morley!" If I may venture the phrase, there was in Morley a sort of honest diffidence and subtlety. The charm of an hour with him touched deepest things, and, as the hour lengthened, the freedom of conversation and the intimacies of relation increased. He was one with all and all were one with him. In taste, he seemed to be an aristocrat, in principles a thorough democrat.

Prophecy is beset with grievous perils. Rash is he who assigns seats on Olympus. Yet I do venture to say that, in the calendar of great men of the last two score of years of the nineteenth and the first score of years of the twentieth century, John Morley will hold a high place. This place will be given to him on at least two grounds, the politcial and the literary. Of the political I do not write. But the literary is more important and will prove to be, I believe the more lasting; and in the literary element of his greatness there are manifest at least two prevailing characteristics, as they are also fundamental in his political career.

The first characteristic which I name lies in his thoughtful reasonableness or reasonable thoughtfulness. Perhaps the adjective in each phrase is unnecessary. Either noun can stand alone. Or perhaps the noun is unnecessary. The adjective can easily be converted into a noun. To Mill, Gladstone applied the phrase "the saint of rationalism." The phrase also belongs to Mill's disciple. The rationalism was quiet in tone and atmosphere, logical in relationship, conscious of its limitations, recognizing its beginning in a fallible brain, and its necessary conclusions. Morley appreciated the inevitableness of the logical categories, and never more than when, as he says, he had listened for an hour to the "thunderings" of Carlyle. His mind was the Oxford type, calm, dignified, restrained. It might be called a form and substance of the Greek mind, rather Aristotelian than Platonic. In many respects he was the Voltaire of English letters and thought. In a few places his style and method are volcanic. But the volcano is covered over with snow-cold reasonableness. The habit of mind, as mind, was dominant. He was Oxford at its best. He unites in many respects Mark Pattison and Jowett. One who stood in many relations to Morley has said of him: "To know him was an intellectual discipline. It was not merely that he had read widely in all literature, ancient and

modern, pagan and divine, but that he had thought
deeply and had trained his mind as an athlete trains
his muscles until he seemed to be always in the
pink of intellectual condition. Some of his earlier
writings, which are not as well known to-day as they
should be, notably, essays on 'Popular Culture' and
on 'The Study of Literature,' are a kind of manual
of mental exercises, as vigorous in their discipline
for the mind as anything that was ever prescribed
for the development of the body. Slovenliness of
thought was as intolerable to him as would be flab-
biness of body to an instructor in physical training;
superficiality of conviction was almost as immoral
as hypocrisy." [3]

The other prevailing element was his sense of
justice. Like his master, he was the incarnation of
fairness. He well embodied the French word of
justesse. His political and literary antagonists—and
of course he had them—he sought to understand,
knowing that to understand one's antagonists is a
primary duty. As Algernon Cecil said of him twenty
years ago: "Not the least of Lord Morley's accomplishments is that he is at pains to appreciate his
opponents' point of view and at the farthest possible
remove from those who scoff without understanding." [4] Believing in intellectual demonstration, he
wanted his demonstration to be made according to

[3] "John, Viscount Morley." By John H. Morgan. p. 2.
[4] "Lord Morley of Blackburn: Six Oxford Thinkers." By
Algernon Cecil. p. 278.

rigorous laws. Believing thought is a method or force in humanity's regeneration, he desired that thought to be sincere, its expression honest, and its mood orderly and scientific. He was a stoic as he faced life, without hardness and with more than the stoic's honesty. His conduct in various affairs reminds one of Mill's remark, "If to hell I must go for doing right, then to hell I will go!"

For Morley may be called the disciple and the apostle of liberalism. He was a philosophic follower of Mill, and, with exceptions, a political disciple of Gladstone. He knew and he felt, however, the perils of liberalism. The last years of his life, and the years which have followed his death, give evidence of the breadth of its movements and of the excesses into which it falls. Liberalism in government has resulted in Bolshevism. Liberalism in the church has resulted in giving us ethics as the substance of religion, eliminating a personal God and lifting humanity to the throne of the divine. Liberalism in the school has resulted in superficial individualism in administration and in the intellectual results becoming either dissipated or depreciated. Liberalism in property rights has resulted in socialism and communism. Liberalism in the family has resulted in divorce and trial-marriages as forms and experiments of social procedure. What the future may bring forth lies in the lap of the gods! If the possible excesses in these five-fold provinces of the institutions of civilization should, however, be united with a general war, the results, governmental, social, civil, ethical, domestic, educational, would go beyond the power of the imagination to conjecture. Such results, the human reason refuses to contemplate. But from such results, in his heart Morley believed the world will be spared. Newman would have said that, as sin is the cause of these results, so by piety will they be ultimately removed. Mill would have said that, as poverty is a primary cause of these catastrophes, so by physical and industrial well-being will they be either prevented or eliminated. Morley would have taken a yet broader ground, and possibly have said that, as general causes have produced these general results, so general causes, such as lie in education and in the discipline of the human reason, will also do away with these direst consequences.

Morley divides historians into three classes, annalists, statesmen, philosophers. Morley, as historian and biographer, belongs not at all to the first class, somewhat to the second, and most to the third. He was a philosopher, for and through justice. His interpretations are based on justice, so far as reason can comprehend, and so far as reason can rise to applications of intellectual and moral sympathy. It has always seemed to me to be striking evidence of his justice that, in interpreting Mr. Gladstone's religious characteristics and loyalty and devotion to the English Church, he never by inference or expressed sentiment seemed to give any intimation of his own religious beliefs or unbeliefs. Yet, be it added, the interpretation is ever uniquely sympathetic. He believes in the moralities of things and of men, and he recognizes that the orderliness of the universe is founded on the principle of justice. His calmness reminds one of Lucretius, as he views the operation or coöperation of atomic forces, either material or human. I was once the willing, and unwilling, auditor of a debate, almost a dispute, between Lord Morley and a friend. The friend was saying that the English people were deteriorating. Lord Morley was declaring that their condition was, at that time, as good as at any period in history. At last the friend left the room in rather high dudgeon. Lord Morley, turning to me, said: "In every chamber of every country house, there ought to be put two books, one a copy of the four Gospels, the other a reprint of Mill's chapter on 'Fallacies.' "

He once astounded me by saying, as I am sure the remark will surprise every reader, that the executors of Disraeli asked him to write Disraeli's official Life. At once, I asked the biographer of Gladstone, "Why didn't you do it, Lord Morley?" His reply was, "I think the result would not have been artistic." I have always questioned, and perhaps the reader will also question, what he meant by the epithet. My own interpretation is that he felt he could not put into such writing his moral earnestness. Artistic results arise from the moralities, as well as from the intellectualities. Does literary history offer clearer evidence of intellectual justice or ethical honesty? At the time, the first volume of Disraeli's "Life" had been published, and he spoke well of it. He also once remarked that the French write better biographies than the English. His judgment is confirmed by Lytton Strachey in saying: "We have never had, like the French, a great biographical tradition;"[5] and by that master, William Roscoe Thayer, in his interpretation, "In one branch of biography, the French have excelled, and that is in critical and analytical lives of public men."[6] Possibly Lord Morley might have been willing to add that the English write better biographies than the Americans. Some would also say that the biographies of Englishmen are better written because their lives are more interesting. Their relationships are greater in number and variety, and nobler in content.

In his great book, though few in pages, on Burke, he says that Burke's life was rich and austere. Such was the life of Morley. It was rich in its forces, materials, opportunities, achievements. It was austere in its devotion to justice, to honesty, and to the virtues. Without denying or affirming the divine origin of Christianity, he yet accepted the *reality* of its truths, and sought to follow the commandment of love and service which its Founder taught and embodied. He was the apostle of the humanities— among which justice is chief—to humanity.

[5] "Eminent Victorians." p. viii.
[6] "The Art of Biography." p. 143.

XV

JOHN HAY

JOHN HAY was born in Salem, Indiana, October 8, 1838; died July 1, 1905. Graduated, Brown University, 1858; admitted to Illinois bar; one of the two secretaries of President Lincoln, 1861-65; Brevet Colonel of United States Volunteers; Assistant Adjutant General; secretary of Legation, Paris, Madrid, Vienna; charge d'affaires, Vienna; First Assistant Secretary of State, 1879-81; president of the International Sanitary Conference, 1881; ambassador to England, 1897-98; Secretary of State, 1898-1905. Author: Abraham Lincoln, a History (with John G. Nicolay), 10 vols.; Castilian Days; Pike County Ballads; Translation of Castelar's Democracy in Europe; Complete Poetical Works.

XV

JOHN HAY

John Hay, Private Secretary of Abraham Lincoln,—John Hay, Secretary of State, under McKinley and under Roosevelt:—the two offices seem to unite a long-ago past with a very near present. The Civil War recedes into a memory far faster, indeed, than the flight of years seems to make necessary. Theodore Roosevelt seems yet to live, to work, to speak among us as a virile, vital force. But John Hay incarnates and unites the diverse experiences.

Between the two dates of 1860 and 1905 lies a unique career, a career made by a man quite as unique. I have just been making notes of the many letters which Hay wrote me, recalling talks with him, re-reading the great Thayer's great "Life," and his own speeches, poems, essays, in order to make myself reasonably certain that my interpretation is fairly sound.

John Hay made rich contributions to humanity in two great fields, literature and diplomatic statesmanship. The cultivation of either field without the other would have been sufficient, in both process and result, to deserve humanity's "Well done!" Yet, these were not his only harvest fields. For, as a competent critic, writing of Sargent's portrait, says: "The attributes of a gentleman, writer, traveler, lover of art, thinker, leader, and diplomat—not each in turn, but altogether, are shown in the Hay portrait. . . . It certainly is a mental or a spiritual delineation of the most elusive of elements—the mind of a great personality."[1] Yet, in these two fields,—literature and statesmanship,—the achievements are the more, and the most, impressive and significant. The union of both calls for interpretation wiser and commendation more ample than his humility would have allowed him to accept. This double contribution was likewise made by a contemporary and friend, Lord Morley. For Morley,—to use a phrase which he once used to me, and which I have just quoted,—made his way, and made his way likewise in these two fields, of literature and of statesmanship. It might be added possibly that for both, the Englishman and the American, the beginning of the way into literature was through journalism. Through journalism each entered into both literature and politics. Hay, like Morley,—in my judgment,—was first a literary man, and secondly a statesman. The political career was, to each, an incident, important though it was in his whole service.

The basis of this judgment touching Hay is found,

[1] "John Singer Sargent: Some of His American Work." By Rose V. S. Berry. *Art and Archæology*, Vol. XVIII, No. 3, September, 1924. pp. 106, 110.

in part at least, in the interpretation made by his son, Clarence:

"John Hay was by inclination an author. He loved to write, and wrote easily. His diplomatic career he considered an accident, or rather a chapter of accidents. When President McKinley appointed him Ambassador to Great Britain in 1897, he was not in good health, and he went from a sense of duty, reluctantly. From that time on, diplomacy and affairs of state controlled his life. The poet sang no more songs, and rhymed no more ballads. . . . It is vain to conjecture what position he would have held in the world of letters if he had followed the inclinations of his youth. Fate took the choice out of his hands and turned the bard to first a writer, then a maker, of history. Though thoroughly suppressed, the poetic side of my father's nature ran as an undercurrent throughout his last years, and helped him in the many serious problems he was called upon to solve. But for the statesman in him, he would have been more a poet: but for the poet in him, he would have been less a statesman." [2]

The inclination toward authorship began early and early showed itself in the form of poetry. Among his teachers at Brown was one who has become known as President Angell of Michigan. In his "Reminiscences," Angell says (as I have before quoted):

[2] "The Complete Poetical Works of John Hay" (Houghton Mifflin Company). Introduction by Clarence L. Hay. pp. xiii-xiv.

"For Mr. Hay one would have predicted a brilliant literary future. I have often said that he was the most felicitous translator I ever met in my classes. He wrote verses of unusual merit for an undergraduate. He was modest even to diffidence, often blushing to the roots of his hair when he rose to recite. In the years of his middle life, and especially after the production of his books on Spanish life, written in so picturesque a style, I used in common with many of his friends to regret that circumstances had diverted him from a purely literary career."[3]

Hay was class poet at his graduation, and wrote verse which long remained in the annals of Class Day festivities unmatched. It will be remembered, too, that James Russell Lowell was the poet of his class, although he did not deliver the poem by reason of his temporary suspension from college. The last verse of Hay's poem is worthy of re-reading:

"Where'er afar the beck of fate shall call us,
     'Mid winter's boreal chill or summer's blaze,
Fond memory's chain of flowers shall still enthrall
     us,
   Wreathed by the spirits of these vanished days:
Our hearts shall bear them safe through life's com-
     motion;
   Their fading gleam shall light us to our graves;
As in the shell the memories of ocean
   Murmur forever of the sounding waves."[4]

[3] "Reminiscences." By James Burrill Angell. p. 109.
[4] "The Life of John Hay." By William Roscoe Thayer. Vol. I, p. 49.

The best known of all Hay's verses, whether of early or late writing, are, of course, his "Pike County Ballads." They are a part of the offering of the poetry which gave Bret Harte's California dialectic epics, or lyrics, popularity. Of the half dozen poems, which are generally recognized, Hay preferred "Jim Bludso." Of it he says: "I thoroughly appreciate a good word spoken for Jim, who is a friend of mine."[5] George Eliot also is said to have called "Jim Bludso" "one of the finest gems in the English language."[6]

There are, however, noble and great verses written in the course of the many and diverse experiences of the years,—poems of strong imagination, of definite touch, of moving sentiment, of pious fervor. Of all forms of his writing, the most difficult, the sonnet, was his favorite. The last poem he ever published, in June, 1904, was entitled "Deathless Death," or "Thanatos Athanatos:"

"At eve when the brief wintry day is sped,
  I muse beside my fire's faint-flickering glare—
  Conscious of wrinkling face and whitening hair—
Of those who, dying young, inherited
The immortal youthfulness of the early dead.
  I think of Raphael's grand-seigneurial air;
  Of Shelley and Keats, with laurels fresh and fair
Shining unwithered on each sacred head;
And soldier boys who snatched death's starry prize,

[5] "The Complete Poetical Works of John Hay." Introduction by Clarence L. Hay. p. xi.
[6] *Ibid.*

With sweet life radiant in their fearless eyes,
  The dreams of love upon their beardless lips,
Bartering dull age for immortality;
  Their memories hold in death's unyielding fee
  The youth that thrilled them to the finger-tips."[7]

Moreover, there are no less than four other forms of the great literary art which he used,—the novel, the essay, the biography, and, with them, let me put the editorial.

"The Bread Winners," for a long time not acknowledged by him, was for the year of its publication—first in the *Century Magazine*—the outstanding novel. It is a story of the town of his adopted love, Cleveland. Read to-day, it pictures another world than the present. It is a sort of a municipal companion to Henry Adams' "Democracy,"—also long not acknowledged in authorship,—the story of the diverse life of Washington. "The Bread Winners" gets its chief value as being a picture of an industrial town, punctuated by industrial strikes, of the beginning of the last quarter of the last century. It takes a place among the greater novels of the decade. One thinks of it, not as a *magnum opus,* but as the outpouring of a noble soul, interpreting life in play and in work. It will live because of its own merit, and also because it is the work of John Hay.

Of the few, too few, essays, "Castilian Days" is the best. It is an etching, made by an artist in his youth, of the beautiful and diverse life of Madrid and of its

[7] *Ibid.,* p. 237.

nation. Once taking up a copy of the book, he said
to me, speaking of life's changes, "I could not write
like this now! This book has feeling, sentiment, a
sense of splendor." It will long remain as one of the
intimate interpretations of Spanish life. With this
essay should be joined his speeches, or essays,—for
the speeches are essays, writ large and spoken aloud.
What variety of themes, what richness of interpretation, what happiness in allusion! They are either
the interpretations by a man of letters of current
phenomena, based on timeless principles, or they are
glimpses and glances of the same principles, applied
to immediate problems. They include themes as
diverse as "Omar Khayyám," "Sir Walter Scott,"
"International Copyright," "The Press and Modern Progress," "Fifty Years of the Republican
Party," and "The Grand Army of the Republic."
No utterances more thoroughly illustrate the breadth
of his understanding or his happy adjustment to the
interests which commanded his thinking and speaking.

Neither, in a literary appreciation of Hay, should
one neglect what is easy to neglect, his service as editor, and as editor of the leading republican journal
of his early day. For five years he served in the
sanctum. The period covered the last days of Horace
Greeley and the early years of Whitelaw Reid.
Greeley called Hay the most brilliant member of his
staff,—a staff which included George Ripley, of Brook
Farm fame, Bayard Taylor, the universal traveler
and interpreter, William Winter, whose career was

to go on for further decades, and Smalley, the editor
and the foreign correspondent. Has ever an abler
staff been gathered? But to Hay, as to many another, the night work proved too heavy a draft on
health. This impairment and his desire to live in
the city of his wife's home turned his feet Cleveland-
ward. Of this editorial service, one is inclined to
ask the question, What permanent effect on his style
did his editorial writing have? John Morley, being
asked whence came his style (the same question which
was asked Macaulay), answered, "Journalism!"

Yet, next to his place as a poet, Hay undoubtedly
would have esteemed his place as biographer chief.
For, into his "Life of Lincoln," with his co-ordinate
secretary and co-editor, Nicolay, he put his best and
largest self. He was thus interpreting a mighty man
with whom he lived for the war period, daily and
nightly. He was also interpreting a mighty movement in which he was at once participant and spectator. No biography ever published in America is
more monumental. It deserves to be compared with
Lockhart's "Life" of his father-in-law. Hay's ten
massive volumes make all other "Lives" of Lincoln
seem puerile, insufficient, inadequate. Like many
other "Lives" of the great man, it is concerned, too,
constantly and intimately, with the War, and, be it
added, not sufficiently with Lincoln himself. Yet one
may say that Lincoln put himself into the War, and
from the War one infers what Lincoln himself was.
The service helps to interpret the man. Happily the

plan of the book was made while Nicolay and Hay were with their chief, and their plan received his approval. To its preparation they gave no less than twenty years of "almost unremitting" toil. Hay once called it "our life-long task." It was written, they declared—and the declaration is needless—with candor and impartiality:

"The material placed in our hands was unexampled in value and fullness; we have felt the obligation of using it with perfect fairness. We have striven to be equally just to friends and to adversaries; where the facts favor our enemies we have recorded them ungrudgingly; where they bear severely upon statesmen and generals whom we have loved and honored we have not scrupled to set them forth, at the risk of being accused of coldness and ingratitude to those with whom we have lived on terms of intimate friendship. The recollection of these friendships will always be to us a source of pride and joy; but in this book we have known no allegiance but to the truth."[8]

The resulting work has had, and will have, a tremendous influence upon the deeper movements of American character. The wish of the authors, expressed more than thirty years ago, that it "may contribute in some measure to the growth and maintenance throughout all our borders of that spirit of freedom and nationality for which Abraham Lin-

[8] "Abraham Lincoln: A History." By John G. Nicolay and John Hay. Vol. I, Authors' Preface. p. xiii.

coln lived and died,'' [9] has been more than fulfilled.
I know that Robert T. Lincoln felt and said that any
other life of his father was unnecessary.

If John Hay would have desired to have been
known rather as a poet than as a statesman, it is yet
true that the people think of him rather as a statesman. Be it added, however, that statesmanship and
poetry are rather historic antagonisms. They represent a medieval antithesis as well as one modern and
immediate. As a statesman, the people think of him
as a diplomatist, whether he be Ambassador in London or Secretary of State in Washington. As a
diplomatist, John Hay continued and enhanced the
literary tradition found in our ambassadorships.
Washington Irving, Edward Everett, George Bancroft, Motley, Lowell, Whitelaw Reid, Andrew D.
White, and Page represent a noble succession, preceding or following Hay, in London and in other
capitals. He enhanced, too, the consideration given
to our ambassadors in social relations. Queen Victoria said that he was the most ''interesting'' of all
the American ambassadors whom she had known, and
she had known many.

Of his service as Secretary of State, there are two
great elements. One is an achievement, the other a
characteristic. The achievement is the ''Open Door''
in China. [10] For Hay saved China unto herself as an

---

[9] *Ibid.*, p. xiv.

[10] The origin of the happy phrase, the ''Open Door,'' is
obscure. MacMurray, for a long time occupying a high office

integral unit, saved her from being made the spoil of the nations, saved her, too, at a crisis when salvation was especially difficult to secure. It is one of the lasting triumphs of and for the world, and for an indefinite time. Of it Henry Adams says:

"For a moment, indeed, the world had been struck dumb at seeing Hay put Europe aside and set the Washington government at the head of civilisation so quietly that civilisation submitted, by mere instinct of docility, to receive and obey his orders; but, after the first shock of silence, society felt the force of the stroke through its fineness, and burst into almost tumultuous applause. Instantly the diplomacy of the nineteenth century, with all its painful scuffles and struggles, was forgotten, and the American blushed to be told of his submissions in the past. History broke in halves.[11]

"In his eight years of office he had solved nearly every old problem of American statesmanship, and had left little or nothing to annoy his successor. He had brought the great Atlantic powers into a working system, and even Russia seemed about to be dragged into a combine of intelligent equilibrium based on an intelligent allotment of activities. For the first time in fifteen hundred years a true Roman

in the State Department, having charge of Chinese interests, and now our minister at Peking, tells me that the phrase may go back as far as the year 1840.

[11] "The Education of Henry Adams." Folio Edition. p. 342.

pax was in sight, and would, if it succeeded, owe its virtues to him." [12]

The second remark, as a characteristic of his diplomacy, is that John Hay told the truth. In the evaluation of reasons for honesty and frankness in diplomacy, one special advantage belonged to Hay. Not only did he tell the truth, but he told the truth with such courtesy and graciousness that its forbidding and sinister revelations and characteristics became much less unwelcome and menacing. Nevertheless, he did not suffer the manner of the diplomat to hide the essential fact. The anecdote, the allusion, were not permitted to prevent the delivery of the message, though they may have hidden the immediate purpose of the messenger. As Thayer says:

"The great diplomatist—and Hay was that—attains his ends, not merely by the business-like methods with which he receives visitors in his office, but by his social contacts. In societies like the English and French, which possess a long tradition of etiquette and manners, the quality of man-of-the-world, which also was Hay's, often counts for more than rank, intellectual eminence, or learning in history and the technicalities of international law." [13]

But more essential for my present purpose than Hay's distinction as a writer and as a diplomatist is his whole character as a man. Of course, the

---

[12] *Ibid.*, p. 440.
[13] "The Life of John Hay." By William Roscoe Thayer. Vol. II, p. 163.

human characteristics determine the elements, and
incarnate the qualities, of the writer and of the
statesman.

Hay's chief intellectual characteristic ever seems
to me, after fifteen years of personal association and
after the more than twenty years since his death,—
1905,—to be his lucidity. By lucidity I mean something more than clarity of intellectual interpretation,
or of intellectual workmanship. In the word I include understanding, and I also include, even in his
writing, that indefinable thing which we call style.
He saw distinctly. He reasoned soundly. He inferred accurately. He analyzed a complex condition carefully,—and, be it added, the power of analysis has been a special characteristic of men trained
at Brown University. He understood the relation
of things. He made the important, important; the
trivial, trivial; the more, more; the less, less. He
saw in proportion. He reasoned through and in his
imagination more than most men. For he was a poet
rather than a logician. In his lucidity was manifest
his wit. For ten years he lived in the city in which
I write. Here he organized a dinner club, known as
the Vampire. James Ford Rhodes, then also a Cleveland resident, says:

"Hay used to come to the dinners primed with
circumstances and anecdotes and, eating and drink-
ing little, he gave himself up to talk and was listened
to with interest and delight. Not infrequently one
of the wits of the club would prod Hay and, with his

rare sense of humor, a witticism of the sort served for an additional display.''[14]

His wit proved, illustrated, and reinforced his lucid style in both speech and writing. I recall several occasions in which wit was added to understanding. I must content myself with repeating only one. The last time I saw him in his office, I made the remark that I believed the American people had confidence in the President and the Secretary of State. Quickly he responded, ''That reminds me. I know that most of the anecdotes told about Lincoln are apocryphal. But this one is true. In the campaign which led, as it proved to his election I was out with Mr. Lincoln on the 'stump.' We had a reception given to us in one of the cities of our campaign. In the line there came up a man who, getting close to Mr. Lincoln, said, 'Mr. Lincoln, down our way, in Buffalo, we kind o' think if we can have you and God, we can pull the old thing through.' Getting close, himself, to the man, Mr. Lincoln replied, 'I kind o' think you are more than half right!' ''

With these intellectual characteristics was joined a distinct charm of manner. The impression and the impressiveness of the gentleman rested upon him by nature and by habit. He had none of the brusqueness or freshness which popular conception gives to the boy born in Indiana and bred in Illinois. As, long ago some one remarked that ―― was ''a man of

[14] ''The McKinley and Roosevelt Administrations,'' 1897-1909. By James Ford Rhodes. pp. 120-121.

the East with the manners of a man of the West,"
perhaps it might be added that Hay was a man of
the West with the manners of a gentleman of the East.
With this charm was united a certain splendor, or
affluence, of bearing and of speech. This splendor,
however, was free from any touch of vanity or arrogance. He was not without selfwardness. But his
selfwardness was free from selfishness. There was
in him, of course, self-respect. But also this respect
for himself was no greater than for every other self.
The bearing did not invite liberties. Some one has
said he would "never think of slapping John Hay
on the back!" I can hardly think of even Henry
Adams taking such a liberty. In such a condition
there were two chief elements: first, his courtesy
toward everyone. I was present when a reporter
came to him asking him virtually to repeat a lecture
which he had just given to a large audience and which
the reporter had missed. The dealing of Hay with
the youth was charming. But this courtesy, be it
said, did not extend so far as the United States
Senate. I never saw Hay irritated except when he
was speaking of Senators who failed to ratify treaties
which he had arranged. The manifestation of this
irritation was constant and hearty. He once wrote
to Richard Watson Gilder, saying:

"The fact that a treaty gives to this country a
great, lasting advantage seems to weigh nothing
whatever in the minds of about half the Senators.
Personal interests, personal spites, and a contingent

chance of petty political advantage are the only motives that cut any ice at present." [15]

It has sometimes been asked, "What killed John Hay?" It might be said that the sudden death of his elder son killed him, or possibly the way in which the news of his death came to him, alone in his house of a summer night. There is quite as much reason to believe that the United States Senate killed him. Perhaps Hay forgot that, as Adams says:

"Since the first day the Senate existed, it has always intrigued against the Secretary of State whenever the Secretary has been obliged to extend his functions beyond the appointment of Consuls in senators' service." [16]

Toward the close of his life, Hay wrote:

"A treaty entering the Senate is like a bull going into the arena: no one can say just how or when the final blow will fall—but one thing is certain—it will never leave the arena alive." [17]

But the Senate had its final revenge:

"In the summer of 1904 the French Government wished to confer upon him its highest distinction—the Grand Cross of the Legion of Honor, 'in recognition of the work done by the American Government during the last seven years in the interest of the

[15] "The Life of John Hay." By William Roscoe Thayer. Vol. II, p. 274.
[16] "The Education of Henry Adams." Folio Edition. p. 370.
[17] "The Life of John Hay." By William Roscoe Thayer. Vol. II, p. 393.

world's peace.' Mr. Hay was for declining, but the President urged him to accept out of regard for France and for the cause which prompted the decoration. When, however, a resolution was moved in the Senate to authorize him to accept, the 'gray wolves' in that body, glad of an opportunity to vent their ill-will against the too unyielding Secretary, voted no.'' [18]

Hay's sense of courtesy could not extend to the legislative end of Pennsylvania Avenue. This limitation, even if it be an almost unavoidable one, was the more remarkable when one considers that the sense of courtesy was joined with modesty and with humility of spirit. His permanent mood was of self-depreciation. He did not think of himself more highly than he ought to think. In fact, he did not think of himself as highly as he ought to think. He shrank from all fullness of praise. Laudation was abhorrent. Especially public addresses gave him a sense of panic. I asked him once, in the month of July, if he could not come to Western Reserve University and give an address at the next commencement. He declined. In declining, he said, ''I should not sleep a night between now and next June!'' Quoting the reply to his sister-in-law, Mrs. Samuel Mather, she observed, ''There is some truth in the remark.'' His elder daughter says of him:

''He had an aversion, amounting to physical suffering, to publicity in any form, and his greatest

[18] *Ibid.*, pp. 393-394.

public utterances were preceded by days of nervous dread that sometimes made him literally ill. His wonderful fund of self-control and balance always came to the rescue at the critical moment, but they could not prevent his suffering agonies of anticipation. He once said: 'Luckily the shakes go to my knees and not to my voice.' " [19]

To his brother-in-law, Samuel Mather, as Hay was reaching England to begin his ambassadorship, he wrote:

"I quake a little in the knees and pale a little about the gills as I am informed the Mayor and Corporation of Southampton are to meet us at the dock and make me an address of welcome and flapdoodle." [20]

To Andrew Carnegie he wrote also at the beginning of his service:

"It is a solemn and a sobering thing to hear so many kind and unmerited words as I have heard and read this last week. It seems to me another man they are talking about, while I am expected to do his work. I wish a little of the kindness could be saved till I leave office finally." [21]

These great qualities,—clearness, wit, modesty, humility, charm,—were both the cause and consequence of his friendships. How many were these friendships and how intimate! Of course, the most intimate was with Henry Adams and also with Clar-

[19] *Ibid.*, p. 66.
[20] *Ibid.*, p. 158.　　　　[21] *Ibid.*, p. 175.

ence King. What a trinity! King I never knew, but
Adams, as well as Hay, it was my privilege to know,
as I am saying in another chapter. How broad were
the friendships of Hay! One can count up scores
of the men whom he knew well. Of course, they include all the Presidents since Lincoln, and with these
Presidents are to be associated all the statesmen of
the last fifty years. In association with them are to
be found John La Farge, W. D. Howells, Richard
Watson Gilder, Horace Greeley, Charles W. Eliot,
Charles A. Dana, Joseph H. Choate. Many Englishmen, too, were among his friends. Kipling, Sir William Harcourt, Morley, Bryce, Joseph Chamberlain
are names that easily spring to the lip. These friendships seem to unite two centuries and two countries.

But with Adams the relationship was one of almost
unexampled intimacy and oneness. I have been trying to think out some comparison or contrast of the
two men, each of whom found in the other closest
friendship. The unity of their two dwelling places
illustrates the personal oneness. In their intellectual
constitution, Adams had a larger historic deposit, a
weightier sense of human values, and a deeper psychology. Hay's mind was the more nimble, the more
witty, the more biographical. Adams was the historian,—Hay, the poet. Adams' mind had a circle
the larger, of larger time-values. Hay's mind was
more immediate, more adjustable to immediate conditions. Adams' mind lent itself more easily to vast
syntheses. He put the "cosmos" into "a nut-

shell.'' [22] Hay's was devoted to more detailed analyses. Adams was the more sober, Hay the more gay
and frolicsome. Adams had an element of raillery, of
a fun, without grossness, approaching the sardonic.
Hay had a raillery more gentle, passing into happy
irony and sarcasm. Adams incarnated the traits,
grace, graces, and severities of the most famous family
in American history. Hay was a man of the world,
without worldliness. Adams was so much an aristocrat that he did not hesitate to be a democrat. Hay
was so much a democrat that he had no reluctance
in being and seeming aristocratic. In each there
was a certain finish and a sense of completeness, and
also a sense of life's fullness. The best had been
given unto them and the best had been their circumstance. Yet each realized that the orbit of their
lives and their power was infinitely small in comparison with the great circles of infinite powers that
surround, and in which they were more victims than
either agents or interpreters. Each dwelt in his own
thoughts rather than in his emotions and his voli-
tions. Each was rather an interpreter than a doer,
a thinker than an executive. Each was a Greek in
his reticence, pieties, and aesthetic appreciations.
Each seemed to dwell in a world apart from the
timely and the common. Each helps one to understands the truths of Wordsworth's ode on Immortality. Adams himself wrote poems which appeal
to the deepest reverence of the soul. The fitting

[22] ''Letters to a Niece.'' By Henry Adams. p. 102.

memorial of Adams is found in Saint Gaudens' masterpiece in Rock Creek Cemetery, made for Mrs. Adams, and where Adams himself rests. The fitting memorial of Hay is found on an historic monument in an historic God's Acre in Cleveland, in a figure of a knight, armed and alert for the fight for humanity.

XVI

ANDREW SLOAN DRAPER

ANDREW SLOAN DRAPER was born at Westford, New
York, June 21, 1848; died April 27, 1913. Graduate of Albany Academy, 1866; LL.B., Albany Law
School (Union University), 1871; practiced law in
Albany till 1885; member of Albany Board of Education, 1879-81, and 1890-92; member, New York
Assembly, 1881; member, Court of Commissioners
of Alabama Claims, 1885-86; State Superintendent
of Instruction, New York, 1886-92; Superintendent
of Public Instruction, Cleveland, Ohio, 1892-94;
president of the University of Illinois, 1894-1904;
first Commissioner of Education, State of New York,
1904-13; elected Superintendent of Schools of
Greater New York, 1898, but declined; member and
chairman, United States Indian Commissions, 1902-
13. Editor, Educational Department of Encyclopedia Americana; editor-in-chief of Self-Culture
for Young People (10 volumes); awarded silver
medal, Paris Exposition, 1900, for monograph on
The Organization and Administration of the
American School System; awarded gold medal and
one of two grand prizes given at St. Louis Exposition, 1904, for unusual service in educational
administration. Author: The Rescue of Cuba;
American Education, and many addresses.

XVI

ANDREW SLOAN DRAPER

ENGINEER IN EDUCATION

THE facts of the life of Andrew Sloan Draper form a mere frame of one of the most powerful of characters, and of one of the most fruitful and diverse of careers. Draper embodied the new American spirit. This spirit possessed and ruled him. He had initiative. The initiative came from his sense of power. He had mental action, activity, achievement, which sprang like a swift arrow from his bow of strength. Directness of aim, simplicity in method, fullness of means, fitness of environment for achieving,—each he possessed, and each came from his forcefulness, native and well disciplined. The military element, strong in the beginning, lasted. "Forward march!" seemed to be a command which he himself obeyed, and which, in case of need, he gave to others. This power of the whole man was expressed in his belief in the people. He was himself a democrat of democrats, both in principle, practice, and in taste. The principle he applied to the education of the whole community, and the principle in turn being accepted, created and made his democracy yet more democratic. In speaking of the nation's purpose, he said:

"There are no 'classes' in education. It is the national belief that the true greatness of the nation and the welfare of mankind depend not only upon giving every one his chance, but also upon aiding and inspiring every one to seize his chance.

"The corner-stone principle of our political theory coincides absolutely with the fundamental doctrine of our moral law. All men and women are to be intellectually quickened and made industrially potential, to the very limits of sane and balanced character. The moral sense of the people is determined by it and the nation's greatness is measured by it. Before this fact the prerogative of a monarch or the comfort of a class is of no account. Before it every other consideration must give way. It is right here that democracies which can hold together surpass monarchies. It is for this reason that the progressive will of an intelligent people is better than the hereditary and arbitrary power of kings. And a sane and balanced and boundless educational system, with a base which is broad enough and a peak which is high enough, will fuse the elements of population and enable a democracy of English speech and sufficient Saxon blood to hold together."[1]

In his interpretation and service as a college president he applied democratic principles to the education of young men and young women, and these

[1] "American Education." pp. 14-15.

principles were, and are, most manifest in the State
university. Of co-education he said:

"Men and women supplement each other; each
supplies the factors in thought and endeavor, in dis-
cretion and stability, in force and progress which
the other lacks; and the great accomplishments in
human society have been worked out by men and
women of character working in coöperation. They
modify and strengthen and regulate and guide each
other. The greatest good of the race is to be attained through the best possible education for both.
Why should they not be educated together? Why
should the men and women who are to be the greatest factors in our democratic society be educated
under conditions which promote self-consciousness
and liking for the life of a club, either a man's club
or a woman's club, rather than under conditions
which make the recognition of interdependent relations imperative and give the best assurance of intellectual equality and similarity of outlook in the
household, and of effective and balanced service in
the state? There is no reason. If there is such
reason anywhere in all the world, there is none in
America. We have made practical demonstrations
and the results are good. We have done more for
woman than any other land has done; woman has
done more for our country than she has been able
to do for any other country. The facts and the reasons are obvious enough. No one, no party or school,
is going to turn the hands back on the great dial

which registers the progress of democratic institutions.''[2]

The type of education which Draper thus interpreted and advocated, as deep as humanity, as broad
as the commonwealth, gives a foundation of education
for efficiency. Education is ever to be aimed toward,
and to result in, service. It is to be manifested in
worthier being. It is to be felt in happier homes.
It is to result in fewer vocational misfits. It is to
cause greater productivity, material, intellectual.
It is to lift the level of society, ethical and industrial. It is to inspire nobler achievement. Leisure
has its place, and to be able to enjoy and to profit
by leisure has been declared to be a worthy purpose
of the higher education. Such an interpretation
Draper would disown. At least he would find it difficult to assent to such a doctrine as a leading principle.
The value of friendships in education, both as cause
and result, he would not despise. But to form and to
nourish friendships, he would not allow is a primary
purpose of the liberal college. He wished the higher
education to create and to discipline the worker,
through and by each faculty of his being. He might
indeed be called, as I have called him, an engineer in
education. How the heat lightning of his humor
would have played about the real lightning of his
wit, and of his affirmations regarding essential educational worths! With a sense of fun and of down-
right earnestness, how he would have spurned the

[2] *Ibid.*, p. 270.

remark applied to Oxford education, that the college is to teach one to be "a good loafer"! Prolonged discussion of recent years has, it may be added, seemed to emphasize the truth of his interpretations. The community is learning to accept primary values in education as primary, and secondary as secondary.

In such efficient education for a democratic people the State university fills important functions. Among these functions are: "It responds to all popular demands and becomes a potent factor in determining educational legislation and shaping education policy. It is free, and all ambitious eyes are turned toward it; it is popular, and all boys and girls in the high schools think about going to it. It naturally comes to be looked upon as belonging to all the people and so becomes the responsible head and guide of the public educational system." [3]

These universities are to become more numerous, larger in number of students, and stronger in educational forces. Draper's prophecy of the earlier time is being proved true in each of the years following his retirement from the Illinois presidency. This proof related, not only to the Illinois University, with an attendance of students numbering ten thousand, but also to other universities with an enrollment equally prodigious.

Yet the colleges which are not of public, but of private, foundation, endowment, and government, are still to fill a great place. With certain qualifica-

[3] *Ibid.*, p. 207.

tions, both expressed and intimated, he says of the so-called literary colleges:

"They are to flourish so long as they can provide the best instruction in the humanities, and do not assume names which they have no right to wear, and do not attempt to do work which they can do only indifferently. They will train for culture and they will prepare for the professional work as of yore. And wherever one does this well and is content to do so, it is to have every sympathy and support which an appreciative public can give." [4]

In this great work of education the public school system is to bear a necessary part. Of the public school system, Draper was a powerful and unflagging supporter,—no less powerful and unflagging when he was a university president than when he was Superintendent of Education in Cleveland. He declares:

"The one great aim of the public school system, as it is well to recall, is to hold us together, to secure the safety of a wide-open suffrage, and to assure the progress of the whole population. Child study, entrance requirements, and all the other things which are discussed often in educational conventions, are only incidental. The law-making power is to enable the people to educate themselves. The public school system is our protection. In the light of the world's experience our experiment in government is a vast undertaking. History does not record a similar experiment which has been permanently successful.

[4] *Ibid.*, p. 197.

The public school system is the one institution which is more completely representative of the American plan, spirit, and purpose than any other. It can continue to be the instrument of our security and the star of our hope only so long as it holds the interest and confidence of all the people by assuring the rights of every one to the best teaching, and by moving the mass to higher intellectual and moral planes.'' [5]

For Draper remembered, as the colleges are prone to forget, that ninety-nine per cent of all the youth of America do not continue their education into the college. In fact, most are obliged to end it with the grammar grades. The public school system has been, is, and apparently is to continue to be, the greatest force for the directing and disciplining, for the enriching and the guiding, of the American democracy.

The efficiency which Draper, as an engineer, manifested, gave a foundation for the discrimination which he made between the universities and colleges of the East and of the West. Through these discriminations, which he intimated and also expressed, runs a vein of humor which characterized no small part of his discourse, both in writing and in speaking:

"Educationally the East is given to wisdom, is deliberate, has quite as much resistive power as aggressiveness, is inclined to be suspicious, and refuses to initiate a movement until it thinks it sees clearly what the end will be. The West is hearty and im-

[5] *Ibid.*, p. 86.

pulsive, plunges into whatever engages its interest, relies upon its resourcefulness, and worries very little about results. The results are never disappointing. If the outcome is good much is made of it; if not, the movement is lightly regarded, for by that time the mind is fully occupied with other things. The Westerners are easier travelers, better 'mixers,' and more enthusiastic and aggressive searchers for information than the Easterners. An eastern schoolman knows much about schoolhouses and appliances, and is reasonably content with what he knows; a western man is never too old or too tired to go to the top or the bottom of a school building in the hope of finding a new appliance or a fresh suggestion in it. The eastern men may go to educational conferences two or three times a year, in the stern performance of a religious duty; the western men want a convention every week, and seldom lose an opportunity to be in at the start and open a discussion of facts and philosophies at a canter." [6]

In Draper's personal character, in his work, in his speaking, in his writing, the principle of optimism was dominant. Like all great leaders, he believed in the power of the right, and that "right the day must win." He believed in the American people; he believed in education as the greatest power for helping the people to achieve the highest civilization:

"The nation is just beginning to realize that the
Ibid., p. 216.

fundamental political principle which holds all men
and women equal before the law, with the now well-
developed national policy which provides free instruction to the very limits of human knowledge to
all who will come and take it, involves an expense
of unexpected magnitude, and presents questions of
grave difficulty in school organization and administration. But there will be no turning back. More
cheerfully than the people meet any other tax, more
cheerfully than any other people ever met any tax
not vital to the national defense and the saving of
life, the American people supply and will supply the
funds for universal and liberal education. The difficulties will not be met in a year; they will never
be settled in a corner. They will be solved by the
rational projection of the political theories which are
the inspiration and the guide of the nation's life.
They will be met with courage and confidence, even
with wit and enthusiasm. They will be settled
through discussion, and yet more through experience. Not all that we plan will come to pass. The
unexpected will often happen, and in time we are
likely to see that the unexpected is better than the
plan we made. The logically progressive purpose of
our millions of freemen, the gradually unfolding
scheme of our nation's mission in the world, advancing in accord with a plan that is more than human,
will overcome difficulties and break out the roads
for a sane and balanced system of education, which
will give most to the nation through the opportunity

it will hold out and the encouragement it will give
to every one."[7]

He has also said:

"It [the nation] is putting its whole self, its political power, its sagacity, and its money, into the work
which it has set itself to do. Of course it has its
perplexities; but it is without apprehension. The
great heart of the nation is conscious of its own rectitude. It will not fear and it will not hesitate. It
will act upon its own thinking. It will mend its mistakes. It does not merely stand for security: it
stands for liberty and for doing. It is not for the
present alone: it is for the future. It will take care
of its own. It will not hide its light. It will not
meddle with other people; but it will deny to no men
and women who would uplift themselves such measure of sympathy and assistance as it may give."[8]

But, though his intellect was on fire for the education of the people, Draper was not blind or deaf
to the misjudgments and mistakes of certain apostles
of education. He was able to discriminate between
theories, some hopeful and some hopeless, both before and in their application. He was fully able to
distinguish between thinkers wise and thinkers foolish. For the college president and other presumed
leaders in the higher education, he had rather a
charming word of interpretation and of description:

"Some university men lose their heads through
their freedom. They go floating around in the up-

[7] *Ibid.*, p. 106.   [8] *Ibid.*, p. 16.

per ether, often in a kind of irresponsible intellectual intoxication. Some of them even soar the higher and dissipate the more recklessly because only fool things get into the newspapers and nothing is so idiotic as to be barred out. But the primary and the secondary schools have to rest upon the earth, and have to respond to very matter-of-fact people who are guided by considerations not ordinarily exploited in the newspapers. To find a way to sustain free thinking and limit fool talk, to protect one in his academic liberty and yet keep him anchored to the verities of life, is a problem of higher education which surely has a very vital bearing upon the helpfulness of universities to a general system of education." [9]

The many years which have passed since these words were written add emphasis to their apt and vivid truthfulness.

As a comprehensive interpretation of the great man, I find a phrase of Bagehot springing to my pen. Bagehot writes of Shakespeare as having an "experiencing" mind or nature. By an "experiencing" mind is meant a mind which has had experiences or is experienced. In the past tense it was used on the occasion, two generations ago, of "experiencing religion." Bagehot's use of the word, however, is most fitting. For the mind of Shakespeare was, above all minds, the mind that was capable of having experiences. He knew without ever having learned. "Shakespeare was a lawyer," say some.

[9] *Ibid.*, p. 174.

"For no one could have known the law as Shakespeare knew it without himself being a lawyer." "He was a doctor," say others. "For he had a knowledge of disease and of cures which only a doctor could possess." "No," declare others, "he was a soldier. For he knew wars as only a soldier knows them, and much had he to say about preparations for war and the need of caution in making preparations, as well as of the spirit suitable for waging war." He recognized, too, war's loathesomeness and cruelty. Yet, as a fact, Shakespeare was neither soldier, nor doctor, nor lawyer. But his was a mind of the type which could respond to the experiences of war without practicing the art, and which knew medicine without possessing a doctor's certificate.

Such an experiencing mind belonged to Dante, to Milton, and to Goethe, but to each in less completeness than it belonged to Shakespeare. Was it not said of Dante by his fellow citizens of Florence, "There goes a man who has been in Hell!"

Draper had such a mind. He was not learned in the learning of the schools. He had not been helped, or hurt, by the enjoying or suffering of certain types of the higher education, types which are supposed to belong to the leader in the service of the American State. But he did have that quality which belonged to Shakespeare and other great ones, of knowing without having learned, and of using powers which he had not consciously acquired or formally disciplined.

In his forcefulness was a large element of emotionalism. His feelings were like the sea, easily and deeply stirred. His reaction to any apparent injustice or unfaithful act was at times passionate. Occasionally he flashed like powder. The spark of wrong doing ignited his anger. But, before striking, he was eager to hear of a method better than his own. Himself an apostle of immediate and direct action, he yet was willing to accept a substitute for his own passionate command. For, he wished only to use the wisest method for achieving the adequate and consummate result.

In any interpretation, however limited, is to be included perhaps a still greater quality than experience, namely, the quality, or element, of constructiveness. For, in constructiveness Draper possessed almost an instinct. He was a doer, and a doer of the highest type. He laid foundations. He was a builder. His achievements, born of vision, founded on hard common sense, bathed in an atmosphere of hopefulness and of optimism, he wished to make of lasting usefulness in and for the commonwealth. The specific Commonwealth might be the State of New York or the State of Ohio, or the State of Illinois, or better yet, it might be the commonwealth of commonwealths. This usefulness in all his administrations was often impeded by the politicians. Of course, Draper himself was a politician in the original sense of the word and, be it added, he knew how to deal with politicians and from them to secure his own higher and highest purposes. I know of an incident in which it was proposed, and determined even, by the authorities to cut down the appropriation to the normal schools of New York State. In controlled anger, conferring with the chairman of the legislative Committee on Schools, he demanded, in a rather thunderous voice and lightning manner, that the appropriation be restored. It was restored. The usefulness might be applied to, and through, the little red schoolhouse (that "ruby fount of knowledge," as Theodore Winthrop called it) or to, and through, the great University of the prairie. But the aim and the result of usefulness were dominant.

The noble building at Albany, the most commanding of any building of its type in the world, dedicated to the education of the people of the commonwealth, seems to be a lasting type of his character. Without, it is impressive. Its pillars have the strength of the hills whence came their marble. Its architectural lines are orderly, continuous, commanding. Its regularity of form intimates strength, and honesty of material and of construction. Within, it is fitted for service, having treasures both for the teaching of the student, for the interest of the visitor, for the research and inductions of the scholar, all assembled under noble conditions of historic architecture. *Si quaeris monumentum circumspice.* The quotation may be applied to Draper, in the capital city of Albany, on the Illinois campus, and in every school district of the Empire State.

XVII

WILLIAM DE WITT HYDE

WILLIAM DE WITT HYDE, born at Winchendon, Massachusetts, September 23, 1858; died June 29, 1917.
Received degree A.B., Harvard, 1879; graduated
from Andover Theological Seminary, 1882; ordained
to Congregational ministry, 1883; pastor, Patterson,
New Jersey, 1883-85; president, and professor of
Mental and Moral Philosophy, Bowdoin College,
1885-1917. Author: Practical Ethics; Social The-
ology; Practical Idealism; God's Education of
Man; The Art of Optimism; The College Man
and the College Woman; Self-Measurement; The
Teacher's Philosophy In and Out of School; The
Five Great Philosophies of Life; In Quest of the
Best, and other books.

XVII

WILLIAM DE WITT HYDE

PRESIDENT WHO TAUGHT PHILOSOPHY,
PHILOSOPHER WHO WAS A COLLEGE EXECUTIVE

A MEMBER of the class of 1879 at Harvard College would have known, in his four undergraduate years, members of no less than six classes besides his own. Among these men would be found several who afterwards came to be recognized as great, or at least constructive and conspicuous in American or world life. Among them would be authors, like William Roscoe Thayer, Edward S. Martin, Henry Osborn Taylor, Barrett Wendell, and George Edward Woodberry. Of the teachers and scholars would be Paul Shorey, Benjamin Osgood Peirce, the physicist, Taussig, Harold North Fowler, Albert Bushnell Hart, and teachers of law like Wambaugh, Beale, Williston, and diplomatists like Strobel. In the company would be found college presidents, or academy principals, like Lowell, Amen of Exeter, and Abercrombie of Worcester. Among them, too, would be enrolled jurists like William H. Moody, Francis Cabot Lowell, Francis Joseph Swayze and James Byrne. In the number, too, would be listed statesmen, or public men, like Roosevelt, F. J. Stimson, Rockwood Hoar, George von L. Meyer, and Robert Bacon.

The list might be greatly lengthened; but with such a group and their comrades, William De Witt Hyde spent his undergraduate years. The emphasis usually put on the formative value of college friendships is in peril of being overstated. But there is one element which does not suffer this danger: the meaning of associations with good fellows who afterwards prove themselves not to be chiefly good fellows, but good workers, of great achieving. Such associations help to form quickening forces, noble ideals, and beautiful memories. Into such associations Hyde was called. To them he gave rich offerings, and from them he received contributions equally rich.

More important and constructive, however, than the group of students who afterward became recognized as great was the group of teachers of Harvard College in those rich and enriching years. That group formed a body which now seems, seen through memory's appreciation, rich beyond comparison. Dear Dr. Andrew P. Peabody was conducting morning prayers, teaching ethics, and quietly manifesting himself as a walking benediction to all. Benjamin Peirce, passing through the yard, was bearing himself as a Jupiter holding up the heavens. Asa Gray, happy man of a white crown, was singing among his flowers. James Russell Lowell was guiding best minds unto the best appreciation of the best litera-tures. Charles Eliot Norton was seeking to give to men, either dull or responsive, a certain understanding of the fine art of Greece, and of the principles of the finer art of wholesome living. Bowen was about to close his great career as a teacher of philosophy, and Palmer and William James had begun their greater careers. Sophocles and Goodwin in Greek, Lane in Latin, Torrey and Gurney and Henry Adams in history, Child and Hill in English, were upholding and enriching the great traditions. Others there were, too, likewise great in name, as well as in worth of service. It was the Augustine age in Harvard College. In such a personal environment, and blessed by such intellectual potencies, Hyde lived his undergraduate life. Would it have been possible to find a richer opportunity for responsive minds, both of professor and student, for giving and receiving a culturing education?

In this experience Hyde was largely a student of philosophy. But also his studies included almost a dozen other subjects,—subjects as diverse as Greek and physics, as natural history, mathematics and chemistry. Like most men who afterward become distinguished, his rank was among the highest. In a class of two hundred and fifty-two (freshmen) members, he stood twenty-fourth in his freshman, sixth in his sophomore, twenty-sixth in his junior, and sixth in his senior year. His general standing was as high as eighth in his class, and at graduation, in 1879, he received his degree, *cum laude.*

The years lying between Hyde's receiving his degree and his right to give degrees were fewer than obtain with most college presidents. These six years were spent in theological and philosophical study at Union Seminary, at Andover, and at Cambridge, and, for two of them, he served as a pastor in Paterson, New Jersey. These student and pastoral years were indeed fruitful in enlarging and deepening his philosophic thought. The results became evident in each of the thirty-two years of his presidency.

Hyde entered into a notable succession. Bowdoin had had, in its hundred years of history, six, and only six, presidents. His immediate predecessor was Joshua L. Chamberlain, who, in the decade between his graduation in 1852 and his entering the army in 1862, had, after studying theology in Bangor Seminary for three years, served as instructor in rhetoric, in oratory, and in modern languages. In the Civil War, his service was outstanding. Grant promoted him to be Brigadier General for excellent service in leading his brigade in a charge. He was assigned to receive the surrender of Lee's army at Appomattox Court House, and he left the army with the rank of Brevet Major General. Following his career in the army he had served for four years as governor of the State of Maine. Preceding Chamberlain, Samuel Harris, a theologian, and Woods,—that mystical figure among all New England college presidents,— were most outstanding. Hyde, indeed,—this young man of twenty-six,—came into a notable succession.

He came also in a somewhat critical time in a no-
torious theological controversy. Two of the chief
participants in this controversy were Egbert C.
Smyth of Andover, and Edwin B. Webb, a distinguished Boston minister,—each a graduate of the
College and each a member of one of the official
boards. Smyth, too, was a member of the committee to choose a president. It would have been easy
to involve the College in what was known as the
Andover-American Board Controversy, a theological
conflict which, intense at the time and apparently
critical, has now become a memory, a memory full
of regret to most. The election of Hyde, himself
remote in his New Jersey pastorate from the immediate field of collisions and of antipathies, was a
wise choice, a choice wiser than any other nomina-
tions which had been informally made. His election
proved to be, as it promised, free from certain theological or institutional embarrassments which at one
time threatened to beset the College. Soon after his
election he wrote me (a Maine boy by birth), saying
that Bowdoin henceforth would be his *alter ego*. Such
indeed it became, and such is the grateful memory
of him in his long, faithful and fruitful presidency.

The president of a college in the State of Maine
enjoys a special advantage. For, his constituency is
the youth of the State. The young men of Maine
are in point of place, country-born and country-bred.
In point of environment, they are blessed with neither
poverty nor riches, but with a competency. In point

of race, they are of a pretty pure Anglo-Saxon origin, with exceptions found in the manufacturing towns, like Lewiston and Waterville, where the Canadian French have settled. In point of church, they are of the orthodox Congregational faith. In point of sports, they are gifted with opportunities for simple fun, such as fishing or baseball. In point of reading and of newspapers, they have formative books in their own little selections and in the small public libraries. In point of general atmosphere, they are environed with healthfulness, physical and moral, and, above all, in respect to the home, they recognize it as the chief altar of their love, loyalty, and devotion. As a result, therefore, the Maine boy, who comes to Bowdoin and other colleges, from the high schools or the few historic academies, comes having a body healthy and vigorous, a character still unformed but forming well, responsive to noblest influences, touched with a sense of diffidence, of wonder, and especially of ambition. Such personalities, thus created, thus environed, constitute the very best college material. No college offers a field more promising to the teacher or to the president.

Several and diverse are the methods which a president uses in making his contributions to his college and, through his college, to the larger human interests. The more important, of course, is the administrative. Side by side with the administrative, in case the college be small, lies the method of teaching. But also, above and beneath and around the

two methods, of administration and of teaching, lie
the books he writes. Each of these three methods
Hyde used. He was both professor and president,
and the world knows that he was an author.

Regarding Hyde as president and administrator,
one of his boys has written me, saying:

"President Hyde was a curious mingling of the
democrat and the aristocrat. In theory and in every
point of view academically considered, he was a democrat. His aristocracy was the aristocracy of scholarship and learning and high thinking. Toward the
students he was cordial, kindly, the friendly adviser.
I once heard Professor —— intimate that his administration was somewhat independent of faculty
advice and faculty coöperation. Yet, I should consider that opinion, given after President Hyde's
death, was not at all a true estimate of the general
relations existing between himself and his faculty.
On the contrary, I would say his faculty was very
loyal to him. The community had great pride in
him. He took a general interest in his town, its institutions, its policies and government." Brunswick
and the State of Maine constitute a very fruitful field.

I am inclined to think, however, that the most precious and the most lasting of Hyde's contributions to
human betterment will prove to be found in his books.
For, he wrote constantly and in many fields. His
books number about a score. From them I shall be
generous in making quotations to illustrate the worth
of his educational and theological principles, the

method of his broad thinking, and the noble effectiveness of his English style.

No one of his volumes seems to me quite so revealing of the man, or so suggestive of rich thinking, as the one entitled "God's Education of Man." The very statement of the principles which he discusses is impressively significant: "The Universal Will of God the Metaphysical and Ethical Basis of Christianity;" "Christ the Historic Revelation of the Universal Will of God;" "The Holy Spirit, God in Humanity, The Doctrine of the Trinity the Unessential Formulation of Essential Truths;" "The Ritualism that is Idolatry;" "The Inadequacy of Law;" "The Priority of Grace;" "Character the Completion, Service the Expression, of the Work begun by Law and Grace;" "The Sense of Proportion and the Art of Subordination Essential to the Highest Character and the Best Service;" "The Bane of Clericalism and Sentimentalism." [1]

These phrases indicate the fulness of his interpretation of the divine method for the education of men. They touch, perhaps, rather the church than the college, rather religious than intellectual education. But Hyde and his friends never forget that he was ordained as a Christian minister. From the pulpit he went to become a college president and college professor. And, while thus serving, he also did not abdicate the clerical function.

The double relation which he held, to the church

[1] pp. ix-xi.

and to the college, he has well indicated in one of the best paragraphs of one of his best volumes:

"This third stage of the spiritual life corresponds to the university stage of education. Law deals with men as the school deals with children; compelling them to do what is good for them though they do not like it at the time. Grace appeals to men as the college appeals to youth; winning them to the spiritual life by the inherent interest and attraction of the Ideal personally presented as the object of their affection. Character treats men as the university treats its graduate students; absolving them from definite rules and specified responsibilities, and leaving them free to do for themselves something which is not exactly like anything that was ever done before. As the university is not content that its graduate student should simply learn and repeat what the university has to teach, but insists that he shall bring to it some contribution of his own; so God admits us to the highest character, not in reward for keeping the moral law, or in recognition of our punctiliousness in the performance of church duties and services, but only on condition that we shall go out into the actual world and make it a healthier, richer, fairer, purer, juster, happier world in consequence of the original contribution that we make to its domestic or social, its industrial or civic, its ecclesiastical or artistic life." [2]

Throughout Hyde's writing, and also throughout

[2] "God's Education of Man." pp. 197-198.

his teaching, was manifest one of his most unique powers, the power of analysis. I know of no teacher, unless it be Mark Hopkins, or Park, or his own master, Palmer, who had this gift in a richer degree. It is felt in each paragraph, in the succession of paragraphs, and in the arrangement of a whole book. Does not the content of the little volume, "Jesus' Way," give an illustration of unique, analytical power: "The Father: The Principle of the Way"; "The Son: The Incarnation of the Way"; "The Kingdom: The Spirit of the Way"; "Faith: The Grasp of the Way"; "Repentance: The Entrance to the Way"; "Forgiveness: The Restoration to the Way"; "Love: The Law of the Way"; "Loyalty: The Witness to the Way"; "Sacrifice: The Cost of the Way"; "Revelation: The Judgment of the Way"; "Blessedness: The Reward of the Way"; "Universality: The Triumph of the Way?"[3]

Yet the volumes, "Self-Measurement," and "Practical Ethics," offer yet further evidence of the analytical interpretation and arrangement of intellectual treasures. I can give only a hint of the scale of human values which the "Self-Measurement" presents. Among the fundamental relations of life, he notes physique, work, property, pleasure, science, art, family, society, country, religion.[4] Each of these ten relations he describes in their fullness or in their lack, under a half-dozen aspects. The family, for instance, on the positive side, is interpreted as stand-

[3] p. xiii.   [4] pp. 23-24 (table).

ing for obligation, affection, and devotion; on the negative side, for neglect, licentiousness, hatefulness. Science, as an example, on the positive side, has the aspects of intelligence, scholarship, and originality; and on the negative, of ignorance, pretense, and falsehood. Country offers on the positive side, the aspects of loyalty, patriotism, reform; on the negative, indifference, corruption, anarchy. Religion, on the positive, is marked by observance, propagation, and redemption; on the negative side, by unbelief, hypocrisy, and blasphemy. In "Practical Ethics," too, the great conditions of knowledge, time, space, fortune, nature, involve duty, virtue, reward, temptation and are accompanied by the vice of defect, by the vice of excess, and by penalties. Time, for instance, involves the duty of coördination, stands for the virtue of prudence, is touched by the reward of harmony, is obliged to suffer by the temptation of dissipation, of procrastination, and is not free from the vice of anxiety, and the penalty of discord.[5]

Thus, interpreting the great forces, materials, conditions, and methods of life, Hyde illustrates his power of comprehensive and of detailed analysis. The result is a practical understanding of life, such as few thinkers have been able to give to student or to reader.

In Hyde's method of reasoning and in his style of writing, it is easy to detect the influence of his early teacher and constant friend, George Herbert Palmer.

[5] pp. vi-vii.

In the fullness and detail of analysis, and in the greater gift and achievement of synthesis and of proportion, one hears Palmer still speaking. In simplicity of interpretation and of statement, a simplicity liable to blind one to the statement's depth and significance, Palmer's voice is still heard. In the lucidity of argument and of method, a method at once Greek and French, Palmer is still recognized. In the persuasiveness of sentence and paragraph, a persuasiveness whose conclusiveness is inevitable, Palmer's power is still regnant. Here are found the sweetness and light of Matthew Arnold and of Palmer, which are touched with a genuine eloquence which neither the Oxford professor of poetry nor the Harvard professor of philosophy were accustomed to use.

Hyde's philosophy of the whole educational process is put forth with a fullness and clearness belonging to few, if to any other, presidents of his time. Its keyword is the proper and much-abused word of "interest." In the five steps of education which he interprets, interest remains a regular and permanent form. In the primary school, interest demands and should receive immediate satisfaction, and, through interest, the child's will is strengthened. In the grammar school, interests, artificially weighed, are introduced, artificial encouragements play their function, manual activities have special value. Promotions, frequent and special, are of much worth, and joy in achievement begins to have a place. In the high school, individual interests assume unique value.

The individual selfhood of the student is to be discovered. Aptitudes are to be found out and to be joined to proper opportunities. In the college, in turn, social interests emerge. The social will comes to play a great function. The various studies form almost a method for developing interests, as well as for giving individual discipline. In the university, in succession, professional interests form the crown of the five-fold educational process. Reverence for truth, the understanding of a subject through research, the commandingness of the professional ideal, represent successive steps in the process. In this five-fold progress, the teacher, the student, and the subject taught and studied, are the dominating forces. But the relation of student and teacher is of special worth. Upon this signal element, Hyde, in great fullness, definite plainness and persuasive conclusiveness, says:

"The college officer should always include the point of view of the student in his treatment of him. This is essential to the teacher's successful discipline in any grade. As long as the student feels that you understand him, appreciate his good qualities as well as his bad qualities, make due allowance for his weakness and temptation, and give due weight to his peculiar point of view, you can say anything to him, however harsh; you can do anything to him, however severe; and he will not resent it. The men you treat most severely will be your best friends; for they know their failings as well as you do, and are willing to acknowledge them. If, along with their failings, you know and recognize their better side, they will appreciate you as their friend even when the attitude you are compelled to take toward their conduct is uncompromisingly hostile. On the other hand, if you have not acquired this power to see and appreciate others as they really are, and to include their point of view in your own, you will find it impossible to live with them in peace on any terms. If you are kind to them, they will despise you as weak, and try to take advantage of you; if you are unkind to them, they will resent it as an intrusion and set you down as a brute. Not to be understood by the person who undertakes to deal with him in any way is, to the student's mind, the only unpardonable sin. However bad he may be, however wrong his acts may have been, as long as there are good sides to his nature which you do not discover and appreciate, he will regard you in his inmost heart as an alien and an enemy; as a smaller, lower person than himself; as his moral and spiritual inferior. In this harsh judgment that he will pass upon you, the worst of it is that he is absolutely right. To deal with persons as though they were things; to deal with the acts of a person as though those acts were the whole personality; not to understand a person with whom you presume to deal,—this is indeed the teacher's unpardonable sin. Whoever lacks that social insight and tact ought either to set about acquiring it in earnest, or resign at once. That person has no more business to be teaching young persons than an infant has to be playing with loaded guns or dynamite bombs.''[6]

It may be said that the several tests of a good teacher may likewise be interpreted as equally worthy tests of a good student: ''Does my study thrill my zeal, and urge me forward to do my best? Do I feel I am developing, through learning and through association, a personality deeper, broader, nobler, richer, and more commanding? Does life seem to me to concern more and more the intellectual, the spiritual, the divine, the eternal? . . . Does law seem to me easier for my obedience, and the more necessary and inevitable, as well as the more beneficent? If these tests can be met, the conclusion is necessary that I, the student, am, day by day and year by year, becoming a worthier son of God, and a worthier member of the race.''[7]

The methods and tests of growth which Hyde lays down for the teacher and for the student, also govern the five great philosophies of life. These great philosophies are the Epicurean, the Stoic, the Platonic, the Aristotelian, and the Christian. The Epicurean stands for happiness, the Stoic for fortitude, the Platonic for serenity, the Aristotelian for proportion, the Christian for devotion. Most apt are these interpretations and characterizations. In them, however, one ventures to suggest whether, in the progress of the development of the individual student,

[6] ''The Teacher's Philosophy.'' pp. 34-36.
[7] Condensed from ''The Teacher's Philosophy.'' pp. 43-45.

proper emphasis is laid upon the element of freedom. Perhaps one might say that freedom is not so much an element as an atmosphere. It represents the condition under which the student, in happiness, in fortitude, in serenity, in proportion, and in devotion, grows and develops. But freedom, though a condition and an environment, is essential. Under the condition of the lack of freedom, there would result no proper growth of the spirit, or a just development of character.

Hyde always impresses me as having at least four constructive elements. They are his intellectual worth, his lucidity, his intellectual and moral forcefulness, and his consequent rational and social theology.

His mind was rich in fact and truth, and in truth of many types. The laying up of stores and the making of resources began early, and continued to the end. The richness of his nature was made manifest in the day's talk and in the classroom presentations. One of his students has written me, saying: "I became a member of his class in psychology, then philosophy, and in the third term of the senior year, ethics. Two things stand out in my recollection of him as a teacher. First, his unusual aptness in drawing from literature, history, and especially current history, illustrations with which to drive home the application of the points he was teaching." The richness which is thus indicated is quite as manifest in his books as it was in the classroom.

A second element is found in the clearness of his understanding and in his consequent style of writing. This lucidity has close relationship to his power of analysis to which I have already referred. Of course, no one knows, yet I do venture to believe that this precious characteristic of clearness was disciplined and enriched by his scientific studies. For, a larger share of his studies at college were in the field of the natural and physical sciences than would normally belong to a man of the philosophic type of mind.

With these two elements or characteristics was joined intellectual and moral forcefulness. His mind was alert, his will vigorous. To him was given a sense of the fullness of life. Leadership was his, both as a gift and as an achievement. If, at times, to some he seemed not to avail himself to the full extent of the counsel of his associates of the faculty, this fact, if it be a fact, and this impression arose from his own worthy sense of power and of initiative. This sense of power was most manifest in the classroom. He was able and forth-putting, so able and forth-putting that he did not seem, in his teaching, to give heed to the views opposing his own which many teachers welcome. A student, himself who has now become a distinguished educator, from whom I have already quoted, says: "His manner of teaching seemed to lack deference toward opinions which differed from his own. The statement of his own position on controversial questions seemed to have what we might almost call cocksureness which did not invite opposition or discussion or even the silent opposition, as worthy. I could probably state that point in better form and better flavor if I might do so without sacrilege, by saying that he taught 'as one having authority and not as the scribes.' "

In his books and in his teaching, Hyde, also, used in the fourth place, a peculiarly able and satisfactory system of rational and social theology. It was among the most human of all systems. Theological writing and teaching is liable to become unrational and apodictic. It is prone to lift itself above reason, even if it does not become anti-rational. Hyde wrote and taught out of his understanding, as did the great Park. His reasoning about the divine was human, as all reason about the ultimate must be. It was also devoted to the welfare of man. His "Outlines of Social Theology" is pregnant with great interpretations. "The world and the self" represent "the Father"; "the real and ideal—the Son"; "the natural and the spiritual—the Holy Spirit." "Sin and law" stand for "judgment," "repentance and faith" for "salvation"; "degeneration and growth" for "life." In the social domain, "The Church," "the redemption of the world," and "the organization of the kingdom," represent the lasting forces and conditions.[8]

Such interpretations are vastly needed in the college class-room, and, be it added, in the lecture-room of the theological seminary. For, some teachers

[8] p. ix.

of philosophy are liable to up-root the religious faith
of students without giving them seeds for bringing forth the plants of a stronger and more fruitful faith. Hyde's system was optimistic, rational,
promising lasting and noblest results.

Hyde died before his time. He was in the sixtieth
year of his life, and at the close of the thirty-second
year of his presidency. Measured by the lengths of
most terms, it was a long presidency, but, under
ordinary conditions, it might have been continued
toward its half-century mark. He does, however, take
his place with the theological, philosophic presidents
of the typical college of New England. He stands
alongside of the foreseeing Wayland of Brown, with
the learned Porter of Yale, with the public-minded
Julius H. Seelye and with the acute-minded George
Harris of Amherst, with the gracious Buckham of
Vermont, and with the beloved Tucker of Dartmouth.
It is indeed a noble race, this race of New England
college presidents, and among them William De Witt
Hyde has a place, high and lasting.

XVIII

JAMES MONROE TAYLOR

JAMES MONROE TAYLOR was born in Brooklyn, New York, August 5, 1848; died December 19, 1916. A.B. degree, University of Rochester, 1868; graduated from Rochester Theological Seminary, 1871; ordained, Baptist ministry, 1871; 1871-72, in Europe; pastor, South Norwalk, Connecticut, 1873-82; Providence, Rhode Island, 1881-86; professor of Ethics, and president, Vassar College, 1886-1914. Author: Psychology; New World and Old Gospel; Practical or Ideal; Before Vassar Opened; Vassar (with Professor Elizabeth H. Haight).

XVIII

JAMES MONROE TAYLOR

PRESIDENT OF STRENGTH AND OF GOOD FELLOWSHIP

ALL the sheaves of the feminine academic harvest make "obeisance" to the sheaf of Vassar. For, Vassar was the earliest of the well-endowed colleges founded exclusively for women. Other colleges for them had been established, but they were poor in endowment, feeble in the instruction they offered, small in number of students, and slight in influence. Co-educational colleges,—private like Oberlin, and of the state establishment, like the state universities,— abounded. But Vassar, well endowed, strong, valiant, stood and must stand first. In his suggestive volume, "Before Vassar Opened," Taylor says of the condition preceding the opening of Vassar in 1865: "A great movement often depends on a great opportunity, and the years of our bitter Civil War were really the open sesame for the budding and blossoming and fruiting of the subconscious demands for larger activities, larger public responsibilities, and a more generous education for womankind. It was one of the happy synchronisms of history which opened the doors of Vassar in the very year which closed those

of the temple of Janus and gave to us a reunited
country with new outlook, new necessities, and new
opportunities. . . . For a quarter of a century opportunities had been offered and they were recognized
by very few. The time for the movement in behalf
of women had not come, but when it came the recognition was swift and the rapidity of the response was
momentous. Vassar really marked an epoch. Therefore to most the foundation seemed new, and the
founder one of the great Originals.'' [1]

James Monroe Taylor came to the presidency of
Vassar after a trying period in its history which
followed, though not immediately, the death of the
great Raymond in 1878. For, Raymond was great,
—among the greatest:—in a period of academic un-
certainty he was firm; in a time when ignorance, or
half-ignorance prevailed, he was wise; in an age when
vision was limited, he had prevision; in a decade when
conservatism was liable to become regressiveness, and
progressiveness radicalism, he properly united both
the conservative and the prophetic power. A great
personality, he yet adjusted himself to conditions of
diverse origin and of momentous consequence. Raymond was, and still remains, among the greatest.

Like most earlier presidents, Taylor came from the
ministry. The ministry, let it ever be said, is an excellent preparation for the weighty, and weightier,
duties of a presidency. For, the ministry, first, represents the quest of spiritual values by means of in-

[1] pp. 83-84.

tellectual atmospheres and forces. Second, it represents the translation of intellectual and spiritual ideals into character and human service. Third, it constitutes a fitting method of the transmutation of personalities into movements for social advancement. Fourth, it represents the adjustment of personalities to each other, and to the gaining of the highest ultimate ends. Fifth, it also embodies the service of the minister himself, through addresses, personal associations and diverse labors, both occasional and constant, given to individuals and to the whole community. From such an experience in two parishes, of fourteen years, in South Norwalk and Providence, Taylor came to the presidency of Vassar. It was a preparation fitting him for the great work of his great life, of pregnant and impressive weight and value.

In the Vassar presidency, beginning in 1886, he continued more than twenty-seven years. The ideal which he set up for himself in his inaugural address, remained his ideal to the end. In that address, he said: "The College will strive, in the future, as it has in the past, to send forth women of fearless intellectual independence, efficient in all the work of the world, thorough in thinking and in action, and possessed of a reverent, God-centered faith. It will not forget that its best may be bettered, and that in its scope and power it may always make progress."[2]

[2] "The Life and Letters of James Monroe Taylor." By Elizabeth Hazelton Haight. p. 95.

His later and permanent interpretation, given more than twenty years after, with even greater emotional force and keener discrimination, in an address made in 1907, is yet more significant: " 'to see straight, to think accurately, to speak exactly'; to arouse his intellectual curiosity; to 'awaken taste, love of good books, art, music,—and so furnish resources for after life'; and 'to create, awaken, and intensify *moral* purpose, with its conviction of *responsibility* to society, and of duty to use all developed power and intelligence for the service of the world.' " [3] These phrases are indeed flashes of truth significant of his constant thinking.

When one attempts to analyze the character of the man, he turns for help, among many evidences, to what he wrote to his son, Hunt, of his own brother who had just died. For one's interpretation of another man is often only a mirror of himself. "He was a man of *duty*. He said, in his last days, to me, 'I have tried to do my duty: I hope I have: I wish nothing else said of me.'

"He was also very courteous in his treatment of all men,—not 'goody-goody,'—but firm, strong, frank and direct in speech,—popular among those whom he opposed because they knew him genuine in his opposition,—and courteous.

"He was a very *'square'* man in his business relations. I have letters about him now telling how he was esteemed. He was fair, honest, strict with himself (I remember noticing how he bought his own

[3] *Ibid.*, p. 234.

stamps for his own private correspondence . . . though a member of the house).

"Above all, he was a Christian man with a well defined hope in Christ. That was his anchor: the rest might have done in prosperous days, but what would all these last days have been but for a calm, deep trust in God and the risen life in Jesus? I know what it was to him,—and you know whether or not Uncle Morg enjoyed life."[4]

The distinguished Professor of Psychology at Vassar, Margaret F. Washburn, wrote of him: " 'There were three qualities which no colleague of Dr. Taylor's, however differing from him in opinions, could possibly or conceivably associate with him, and those were vacillation, underhandedness, or egotism.' "[5]

Miss Washburn goes on to interpret, and with much truthfulness, the three great qualities, the opposites of which she intimates:

" 'His was a mind of great clarity and definiteness. When I say that he did not vacillate, I do not mean that he was impulsive, or that he could not suspend judgment when deliberation was in his opinion necessary. But he always understood his own position; the moment of decision was a sharply defined one with him, and once having reached a determination, he did not readily change his opinion. With this intellectual quality the moral quality of his straightforwardness was closely associated. No mem-

[4] *Ibid.*, p. 110.   [5] *Ibid.*, p. 309.

ber of the Vassar faculty was ever in doubt as to
Dr. Taylor's policy on a matter which he had time
to consider. The conjectures and rumors which are
rife in some institutions as to the presidential attitude
would have been ludicrously misplaced in the atmosphere which he created; plots and schemes and
suspicions could not flourish in relation to his office.
So marked was this transparent honesty and out-
spokenness of his that I believe it was the chief characteristic associated with the thought of him in the
minds of the academic world at large. Decision and
straightforwardness had their roots in the nature
of his thinking processes; the third quality I have
named, the absence of egotism, had a deeper basis in
his character. Dr. Taylor was intensely human. He
desired intensely the things he desired; he had strong
personal likes and dislikes. He was, I feel sure, sensitive to the joy of seeing his plans succeed and
realizing that it was his own power which had thus
found expression. But he was not interested in himself. The world around him and the people around
him were so intensely interesting to him that he had
no attention to bestow on himself as a spectacle.
Hence, while he was vulnerable through his feelings,
he could not be reached through vanity. This ob-
jectivity, helped by his steady sense of humor, was
a happy trait rarely found in a personality with so
much reason to find itself interesting, with a temperament of so much vigor and fire, and an achievement
so notable. It does not often happen that so power-

ful a will is associated with 'a heart at leisure from itself.' " [6]

With these and other elements was united the element of sympathy, the sympathy which, in certain respects, became in him a sense of geniality and of informality. It is a sense which appeals alike to students and to children, as well as to their seniors. One of his oldest and dearest associates has written me regarding this beautiful quality:

"It was a similar sort of sympathy and adaptability that enabled him to understand the student point of view. He urged us older people, many times, to remember that no matter how we might change, the students represented practically a stationary age, and that *their* problems were constantly those of youth. Also he reminded us over and over again that the college was primarily for the students and that they furnished the reason for our being there. He believed in the student's honesty of purpose and ability, and when he objected to any *great* extension of their responsibility, it was chiefly because he thought it unwise and unfair to let them assume administrative burdens that taxed too heavily the time and strength that belonged to the academic work.

"It was in the summer of 1887 or 1888, after the preparatory department had been closed, that he wrote, 'I wonder if we shall have many students. I have sixteen names down since Commencement and eighteen more have beer marked doubtful. I hope!'

[6] *Ibid.*, pp. 309-310.

It was a far cry from that time to the spring when he decided that we must begin to turn away many of those knocking at our doors, but the greater numbers seemed to find him with greater capacity for acquaintance with names and with the individual characteristics and deeds. Truly his knowledge of, and interest in, the individual, were marvelous. Once when there was a serious case of discipline before us, he wrote, 'Can't we save her? Isn't there a better side to bring out? I know she has been a nuisance, I know we are tired of her, but that is nothing. I hate to give up a girl as long as there is a chance of our being able to help her.'

"Along with constant thought and effort for better and broader opportunities for intellectual work, Dr. Taylor was always interested in the play of the students, I might almost say their nonsense, and regretted any absence from their entertainments, especially those that were original. Their happiness as well as their problems he shared in great and small things. For instance, I can see him now with a most happy expression on his face, standing by the office window (at the end of third hour,) at the beginning of a vacation, when the campus was full of girls with suit cases, flocking to the cars. Again in September he always commented with pleasure when the happy shrieks in the corridors announced that friends were meeting after the long, long separation of the summer vacation."

I recently asked one of his students who was both

a graduate and afterward an executive colleague, what was her impression of Taylor? Her informal and oral reply was,—and perhaps a reply all the more full of meaning because so informal,—"He made fundamental things as interesting as the superficial, and serious things as exciting as the frivolous. He gave breadth of vision and vitality to solid things. His own vision, keenness and personality put him in touch with all students."

I have many letters from Taylor which indicate the informality, sympathies, and happy relationships which may exist between two presidents. For some reason or other, and with our mutual acquaintance with the writings of Jacob Abbott, I adopted him as my "Rollo," and he me as his "Uncle George." From time to time, "Uncle George" wrote to him giving proper counsel, and he replied in a typical Rollo-like spirit. From the letters of "Rollo" addressed to his "Uncle George," written through many years, I venture to make certain extracts. The personal allusions may find possibly a certain apology in the playfulness and the fun. In 1911, he wrote me asking: "When do you get together your circus . . . you have so kindly asked me to attend with you? Is there a fixed time in the spring—and fall? What fun it will be to have you point out to me the side-shows,—and how shall I appreciate your guidance thro' the pitfalls of such a show!" Two years earlier, "Rollo" wrote saying: "Uncle George, your letter has a cheering ring. I woke up this morning at half-

past four, and have done a day's work here at ten
o'clock, and I could not get asleep again because my
unhappy mind began working on these problems.
. . . Your word is my first note of cheer this morning, and it draws out my heart toward you as a
nephew's ought to gush toward a mature and helpful
uncle.'' At the time of his resignation, which came
out of his own wish and will, he wrote: ''The latest
[report] is that I am being driven out by the suf-
fragists! I think if anything could have kept me
here for a while it would have been an attack of that
sort. Alas! dear uncle, there is some fight in the old
man yet, notwithstanding the fact that I find myself
referred to in the prints as retiring on account of
my 'advanced age!' '' Indeed, the dear and great
Jacob Abbott still lives!

Taylor, the person, was also a teacher. He was
one of those presidents,—and the number, alas!
diminishes,—who was willing to teach, who often even
demanded of himself this right. His conception of the
college teacher was of the highest type, and his interpretation of this type was dominated by the power
of the personality of the teacher himself. In the
year 1898, in the very midst of his career, he wrote:

''I have no hesitation in saying regarding the two
or three greatest teachers whose influence I felt in
my own education, notwithstanding their brilliant
intellectual powers and their keenness as mere instructors, the force which they left upon my own life was
the impelling power of their great personalities, the

power which somehow in a man takes hold of the life of another man and brings him to sight and to insight, which becomes an impulsive force in his life, and which brings into our own lives the joy and the strength of the vision which he has looked upon. That is the force of the teacher's life after all, whatever his intellectual keenness and greatness. That is the secret of the power of Socrates, of Comenius, Pestalozzi, Wayland, Robinson, Anderson, or of any of the greatest names that you have known in your own history or in the general history of education. It is true of every one of them. It was their personality, the power of a heart and a soul that believe in truth and believe in communicating that truth, whatever it was, to the hearts of other men. It was not because Arnold was a great master of Latin that he accomplished what he did at Rugby; it was because Arnold got into the hearts of the boys before him that he made them greatest in church and state in England. Every one of us feels the impulse of some life that has influenced us to some extent and made us feel the power of its own visions and the power of its own truth. Unless lives have that, whatever may be' their intellectual attainment, they must fail as teachers. No teacher can be great without this, and no great teacher can fail to communicate part of this to the souls of those to whom he speaks. No advanced course can take the place of it, and no pedagogical training, however thorough, can stand instead of it in that great work which it is our highest privilege to be engaged in, the teaching of the young how to live."[7]

The value of his own teaching, and especially his teaching of ethics, is illustrated in some nonsense verses once sung to him on the completion of the annual course:

> "Now our Exam is over,
>   It's not utility
> That makes us serenade you,
>   But Social Sympathy.
> The motive that controls us
>   Is a force that is innate;
> It's natural affection
>   Not pre-ordained by Fate.
>
> That we can now distinguish
>   Pushpin from Poetry
> We owe to you, dear Prexy,
>   Our Moral Faculty.
> Though Hedonists by nature
>   You and Conscience teach us still
> To cultivate our Reason
>   And Freedom of the Will."[8]

In the teacher, however, he did not wish to find personality only. He had a belief in the worth of intellectual studies, pursued faithfully day by day, as a method and means for the growth and development of character. No finer illustration of the use of this method can be found than in the career of his

[7] "The Life and Letters of James Monroe Taylor." By Elizabeth Hazelton Haight. pp. 155-156.

[8] *Ibid.*, p. 158.

colleague, the great Maria Mitchell. The mathematician and astronomer used her tools and her formulae to teach moral soundness, as well as intellectual accuracy and understanding. Her fearless pursuit of truth in science inspired every student to be likewise fearless in the quest of religion and in the struggle for noble womanhood. Her observatory was the birthplace of souls, as well as the laboratory of mathematical astronomy. Maria Mitchell had an influence over Vassar girls akin to that which Albert Hopkins, also an astronomer, had over the more reverent type of boys at Williams.

Yet one does not forget that it was the President, and not the Professor, who represents the lasting power and influence. In Taylor were incarnated the enduring qualities of a great president,—patience, energy, foresight, thoughtfulness, height and definiteness of purpose, comprehensiveness of understanding, and a sense of opportuneness. On that difficult relation, however, the relation to the board of trustees, I wish especially to comment. This relation was marked by confidence, personal and administrative, shown on many occasions, as well as in the daily routine. In this confidence, the element of friendship had a large and unique place. One of the trustees, who was also a graduate, wrote on the Twenty-fifth Anniversary of Taylor's presidency, saying:

"I am only one of many who are thinking of your coming to the College twenty-five years ago this month, when Vassar was a young thing. There is a choir invisible of old girls thinking tonight of your constant devotion, ready to sing of Prexie and the lady behind her miraculous cruse of welcome. I wish it were possible to pass under the yoke, with the lodge-clock above it and join the white processional of undergraduates tonight. But . . . from Sparkill I send you both many thoughts, grateful for the past, wishing you joy in your present and the happy tomorrows. This is a day of our beautiful September weather, with river, sky and trees under the spell of mellow autumn. I can see the campus trees, sunset light on the old brick front and my dear friends facing the long year together.''[9]

These results, so beautifully set forth, won in these many years of service, came from a life which was inspired by the unseen forces. He saw and he felt the invisible, but he also saw and felt the visible. Both the human and the divine, the natural and the supernatural, were his constant ministers. The world above and the world without helped to make the world within. Books were his constant companions. He was the reader of many books, and of diverse themes. In his own handwriting, there lies before me a list of his books of a single summer vacation:

> "Mss. written, Ethical Syllabus,—43 *large* pp—
> Read much . . . on Aristotle, Welldon,—a new book.
> *Marshall's:* Theory of Conduct.

[9] *Ibid.*, pp. 254-255.

Huckel: Modern Study of Conscience (a little book).

Davenport: Primitive Traits in Religious Revivals (capital).

Maitland: Life and Letters of Leslie Stephen (500 pp.).

Rhodes: History of United States,—two vols. (6 and 7).

Church: Nicias and the Sicilian Expedition (suggested by my interest in Sicily, and recalling *Syracuse* most fully).

Mrs. Brookfield and Her Circle (500 pp.).

Several of *Macarthur's* sermons in his new volume.

Glanced thro one (of two) vol. on *Old Provence,* chiefly on Roman and Greek times, and not very interesting just now. But what a country to visit, Arles, Nimes, etc.

I have partially read two or three other books, but the above is my three weeks' record, and now I can rest a little."

In sending this list to his friend, who is also my friend, he wrote, "Books are a great resource and companionship." He found in books, as he said, "the pleasure of cultivating his mind and soul." It may be added that he made a special point of reading on Sunday, as a dear friend said: "Something that bore especially on the religious and spiritual life, for he thought, as he expressed it, that 'Sunday ought to mean to us some glimpse of the broader, higher relations of life that sweeten the common things, and make it all worth while. You know that I *do* reach up

above the tangible and visible, and do love the
things that are unseen.' Probably this constant enriching of his life had much to do with the impression of many as expressed by one friend when she
said, 'Dr. Taylor radiated a kind of spiritual force
which does not cease to act. How hard it is to describe just what he had that most people have
not! It was rare, rarer than most of the qualities
that one can call by name.' "

After twenty-seven and a half years of devoted
service, he asked to be allowed to resign. His was a
model way of retiring. The two most serious periods
of a college presidency are the beginning and the
ending. In this respect a college presidency is like
the departing and the landing of the ship. Between
the periods, almost any captain and president can in
fair weather manage the craft. Taylor's letter of
resignation is worthy of special note. It is too long
for quotation. I must, however, include its first
paragraph:

"I wish to consult with you regarding my resignation of the great trust committed to me by the Board
in 1886. Our relations have been so unbroken in
coöperation and friendship that I cannot send you
a merely formal renunciation of my privileges and
powers." [10]

But the whole letter, worthy of reading by the
president engaged in actual service, and with many
years before him, is specially rewarding to the presi-

[10] *Ibid.*, p. 273.

dent who is about to retire. For, the letter was given,
it is to be noted, first, with a length of time in advance
sufficient for making necessary administrative adjustments, or for finding a successor: it gave warning of
a year, as well as a definite date. It was also a personal note, without being too personal, suggestive of
service rendered, rather intimating than naming results accomplished. Free from selfwardness, it
furthermore offered reasons for the request which
appealed to the rational understanding. It was also
filled with an atmosphere of gratitude to the board,
with personal affection for its members, and, lastly,
it breathed optimism and confidence in the future
of the College.

The personal end came not long after the sunset
of the long college day,—two years. To him may be
applied the Greek eulogy, as is done in the biography,
from which I have freely quoted:

"Hard it is to find a man truly noble, four-square
in hand, foot, and mind, wrought without reproach,—
a blameless man. So I, having found one, proclaim
him, and praise him and cherish him,—one who
voluntarily did nothing base." [11]

[11] *Ibid.,* p. 379.

XIX

SAMUEL HARVEY TAYLOR

SAMUEL HARVEY TAYLOR, born on the farm of his Scotch-Irish ancestor, Matthew Taylor, in Derry, New Hampshire, October 3, 1807; died January 29, 1871. At fourteen, he became largely responsible for the running of two farms, and expected to devote himself to farming. At eighteen years, by reason of an accident, he decided to follow a literary life. He prepared in Pinkerton Academy and Atkinson Academy for the sophomore class, Dartmouth College, in two years. Graduating from Dartmouth, with honor, in 1832, he at once entered Andover Theological Seminary, but withdrew to teach in Phillips Academy. He was the next year asked to become assistant principal, but declined. He served as tutor in Dartmouth College, 1836-37. In this time he pursued theological studies, and received a diploma from Andover in 1837. In this year, he was chosen principal of Phillips Academy, —a place he held till his death in 1871. For thirty-three years, he was member of the Board of Trustees, Andover Theological Seminary, and clerk of the Board; librarian of the Seminary; member, Examining Committee, Harvard College; member, Oriental Society; member and president, Board of Trustees, Pinkerton Academy and Adams Female Seminary, Derry, New Hampshire.

Author: Guide for Writing Latin, translation from the German of John Phillip Krebs; Grammar of the Greek Language, with Professor B. B. Edwards, translation from Dr. Raphael Kühner; assisted in editing The History of Londonderry, and wrote a Memoir of Reverend Edward L. Parker as a preface; Method of Classical Study; Memorial, of his brother-in-law, Joseph P. Fairbanks, 1865; Classical Study, Its Value illustrated by Extracts from the Writings of Eminent Scholars, with Introduction; editor of Bibliotheca Sacra, 1851-1871.

XIX

SAMUEL HARVEY TAYLOR

TEACHER, WHO TRAINED BOYS

THERE were great teachers on Andover Hill fifty and more years ago. There was Phelps—warm of heart, splendid and moving in eloquent lecture or sermon, impressive to the imagination both by reason of, and despite, a certain personal elusiveness, father of distinguished children. There was Thayer—a soldier in the Chair of New Testament Greek, a gentleman of the manner, and the manners, of a chevalier, with the heart of a hero, without fear and without reproach, quickening to intellect and to soul. There was Park—a Dante in the close-drawn intensity of face, a giant of swinging gait and of stature, possessed of a mind, massive, or possibly having a mind mightily possessing him, analytical and logical, of the highest type. There was also Taylor, Samuel Harvey Taylor, Principal of Phillips Academy, a teacher about whom, in grateful remembrance, I wish to write.

The academies of New England, in the last decades of the eighteenth and the first half of the nineteenth century, performed great functions in the permanent

education of American youth. The high schools of
the later decades had not come to their present commanding place in either their number or multitudes
of students. Undoubtedly, the two most conspicuous
academies of the time were Phillips Exeter and Phillips Academy of Andover. Their foundations were
laid by the early members of one of the most useful
of American families. The two most outstanding
heads of these Academies, in the later period, were
Gideon Lane Soule of Exeter, and Samuel Harvey
Taylor of Andover.

A form plump, a face fair, approaching undue
fullness, vigorous bearing, a sense of power and of
forth-puttingness, a voice strong and low, yet intense, usually without harshness, bespectacled eyes
that looked right into you, lips firm, yet not too firm,
bearing a smile that seemed to give peculiar happiness, both to him who wore it and certainly to the
one for whom it was meant—such was "Uncle Sam."
And yet "Uncle Sam" was more, much more, than
these simple and awkward phrases betoken. He was a
personality, a principal, a teacher.

Yet, though most outstanding as principal of
Phillips Academy, Samuel Harvey Taylor was more,
and most, powerful, and far more deserving of
memory, as a teacher.

For, Doctor Taylor was a teacher of mighty forcefulness. The stream of his teaching ran full and ran
swift. The sense of progressiveness moved him, and
therefore moved his students. In the recitation-

room no delay was suffered. Procrastination was a sin, and not only a sin, but also an academic crime, a crime meriting, and usually receiving, academic punishment and creating personal regret or remorse. The assembling of the forty-five men of the Senior class was timely, the settling down to work prompt, the beginning of the recitation,—a contest and a struggle,—immediate.

"Smith, read the Greek." Smith reads.

"Sufficient!" Smith realizes it is sufficient.

"Translate." Smith translates.

"What tense is——?" "It is the imperfect tense," answers Smith.

"You waste words. 'Imperfect' is enough. Sufficient!"

In swift succession, the cards on the desk, each bearing a name, are turned over and each man is called up to recite. For an hour and a half the battle rages. The weapons are the Æneid, the Anabasis, the Iliad. The method of attack is simple, direct, at times seemingly fierce. The scholastic aim is as direct as a soldier's rifle, the onset as full as the machine gun's blast. The sweep of the movement is Niagara-like, and yet in quietness. The pull of going forward is like the force of the electric locomotive. In his memorial address on Doctor Taylor, Professor Park said:

"His rapidity of thought may have been the result of his hard work, and his familiarity with his lessons; but it surprised his pupils. The celerity with which he detected an error, analyzed a sentence, compared different constructions, appeared magical."[1]

"The scene in his recitation-room reminded one of a torrent rushing onward to the sea; one wave not waiting for another, but every wave hastening forward as if instinct with life. Every mind was on the alert. Those who were naturally quick learned to be accurate before him; those who were naturally slow spurred themselves onward before him."[2]

A pupil of Doctor Taylor has also testified:

"We were called up with great rapidity, and trained to tell promptly and concisely what we knew. Woe to the boy who professed to understand what he did not! No matter how smoothly he could repeat it, the fraud was instantly detected, and exposed without mercy."[3] Another student, who became himself a teacher, has said: "I remember the first recitation when he had flunked every high standing man in the form. We shook in our shoes at the future, and nearly died when he pushed back his book, took off his spectacles and said, 'These are the questions which I propose to ask during the year.' And then he gave us a talk on studying and teaching which could not be bettered."

In this football struggle of forces was heard and felt the worth of accuracy. Experiments in the chemical or physical laboratory are examples of ac-

[1] "Memorial of Samuel Harvey Taylor." p. 24.
[2] *Ibid.*, p. 28.
[3] "Reminiscences by a pupil of Dr. Taylor." *Ibid.*, p. 114.

curacy. But the understanding and the analysis of a single Greek sentence, or even of a single Greek verb, represent an accuracy quite like that of the scientific experiment. A Greek particle is as exact and significant as a chemical particle. Under a proper teacher it can be made as explosive. Can any one of Dr. Taylor's pupils ever lose the significance of kai gar? Can any one forget the inevitable rendering of a verb in a certain paragraph of the Anabasis to the effect of the way the battle "eventuated?" Nothing was about right. Each thing was either right or wrong. His mind was perpendicular, his teaching straight, straight up and down. Professor Park has also said:

"Accuracy is essential to the success of a teacher, but does not insure it. Our friend was correct in the minutiæ of the Latin and Greek languages. In his view, no error was trivial. With scrupulous care he exposed the slightest mistake of a pupil. . . . He did find a pleasure in interpreting the Greek particles. When he first studied the Greek accents, he was transported with delight, as if he had been reading a romance." [4]

"It was obvious that he loved the Greek verb; that he felt a personal interest in the Greek syntax. An offense against the laws of the Latin language seemed to be a personal injury to himself; and, on the other hand, he was wont to speak as if he felt a personal gratitude to some of his pupils for their neat or exact

[4] "Memorial of Samuel Harvey Taylor." p. 23.

renderings of the classics." [5] The value of Greek particles has intimate relation with the value of connectives in English style; these connectives largely constitute a good style.

This intellectual accuracy had close affiliation with moral honesty. Veracity was ethical as well as mental. Mount Sinai again thundered at any deception. The apparent use of a "pony" in a translation laid the whip of scorpions, and even of scorn, on the back of the stricken student who tried to ride the poor beast. It was usually easy for him to detect the use of the help. For he knew the student's pace. Such a man could not escape, as did the Rugby boy, who replied to Doctor Arnold's reprimand, "I am doing the best I can, Sir!" If he desired to escape, he knew he could not. He knew he deserved not to escape. He was not doing the best he could.

These elements of force and of accuracy were accompanied by a sense of relationship. Each new lesson was a review of every preceding lesson. To-day's text referred back to the foregoing pages, and the foregoing pages of the text referred back to the grammar. Each page in the Æneid stood for lexical, grammatical, literary, historical values. Each verse, too, was a training in English speech. Certain lines in the Æneid called up lines in "Paradise Lost:"

"Now Morn, her rosy steps in the eastern clime
Advancing, sowed the earth with orient pearl."

[5] *Ibid.*, p. 28.

The sense of relationship went forth into high and noble atmospheres. Again we retreated with the ten thousand. Again we were wrathful with Achilles.

The effect of such teaching on a class of half a hundred men was simply tremendous. Intellectual alertness in the great teacher quickened intellectual alertness in the class. There was no somnambulism in that room, neither was there dreaming. There was a mastery over the boys such as Andrew Carnegie had over his business associates. Each had to mind his business, or presently he had no business to mind. Such mindfulness had close connections, moreover, with fear, either actual or potential. We were all afraid of that man. We were told that, really in his heart, he was kind. I believe he was. But class-room No. 9 gave little evidence. To the conscientious this fear even became contrition, a contrition, however, touched with hopefulness. We could, and we would, do better tomorrow. To the unconscientious, such castigations might create rebelliousness. But of both the conscientious and the unconscientious, it could be said that many lay dead on the seashore of No. 9 at the close of the battle. As Professor Churchill, himself a student, and afterwards a colleague, has said:

"With the dullest of us he was patient and helpful, if he could be assured that we were doing our best; but for the geniuses of the class, who 'got along' by the light of Nature, without study, he had no mercy. He taught us that true study was the very soul of

genius. Mere smartness with him was of little account. He wanted to see it united with sterling
character. From genius to dullard all he required
was faithful work, high principle, and gentlemanly
conduct. The business-like manner of conducting a
recitation, the quick glance of the eye, the rapping
of the pencil, the pleased look and simple nod of the
head which followed a good recitation, the deep, and
severe-toned 'sufficient' which followed a poor one,
which he knew might have been better,—all these
little traits of manner,—how often will they be recalled and talked over now that he is gone!'' [6]

Outside the classroom, as well as within, the influence of this personality and the effect of this teaching was intellectual laboriousness. We fellows studied. We got our lessons. We had to. No eight-
hour day for us! That academy bell rang out its
short, sullen tones, at six every morning. As I remember, there were no gentle, soporific tones issuing
from the same bell-throat at nine or eleven o'clock
of the night. Early breakfast was followed by study,
by prayers, by recitations, till the simple noon-day
dinner. The early and middle afternoon was given
to study, the late hours to gymnastic exercise, to play,
or other sorts of freedom. The evening, too, was
spent in study, till sleep put its soft and heavy hand
on the tired boy's head.

All this life of study was designed by the great
master to make the individual boy into a reasoning

⁶ Sermon. By J. W. Churchill. *Ibid.*, p. 88.

and moral man. He worked to make the boy a thinker and a good man who would love and do the right. The education which "Uncle Sam" inspired, and used, was an education which, if it ended with the Academy, would have given this boy of seventeen or eighteen a first-rate equipment for life and for life's duties. The Latin and the Greek, though apparently made so important in themselves, were to him merely means and never ends. He had little thought of college entrance examinations. He did not prepare for Harvard, then having the reputation of setting the hardest papers for admission for each freshman class. He foresaw no College Entrance Examination Board. He sought to transmute these callow youths into men, fitted to endure hardness as good soldiers in humanity's battles.

As Professor Park has again said:

"He valued his pupils, not so much for what they knew, as for what they could and would learn. He did not love to crowd their memory with thoughts, so much as to enable them to think. He was careful not to overload their minds, and equally careful to develop them. His aim was not to give them knowledge, but to qualify them for getting it." [7]

Professor Churchill has also pointed out:

"He made us feel most sensibly the difference between mere instruction and education. It was the difference between the means and the end to be secured by them. He seemed to teach as if it was not

[7] "Memorial of Samuel Harvey Taylor." p. 31.

his business simply to impart knowledge, but to teach the way of getting knowledge. It took us a long time to see, perhaps we never did see, in 'No. 9,' how our hours of study and the recitation-drill were slowly, but surely, forming mental habits valuable for any sphere of future action. What we had to do must be done accurately. It must be done with all the speed possible and consistent: this required the concentration of our attention. We must be ready with our reason for the faith that was in us. This cultivated logic. Facts must not only be collected, but weighed, compared, and classified; and this taught us method. With a start in these four things,—accuracy, attention, logic, and method,—he equipped us for college. These, he told us, were the intellectual instruments that every man needed, no matter what might be his calling in life." [8]

That Doctor Taylor accomplished the sublime and far-off purpose is proved by the subsequent biographies of his boys. As I remember my own class of some forty-five men, more than a quarter gave significant accounts of themselves in their following life. There was Walker Blaine, who became an Assistant Secretary of State under his great father. There was "Jack" Patton, who was made by the Governor's appointment, a United States Senator from Michigan. There was Guy Howard, son of General Howard, who became a United States Army officer, and gave up his life as a brave man in the Philip-

[8] *Ibid.*, p. 87.

pines. There were the Ishams, Charles and Sam—
Sam, the painter. There was Harry Johnson, who,
from the middle class, went to Bowdoin College, and
who, for forty years, as a teacher and friend,
enriched the life of all Bowdoin men. He lives, too,
in his poems, and in his translation of Dante. There
was also Almet Jenks,—dear Almet, handsome fellow,
and charming, whose early promise was more than
made good by a great career at the bar, and by a long
and rich service as a member, and, indeed, for a
time, as Presiding Justice, of the Supreme Court of
New York. These names are among those that are
starred. Among those unstarred are great lawyers
and great justices in New York, a governor of a
New England state, outstanding school superin-
tendents, and college trustees. It is a long list of the
able men that could be made up of the members of
the ordinary class.

Dr. Taylor's power as a teacher sprang from the
vigor, force, and determination of his personality.
It was not a teaching broad, or deep, or rich in
scholarship. It was direct, forceful, rapid in movement, bare of ornament. I might call it rather psychological than scholarly teaching. In writing this
sketch, I have had the advantage of reading the diary
which he kept in a prolonged journey in Italy,
Greece, and neighboring parts, in the year 1856.
Places and scenes most intimately associated with his
life's work, as I read these pages, call out no personal
or scholastic comment. The new knowledge and ex-

periences make slight appeal to his mind. The written record is the description of the guidebook. Perhaps, indeed, the force of the teaching of Dr. Taylor came, in part, from its simple narrowness. The Niagara Gorge is necessary for getting the accumulated force of the wide-spread Great Lakes.

By these results, by these methods and under these conditions, Samuel Harvey Taylor triumphed as teacher, despite his service as principal. I often think that great teachers are not, and should not try to be, educational administrators, and that first-rate administrators should make no attempt to be proper teachers. As a principal, I find my pen writing reluctantly and slowly of "Uncle Sam," and going swiftly and enthusiastically as it is writing of him as a teacher. For, as a principal, his government was apparently founded on what ever seems to me to be a false basis. For the evidence compels the conclusion that apparently the great man regarded every boy as an embodiment of the doctrine of New England theology of total depravity. Doctor Taylor was, like all of us, in every age and clime, more or less the product of his own time and environment. Each boy was apparently to be regarded as bad until he had proved himself to be good. The preliminary supposition was against the lad. I recall one of my dear friends, now a Bishop of the Protestant Episcopal Church, who lately confessed to me that his first intimation that he was not doing right lay in the accusation by "Uncle Sam" that he was

doing wrong. The sense of fear which we all had
of him in the classroom was not confined to the
classroom. We were afraid that, even if we were
honest and laborious, we were in peril of being mis-
judged as dishonest and lazy. Perhaps he knew
us as we did not know ourselves! Perhaps, let me
now say, he was right and we were wrong. Let
me also say that I know of at least one Andover boy
who tells me of "Uncle Sam's" personal kindness,
considerateness, and helpfulness to him. However,
most of us were afraid that he would believe we
had been over to Lawrence without permission, even
if we had never been there; that he would believe
we had walked in "Love's Lane" to catch sight of
a "Fem. Sem.," even if we had not walked there at
all; that he would believe we had cut down the inter-
fering tree on the baseball field, even if we had not
crossed the diamond for a week; that he would believe we had visited "Pike's" (Restaurant), even if
we had not tasted ice cream for a month; that he
would believe we had smuggled a book into the chapel
service, Sunday morning, or that he would believe
we had gone on a sleigh ride, although we had not
read a novel or stepped into a vehicle for a whole
term. A member of the class of 1863, Mr. William
H. Morse, Assistant Librarian of the Law Library
of Congress, writes me, saying: "When I first went
to Andover in 1859, I never shall forget 'Uncle'
calling me up one morning and asking me if I was
in the habit of going late at night with a rabble of

fellows to Lawrence. Upon my replying in the negative, he asked me if I would turn over a new leaf. I replied if I had not been to Lawrence why should I be called upon to turn over a new leaf. 'Uncle' was so insistent that I should turn over a new leaf that for the sake of his instruction and the desire to get his wonderful teaching I said 'Yes, I will turn over a hundred leaves.' But I always had from that day a sense of fear of him and the thought would frequently present itself that he believed I had gone to Lawrence. His belief that each boy was bad until he had proven himself good; that he was guilty until he proved his innocence, was a wrong way in which to deal with the majority of boys.'' The morning chapel service ''Uncle Sam'' used as occasion for punitive discipline. At the close of the service the following announcement, given in a deep bass voice which I still hear, was not unusual, ''The following individuals are requested to remain.'' Of this procedure, Mr. Morse makes an interpretation. He says:

''This solemn announcement came as a thunderbolt to many a student accused of acts of which he was not guilty. The student only had a short time to think of why he was called up before he appeared before 'Uncle' wholly unprepared to combat the questions as to why he was seen going to Eagle Rock on the afternoon of —— with two girl companions. (This, if it did occur, happened several months ago and was entirely forgotten by the person called up.)

'Uncle' always seemed to make it a point to call a student up a long time after the occurrence and when most persons would have forgotten about the circumstance.

"I never was called up but once and that on the second term Senior year to give an account of why I was seen out driving in the afternoon of Wednesday with a carriage full of persons. It took me some time to convince Dr. Taylor that I had his permission to go out driving on the day mentioned, and that the persons in the vehicle were none other than my parents and my brother, who were on a visit to Andover at the time. 'Be careful not to do so again' was his only reply.'' Another old boy has written with grateful pleasantry of these far-off times, saying:

"I look back upon my three years at Andover with amusement and pleasure: amusement at the utter ignorance of Uncle Sam of proper methods of winning boys: pleasure at being under an inspiring teacher who compelled you to think on your feet.

"How the dear man lied to you! How you knew that he lied! How he was aware that you knew! It all comes before me as I review the many times that I was 'the worst boy in the school.' "

Such doings, or apparent doings, were transgressions of school laws which were easily translated into offenses against the moral commandments. Such experiences were moral backslidings, and such indulgences, ethical weaknesses. Such actions, committed or contemplated, bad in themselves, were guide posts pointing the way to unspeakable evils, encouraging the boy to walk in the way of the transgressor, a way in which, at its end, he was sure to perish. In the words of Professor Park:

"He believed that one of the dangers to which this democratic land lies exposed is a disrespect for law: he therefore believed that he was performing an act of kindness to his pupils when he was accustoming them to obey." [9]

Though the government of such a ruler was not, and is not, I believe, good for most boys, we stood it. This atmosphere, too, was not so structural of character as were the principles and the methods of the classroom of the great man. Boys have a way of defending themselves. Mr. Morse, from whom I have already quoted, also says:

"And yet Dr. Taylor was always very loyal to each one of his pupils. I remember my cousins, who came later to the Academy, when asked if they were related to the 'Morses' that had graduated in the sixties and upon their answer in the affirmative were told, 'See that your conduct is as exemplary as theirs.' His knowledge of each student that graduated under him, his whereabouts, just what he was doing, etc., was very remarkable. I remember one of our Class who happened to be in Andover five or six years after graduation called on 'Uncle' and told him that he supposed he did not know him,

[9] "Memorial of Samuel Harvey Taylor."   p. 20.

whereupon 'Uncle' related everything he had been doing since he graduated and just how he was situated."

Keate of Eton, who helped to educate most of the English statesmen of the middle decades of the nineteenth century, is not remembered gratefully as is Arnold of Rugby. Taylor has been called the Arnold of America, as other great masters have also been called. As a teacher he deserves the tender and noble name. For he maintained the classical tradition. As a principal he belongs fully with Keate, the ruthless, and far less with Thring of Uppingham, or with Temple. To Taylor, the teacher, I would pay my filial respect of gratitude, of admiration, and of affection. Says one who was himself a teacher, "I owe him all I ever did as a teacher." He was one of the great teachers of a generation great in teachers; one of the noblest creators and inspirers of manhood, in a school whose aim from its foundation has been, as says one of its formal instruments, to teach the "great business of living."

XX

EDWARDS AMASA PARK

EDWARDS AMASA PARK, born in Providence, Rhode Island, December 29, 1808; died June 4, 1900. Graduated at Brown University, 1826; Andover Seminary, 1831; Ordained to the Congregational ministry, and pastor at Braintree, Massachusetts, 1831; professor of Moral and Intellectual Philosophy, Amherst, 1835-36; Bartlett professor of Sacred Rhetoric, 1836-47, and Abbot professor of Sacred Theology, 1847-1881, Andover Theological Seminary. Trustee, Abbot Academy, and Smith College. Editor, with Dr. Samuel Harvey Taylor, of Bibliotheca Sacra, 1844-84; one of the editors (and translators) of Selections from German Literature, 1839.

Author: Memoir of Life and Character of Samuel Hopkins, D.D.; Memoir of Nathanael Emmons; Memoir of Professor B. B. Edwards, 1853; Memoir of W. B. Homer; A Life of Samuel Harvey Taylor; The Atonement: Discourses and Treatises; Discourses on some Theological Doctrines as related to the Religious Character; besides other discourses, sermons, essays, etc.

XX

EDWARDS AMASA PARK

APOSTOLIC THEOLOGIAN, DISCRIMINATING TEACHER

"IT is told of Saladin, the champion of Islamism, that—after he had retaken the Holy City; subjugated numerous fortresses in Syria, Arabia, Persia, and Mesopotamia; performed so many exploits in the crusades as to be designated 'the Great'—he was seized with a disorder which threatened to wither up at once all his garlands of victory. When he saw that death was inevitable, he called his herald who used to carry his banner before him, took his lance, which had so often been shaken in battle, tied his shroud to the top of his lance, and then said to the herald, 'Go unfurl this shroud in the camp. It is the flag of the day. Wave it in the air, and proclaim, "This is all that remains of Saladin the Great, the conqueror, the king of the empire; all that remains of his glory!"' But, when a good man dies, we cannot say that all which remains of him is the coffin and the shroud. He has lived in his thoughts and deeds; he still lives in the remembrance of them. They are like seeds planted by the water-courses: they spring

369

up, and bear fruit; and he lives in their perennial life." [1]

Thus spoke Professor Park in an address delivered in 1871 at the funeral of Samuel H. Taylor, of whom I have written in the preceding chapter. Professor Park was a teacher of theology for thirty-four years (1847-81). This prolonged and conspicuous service as a teacher of theology followed a similar service in homiletics of eleven years. His theology, following his teaching of it, suffered a collapse—which one of his favorite and able students declared was, in a large degree, "sudden and complete." It was like the fall of Saladin. But of his theology, whether in "collapse" permanent or transient, I do not write. To write of it, I am not fitted. For my present purpose, his theology has little or no meaning, excepting as it serves to shed light upon Park as a teacher, and as a man of commanding intellect and of virile character.

Park's career began in that great fourth decade of the nineteenth century. It was indeed a time of beginnings: it was a period of newness. The Westward movement of population was slowly pressing its way over the Eastern mountains and across the continental river, and passing beyond. Mighty anticipations of mighty powers were filling the hearts and minds of men. In the middle year of the decade, Morse set up his telegraphic apparatus in his room

[1] Memorial Address. By Professor Park: *Memorial to Samuel Harvey Taylor.* pp. 9-10.

in New York University. Visions of wealth were
filling the public eye and moving the community's
heart. Values in certain lands touched a figure which
they have never since reached. Reforms were in the
air. Apostles of newness abounded. The Fifth Mon-
archy was indeed to be re-established. It was the
age of transcendentalists, *Redeunt Saturnia regna:*
it was the age of antislavery, of temperance, of non-
resistance, and of "come-outism." Everybody had
a mission; and, as Lowell says, his mission was spelled
with a capital M.

In its earlier years, Park's career covered the
careers of great statesmen, thinkers, writers, preachers and teachers of the middle decades of the nineteenth century, and in his later years it touched upon
the lives also of great statesmen, thinkers, writers,
preachers and teachers whose services beginning with
the last decades of that century entered into the
first decade of the twentieth. Daniel Webster died
in 1852. Charles Sumner was first elected to the
United States Senate in 1851, and he died in 1874.
Emerson gave his Phi Beta Kappa address in 1837.
Longfellow went from Bowdoin to Harvard in 1836.
Longfellow died on March 24, 1881, and Emerson's
death followed in a little over a month. Lowell
wrote "The Present Crisis" in 1844. In ecclesiastical
circles—Henry Ward Beecher became pastor of
Plymouth Church in 1847, and died in 1887. Richard
Salter Storrs ascended his pulpit-throne a year earlier,
in 1846, when he became pastor of the Church of the

Pilgrims. It was a noble, intellectual and spiritual environment and tradition into which Park's life and teaching were cast. The exterior circumstance was fitting to the great personality himself. He was a giant among giants.

Park made his great contribution to and through the Andover professorship of theology. A professorship of theology bears the relation to other chairs in a theological school which the professorship of philosophy in a college bears to other professorships: it is the foundation on which they are built, it is the capstone of their ultimate mission and teaching. This chair Park filled from the year 1847 till his retirement in 1881. He filled it as no similar chair in American schools of divinity has been filled. Of Park's service, Richard Salter Storrs, in a memorial address read at Park's funeral, but prepared a decade earlier, has said:

"Certainly the fame of the lectures, when delivered, went every-whither, as the *vast enthusiasm* excited by his work in the department of Homiletics was continued, if not surpassed, in the department of Theology. The lecture, with questions and answers, often occupied from an hour and a half to two hours. Sometimes the questions were so many, the answers so incisive, energetic, rapid, far-reaching, leading to prolonged discussion, that no room whatever was left for the lecture. The examinations at the end of the terms brought ministers hither from near and far. Each of these examinations occupied

an entire day, eight hours being assigned to it; and
the students and their clerical examiners came not
unfrequently to as animated discussions as any that
had been waged in the class-room. No political de-
bates, no discussions of questions of social reform,
have stirred an interest livelier or an inquisition
sharper than did the discussion of questions here
at that time in the Seminary, on subjects which man
may not wholly master till he goes up higher, but
which always will search his mind and conscience
with profoundest appeal; and the echo of such lectures and discussions went continuously, for thirty-
five years, into the pulpits of New England and the
West, into the religious life of the land. The Theological chair in any Seminary has vast responsibilities. An angel might ask for special illumination
before he undertook them. It may certainly be said
of the friend now gone that he saw and felt them
to the full, and did the utmost that in him lay to
meet and fulfill them. He desired and sought, with
all his soul, so to present the truth of God as to
touch with it the forces which afterward were to
touch great multitudes of minds, in this country,
and beyond the breadth of the seas.'' [2]

Park came as near being an intellect and a reason
as any man I have known. He was primarily a
thinker. Inheriting the traditions and bearing the
name of one who has been called the first of Amer-

[2] Edwards Amasa Park, D.D., LL.D.—Memorial Address.
By Richard Salter Storrs. pp. 59-60.

ican philosophers, both in time and in ability, he maintained the great tradition. Some (not all) would say he magnified and enriched all that he had received. Of him Dr. George A. Gordon has said: "Aside from his prejudices, which were strong, and sometimes deplorable, he had the widest intellectual sympathies, the keenest interest in the things of the mind."³ He was more of an Aristotelian than a Platonist, and yet, in both wit and humor, as well as in wisdom, he was not unlike Plato's master. He was more of a philosopher than a psychologist, though as psychologist he possessed a unique understanding of the workings of the human mind. At times his students have been charged with being his imitators, or victims, in respect to the mere memorizing or adoption of his system. The charge, if true at all, is only true partially. But he himself never sacrificed intellectual power, alertness, vision, reasoning, to the accumulation of knowledge. In fact, he never seemed to be learned as was Professor H. B. Smith or Schaff. Rather he reasoned, and again reasoned, as did John Stuart Mill. He was far more of a thinker than a scholar. His reasoning was at once inductive and deductive. Principles he arrived at by induction, at times almost by unconscious induction, and from these principles, he reasoned out into derived processes and inferences. His assumptions or prolegomena made a direct, instinctive appeal to the

³"My Education and Religion." By George A. Gordon. pp. 274.

reason. Theological conclusions were supported by rational arguments, or by statements primarily interpreted by reason. Professor of Systematic Theology, he transmuted the adjective into a noun. He was the master, and projector as well, of a system. That system he made as an architect, not as a landscape artist; as a builder, not as a gardener. Christ's figure, "Behold a sower went forth to sow," would not be applicable to Park. For germination and growth are, and represent, a certain quality of irregular adjustments. Park's system was a regular, orderly and precise adjustment of part to part, of proportion to proportion, of major premises to minor, of minor to major, and of both to a conclusion. Yet his reasoning did not seem narrowly syllogistic. It was rather a series of statements with each link welded into every other link unto a chain of argumentation. His lectures often seemed, however, to be a *series* of well-ordered reasoning, comprehensive and definite. "Q. E. D." might have closed many a lecture. The process often impressed one as mathematical. The orderliness of thinking might be called arithmetical. It added and subtracted, multiplied and divided rational values. It might be called, superficially, algebraic. For it dealt, in its arrangements, with letters—big A, little a, and other symbols. It certainly could be called geometrical in its sense of large relations of truth and of being. I might say, it was a theological analytical geometry.

One of his students, himself a distinguished theologian, Professor Frank Hugh Foster, from whose history I already have quoted, in a personal letter to me, has said:

"Professor Park deserves to be ranked among the very greatest teachers of theology of all time. It was the fortune of the writer to study in Harvard College, and to have great teachers there: later to study at Göttingen and Leipzig, Germany, where he heard the greatest German Philosopher of the day, Hermann Lotze, and the most influential Theologian at that time in Germany, Albrecht Ritschl, and the three great masters in Leipzig, the most famous Faculty since that of Hegel and Schleiermacher at Berlin, Delitzsch, Kahnis, and Luthardt, and he says emphatically that the Andover Three, Park, Phelps, and Thayer, were the equals of any in Germany, and Park by far the greatest teacher of Andover.'' (With much definiteness Foster points out Park's excellences.)

He made men thinkers:

"(1) By the clearness of his own thought. He held the Scotch Philosophy of 'common sense,' which is level to the understanding of the common mind, clear and cogent (I do not say, altogether correct), and upon the basis of this he spoke himself with extraordinary clearness and analytical keenness. Hence he *taught what clearness is,* and the value of it.

"(2) Out of this sprang the cogency of his proofs. They were elaborate, and comprised a careful review of objections, stated with perfect fairness to oppo-

nents, and then trenchantly refuted. He even gave
a certain proof to his axioms, such as 'Every event
has a cause.'

"(3) He impressed his pupils with the nobility
and greatness of thinking. There was a certain
scorn in him of many low things; but his chief scorn
was of confusion of thought, of compromise in intellectual matters, the taking of middle ground between
two positions either of which may be true or false, the
middle ground, however, certainly false; of intellectual cowardice which refuses to say what the man
thinks out of fear of consequences.

"(4) He taught specific features of the art of
thinking by example. For instance,

"(a) He made clear definitions of what he was
going to prove. This led to the habit on the part of
his pupils, of trying to get a vista through any tangle
of strenuous investigation as a preliminary to the
work. The definition was often the equivalent of a
proof, and often of a refutation. [Of course, such a
method has both excellences and defects.]

"(b) He analyzed his thought with great minute-
ness, and thus taught the art of analysis.

"(c) He taught the art of weighing premises by
his careful discrimination between their respective
values as elements of proof.

"(d) He taught the art of inductive reasoning
because he practised it, and because

"(e) He so often carefully explained the course
of the argument at some difficult point. One of the

best illustrations of this is his argument for the benevolence of God.[4]

" (5) His final evidence for the truth of any position was its self-evidence. This was sometimes, perhaps, fictitious, as in the case of the proposition that miracles are necessary to attest a divine revelation. But this seemed to him well nigh as axiomatic as the principle that every event must have a cause. Like Descartes, he saw in the *clearness and distinctness* of ideas a proof of their truth.

" (6) He taught a *system*. This was not merely an orderly arrangement of ideas, but an arrangement where every truth advanced rested upon the basis of other truths previously proved, as the layers in the wall of a cathedral lie each upon the layers which have been previously put in place. Such a system is one long and steadily maintained course of argument: and he who faithfully follows it cannot fail to become himself a thinker.

" (7) He encouraged independence of thought because he was himself completely independent. He followed his teachers, and summed up their best work, but he was never *addictus in verba magistri jurare*.

" (8) He taught the unity of theology and ethics, as both founded upon the principle that God is love. This broadened the thinking of his pupils.

" (9) He possessed the art of firing the enthusiasm of his pupils. Men often went out of the lecture-

[4]See "A History of the New England Theology." By Frank Hugh Foster. pp. 477-487.

room with their hearts burning within them." [Personal letter of Professor Frank Hugh Foster to the author.]

Such an unfolding was made in an English style, distinguished by succinctness and absolute clearness of diction. It had no or little room for ornamentation. It discarded the adjective. It eliminated the adverb. It was simple, direct, plain. It was beautiful, and its beauty lay in its perspicuity. It represented Herbert Spencer's law of mental economy. It stood for the simple Greek type of literary architecture, and of the severe form, too. Yet, in certain parts of his writing, both of essay and of sermon, are found a wealth and a sense of rhetorical luxuriousness which his algebraic analyses do not at all connote. As an illustration of such writing, let me quote a paragraph found in his Memoir of his kinsman and colleague, Professor B. B. Edwards. The paragraph is drawn from a passage describing the funeral service.

"And *so* we buried him; and wended our way back slowly and sadly to his house. There we watched, as he had so often watched there, the setting sun. It went down in more than its wonted glory. A few clouds were floating about in liquid amber, reminding us that the most cheering light comes sometimes from the darkest dispensations. The beauties of the world fade not away, when our strong staff is broken and our beautiful rod. The government of Jehovah moves on as it moved aforetime, and he will sustain his own cause, and is dependent on no child of mortality.

And far beyond that setting sun, our brother lives and speaks the language of Canaan. All his germs of thought have blossomed out and are bearing fruit. All his treasured hints have expanded into a science, of which he had no conception in this dark world. The plans from which he was cut off have ripened into unexpected means of joy. His endeavors are rewarded as if they have been accomplished. With his Redeemer, a good intention is a good deed, and baffled efforts are as a glorious consummation. A disappointment here is but a preparative for new service there." [5]

The simplicity of his style, however, was relieved by the wit and the humor which illustrated and distinguished the statements of principles and the orderly unfolding and up-building of the argument. His phrases captivated. His allusions, happy themselves, gave intellectual delight. His stories quickened the intellect, as well as broadened the listener's face. I recall that, in the lectures on divine decrees, he once asked a student, "Suppose a man should succeed in defying a divine decree, what would be the result?" The student looked around for aid. He looked down for comfort. He looked upward for intellectual help. Failing to get relief, he answered, "I do not know, Professor Park, but I think there would be a general crash!" Dr. Storrs tells that "When some one asked him [Park] why he had de-

[5] Writings of Professor B. B. Edwards, with a Memoir by Edwards A. Park. pp. 363-364.

clined a proposal to give him a free passage to Europe in a sailing vessel, his reply was, 'Oh, but you know it never would have answered! How it would have looked, going down into history: "Professor Fisher, of New Haven, lost in the *Albion;* Dr. Cookman, of New York, in the steamship *President;* Professor Park, of Andover, lost in the brig *Nancy Stevens!*" I couldn't take the risk.' "[6]

Whatever may be the worthiness or unworthiness of Park's systematic theology, his teaching of this theology was to the student an intellectual discipline of highest value. The teaching possessed the first requisite of such discipline; it was a training in method. It was, like all education, a weighing of evidence. It represented an evolution of statements in reference to a distinct conclusion. It stood for thinking, thinking closely articulated, quickening to the heart, comprehensive and honest to the conscience, having cubical relationships. It possessed the essence of a liberal education. One might say in objection that it was a formal education, like the logic of the Jesuits' discipline. If it were open to this objection, I should reply that the formality of the teaching pointed to a certain intellectual formula into which most good thinking falls. Algebraic formulas have their place! Chemical formulas are not useless! Reasoning, the weighing of evidence, is the first thing—I frequently think that reasoning and the

* Edwards Amasa Park, D.D., LL.D.—Memorial Address. By Richard Salter Storrs. p. 62.

weighing of evidence is the only thing—in education. Of course, the remark is false. It goes too far. If a student of medicine as a diagnostic science, or a student of law as a practical art, based on the veracities and the verities, could have taken a course with Park, he would have reasoned in the practice of his profession, either medical or legal, with a logic more exact, vigorous, rigorous, and to conclusions more solid, sound, inevitable.

In the light of Park's fame as a master of theological thinking, one is inclined to forget that he was among the greatest of preachers, as well as one of the first of professors of the art and science of preaching. The popular titles of some of his sermons, as "The Peter Sermon," and "The Judas Sermon," are still regnant. His preaching was a preaching based on fundamental principles, developed in logical sequence, weighted with massive truths, and was given with a quiet force which burned into the heart and illumined the mind of the hearer. Who forgets the force of that forefinger which pointed directly at "me," or the fire of that eye that saw right through "me"? As Arthur Symons says of George Meredith's novels, his sermons were flame-like: they burned. A mighty preacher himself, Storrs has said of Park's preaching:

"Those sermons were as carefully planned as were ever the bastions of any fortress. It used to be the wish of students, who had perhaps smarted under his criticism, to find in his own plans some weakness

or incongruity, some want of concinnity in parts, or
some failure to enforce his theme; but they never
succeeded. Each part was in its just relations. The
whole was as completely organized as were the members of any sentence. The style of expression was
perspicuous, energetic, with images suggested in a
word sometimes, or a half sentence, fine as a cameo,
vivid and lustrous as a picture; with passages of marvelous literary charm, which beguiled the enchanted
attention.'' [7]

Since Park's days in the pulpit, the movement of
preaching to college students has taken firm root,
and has developed. But Park, for three decades,—
fifth, sixth, and seventh,—of the century, was one
of the greatest and most commanding of such preachers. Of this preaching, Dr. Storrs himself has again
said:

''To students especially, above all to theological
students, he was, and before their minds he remains,
the very prince and king among preachers. His mere
presence in the pulpit was majestic and fascinating,
in the weird abstraction, concentration, solemnity of
face, voice, mien, and manner.'' [8]

The students who went from Andover in Park's
time were distinguished, so far as they were distinguished at all—and not a few won high places in the
American pulpit—for their reasoning power. His
graduates did not substitute emotionalism for logic,
feeling for intellectual content. Their sermons had

[7] *Ibid.*, p. 47.　　　　　[8] *Ibid.*, p. 46.

pointedness and application, because the thinking proceeded by orderly steps in the presentation of moral and religious truth. Their discourses were not disquisitions, to be read. They were not homilies, commonplace and empty. They were not vague essays on subjects which do not compel rigorous thinking. Their sermons embodied doctrines, as all good sermons do and must.

There is, however, yet another side of this man of many sides, and that is the side of friendship. One who stood in close relations to him has, at my request, sought to interpret this element. He says:

"In endeavoring to sketch Park in the relation of a friend, it is necessary that we should first understand his personal temperamental traits. He was of the old high-strung, proud and very sensitive New England type. And he was exceedingly quick in reaction to whatever offended him, and implacable when he had once taken an unfavorable view of a man's character and attitude towards himself. Although the valedictorian of his class at Brown, he refused to be present at Commencement on account of some action of his class of which he did not approve. He would not condescend to defend himself against what he believed to be malice. Littleness of soul he despised, and when a man had once shown it in dealings with him, he was done with that man forever. But he was also very affectionate and tender, particularly with children.

"Very many, probably most, of his friendships

were with younger men, for they originated in the relations of teacher and pupil. Towards all his pupils he was accessible, patient, ready to listen and to instruct, provided he found a real grappling with the subject in the inquirer. But I do not think that the stupid, and especially the self-conceited and self-assertive, found very much hospitality in his reception of them. Those who were able, keen, inquiring, and genuinely docile, he received into his friendship; and I do not think such friendships easily perished. He did not demand that his pupils should agree with him, and he did demand that they should think things thoroughly through. Such friendships were the meeting of two thoroughly intellectual and strenuous souls in interchange of their spiritual acquirements.

"Park was so good a fighter that it was often thought that to disagree with him was to lose his friendship. This was, however, an entire mistake. If disagreement led to a severance of friendly ties, it was because there was something more than disagreement there, some falseness of some sort which Park detected and which he highly resented. Dr. R. S. Storrs wrote in that funeral address which was delivered when both subject and writer were lying in their coffins,—'As one who differed from him sharply, on more than one question of importance to us both, and who was stubborn against his argument and strenuously set against his remonstrance, I can bear an unimpeachable witness to the sincerity and the generous sweetness of his continuing friend-

ship.' [9] The writer can do the same. Refusing once
a request, with the feeling that the refusal might be
regarded as a break in our friendship, which had
been one of peculiar intimacy and mutual confidence,
and was therefore made with the greatest hesitation
and apprehension, I found no such result to follow.

"His was also a loyal friendship. Critical in temper as he was, and slow in forming friendships, he
gave his confidence, when he did give it, whole-
heartedly. He did not hedge, and he did not qualify.
A young man, whom he once favored for a high position, failed to receive it. Some may have thought
that Park had 'mentioned' him along with others,
and some may have wondered, as the young man
himself did, whether the Professor did not later
change his estimate of his young friend, or wish he
had favored some one else. But not such was Park.
Twenty years later he said to the friend, '*You* ought
to be in such and such a place!' and added a little
later, 'I recommended you, and I never recommended
anybody else.' If it was one of the young man's de-
feats in life, it was Professor Park's also.

"But if a man lost Professor Park's friendship—!
His relations with a certain man, so associated with
him that they ought to have been those of intimacy,
and I think were such on his side, although I do
not think that Park ever had a very high estimate of the gentleman's ability, were ruptured by
this man, who went so far as to cut the Professor on

[9] *Ibid.,* p. 64.

the street. Park never recognized him again. I do
not think he ever *saw* him, however near he may have
been to him. Treachery, meanness, and littleness, he
could not abide.''

Park died in 1900. His system, as I intimated in
the beginning, in a sense died before him. He ceased
teaching almost a score of years before the end. Foster, in his great book, ''History of the New England
Theology,'' says that the reasons of the fall of the New
England theology lay: (1) in sacrificing ''freedom to
the Calvinism of the old system''; (2) ''in the *a priori*
character of much of the reasoning with which the
system was defended''; (3) in not ''answering fully
the questions put it within its own circle as to the
central doctrines of the Christian system.'' [10]

But the system does live in the character of the
students who studied under and reasoned with Park.
It is felt in each sermon they preach and in all the
pastoral work it becomes them to do. ''There were
tones in the voice that whispered then, you may hear
today in a hundred men.'' His lectures were never
published and never will be. They have been called
''wooden.'' His theological system which they embodied has been charged with being ''dead.'' Such
interpretations intimate that those who make them
have failed to be quickened by the intellectual forces
and the human vitalities of the man himself. His
lectures can be found only in the notebooks of students. It was said among us students, while we sat

[10] See pp. 549-551.

on those green benches in that middle lecture-room, that Park was always revising and re-revising his lectures. Publication meant finality. His desire for improvement forbade the printed and unchanging result. I know not how true is this reasoning. Interpretations of his system are, however, not lacking. His published sermons, altogether too few in number, and his essays, give certain interpretations and conclusions. But Park still lives in the intellectual power of his students, and will live so long as the truth of his metaphor, with which I began this chapter, lasts: he lives in the perennial life of his students and their successors, generation after generation.

XXI

WILLIAM JEWETT TUCKER

WILLIAM JEWETT TUCKER was born in Griswold, Connecticut, July 13, 1839. Died September 29, 1926; A.B. Dartmouth, 1861; graduated from Andover Theological Seminary, 1866; ordained in the Congregational ministry, 1867; pastor of Franklin Street Church, Manchester, New Hampshire, 1867-75; Madison Square Presbyterian Church, New York, 1875-79; professor of Sacred Rhetoric and lecturer on Pastoral Theology, Andover Theological Seminary, 1879-93; president of Dartmouth College, 1893-1909; president emeritus, 1909-26; associate editor of Andover Review; founder of Andover House (South End House, social settlement), Boston; lecturer at Lowell Institute, and Union Theological Seminary, Yale Lyman Beecher Lecturer. Author: From Liberty to Unity; The Making and the Unmaking of the Preacher; Public-mindedness; Personal Power; The Function of the Church in Modern Society; The New Reservation of Time; My Generation, an Autobiographical Interpretation; and many articles for magazines.

XXI

WILLIAM JEWETT TUCKER

BELOVED, A LOVER OF STUDENTS

IT has always seemed to me significant that three New England colleges, in their early decades, in times of scholarly feebleness, sent out as their graduates commanding leaders whose spirit is still regnant or the traditions of whom still linger. Bowdoin gave us—and in one class, too—the most popular poet and our noblest romancer, Longfellow and Hawthorne. Amherst gave the world two of the greatest preachers, Storrs and Beecher. Dartmouth graduated Rufus Choate, whose name still conjures, and Daniel Webster, whose rugged figure still remains dominant as an interpreter, if not a leader, of a generation in the nation's crisis. These graduates seem quite as impressive as the names which Yale, of longer history and ampler resources, enrolls,—Jonathan Edwards, Lyman Beecher, Horace Bushnell of the pulpit, Eli Whitney of the cotton gin, and Morse of the telegraph. They are also as outstanding as Harvard's historians, Bancroft, Prescott, Motley, and Parkman, or as her poets, Lowell and Holmes, her Concord essayist alone overtopping all.

Above most colleges, Dartmouth seems to be an incarnated personality. In its first years, it was Wheelock, a voice crying in the wilderness, yet a voice coming forth from a great man. In its middle period, it was Webster, its savior or at least its second founder. In its last decades, it has been Tucker, —Tucker, the Beloved, and the Lover of Students, and, therefore, beloved by and the lover of all graduates.

In his autobiographic book, "My Generation," Tucker says that, in an examination on the Colonial Period, a Dartmouth teacher asked for a comparison between the early history of the College and its latest development. One student compared Wheelock and Tucker, and remarked that both "were gamblers by instinct." The comment of Tucker is that he himself was as much pleased as amused with the student's insight.[1] The foundation of Dartmouth by the elder Wheelock in the northern wilderness was an adventure,—an adventure of religious and institutional faith. The reconstruction of Dartmouth by Tucker was also an adventure, primarily of institutional, and secondly of religious, faith. Tucker had begun his life work as a preacher in an historic church in New Hampshire, had continued it in a still more historic and outstanding church in New York, and had enlarged that work by accepting the great chair of preaching, filled by Austin Phelps for a generation, in the most historic theological school in America.

[1] p. 268.

Andover Seminary was moving, at the time of his professional service. (1879-93), in a theological and legal crisis. For other seminaries as well, and in a period of general theological unrest, the condition was critical. Andover demanded for that period a great teacher and an irenical theologian. Tucker became its most commanding personality as a member of a faculty which included George Harris and Egbert C. Smyth. But, at this very time, in the years of the ninth and the first years of the tenth decade of the last century, Dartmouth, too, was calling for an interpretative and constructive leadership.

For, though the development of Dartmouth College, under the presidencies of wise men and cautious, like Lord and Smith, and of an acute scholar like Bartlett, had been normal, yet that development had not kept abreast of the exceptional advances which, under the forces of enlarged learning, and the leadership of strong executives, other New England colleges were making. Dartmouth had come to the critical point at which its curriculum should receive noble enrichments, its equipment vast enlargement, and the teaching staff an increase in numbers and forcefulness. The high schools and academies of the whole country were beginning that prodigious growth which has since gone forward at a yet faster rate, and which were giving to Dartmouth, and to every college, a new and broadening constituency. It was also evident that a reservoir of strength lay in her graduates who had not been properly drawn

upon for the benefit and enrichment of their Alma
Mater. With such changes impending in the college
invisible and intangible, it was also evident that the
college visible should receive enlargements. The
whole college plant, in fact, called for thorough reconstruction and manifold improvement.

At the close of his service, Tucker made to the
Alumni a report of his administration. In this interpretation, masterly and gracious, he said:

"As I interpreted the needs of the college, when
I assumed the presidency, the policy of reconstruction with a view to expansion seemed to me to be the
only adequate policy. There were at that time certain facts of very great educational importance to be
considered: the vast extension of the subject-matter
of the higher education, involving corresponding advances in the methods of instruction; the rapid
growth of high schools as fitting schools for the colleges, virtually creating a new college constituency;
and the sudden increase of endowments and appropriations for colleges and universities, making itself
felt not so much in competition as through an enlarged scale of expediture. It was impossible to
ignore or evade any one of these facts. The obligation resting upon an historic college like Dartmouth
to preserve its well-recognized individuality was no
more evident nor imperative than was the require-
ment that it should relate itself efficiently to its new
educational environment." [2]

[2] p. 2.

To his service, which lasted for sixteen years—1893-1909—Tucker brought many great, and several rather unique, elements of power. These elements of power, of course, had relationship to the office of the president itself. He has himself given an interpretation of that office, which deserves full statement, not only for his College, but for every other also. Tucker says:

"The college presidency is an anomaly among the professions. In and of itself it has no professional standing. Whoever occupies it must furnish his own professional guarantees. . . ."[3]

"It is, of course, an infelicity that there is no authorized academic approach to a college presidency, not even through the faculty. Neither teaching nor research can give the requisite training for administration. There are indications of the growing recognition of the normal path to administrative responsibility through some form of direct administrative training. . . . Doubtless in due time a college presidency will evolve or acquire its own professional standing. Meanwhile the distinguishing feature of a college presidency in the place allotted to it by courtesy among the professions is the ground it covers. No profession has the same variety of semi-public duties assigned to it or expected of it. The public expectation is not infrequently embarrassing as it finds expression in the neatly turned compliment. In introducing me, soon after my advent at Dart-

[3] "My Generation." p. 362.

mouth, as a speaker at the dedication of the new state library building of New Hampshire, the presiding officer made use very graciously of the epigram of Macaulay on Sir William Temple. 'I think,' he said, 'that I may adopt the words of the brilliant essayist and historian in introducing to you Dr. Tucker, President of Dartmouth—'a man of the world among men of letters, and a man of letters among men of the world.' However much I might have been disposed to disclaim the right to a place in the historic succession to this epigram, I could not deny its pertinence as expressing the public estimate of the supposed fitness for the position I had assumed.''[4]

At the very beginning of his career as president, in his inaugural address, Tucker said:

''The life of an individual cannot attain to the dignity of history. The approach to that dignity marks the lessening of one's future. It is not so with the life of a great institution. The historic college moves on from generation to generation into its illimitable future. Each generation waits to pour into its life the warmth and richness of its own, and departing bequeaths to it the earnings of its strength. The college lives because nourished and fed from the unfailing sources of personal devotion.''[5]

Under these conditions, which are set forth with

[4] *Ibid.*, pp. 363-364.
[5] ''The Historic College: Its Present Place in the Educational System'' (1893). pp. 38-39.

charm and truthfulness, it is proper to ask and to seek to answer the question, what were the qualities and elements which Tucker brought from his pastorates and professorship to Dartmouth, fitting him for an office which was already historic, and to which his filling gave greater historic worth?

Tucker was gifted with a large sense of intellectual and administrative altruism. He had imagination. He saw the past of Dartmouth, and felt its traditions. He foresaw Dartmouth's future, and was moved by its visions and pre-visions. Dr. Johnson said of a sympathetic friend, "He puts his mind to yours." The remark could be applied to Tucker, and to the causes, too, to which he was pledged. In him was a certain selflessness which does not belong at all to small natures, and also is lacking in some great ones. This altruism took on the form of intellectual imagination. His ability to create lay in the field of thought. He saw Dartmouth as a great, constructive, formative personality. His imagination also took on the terms of feeling, and in this feeling lay the unconsuming love of Alma Mater. The imagination was also an altruism of the will which gave a sense of loyalty, a sense so deep, so broad, and so high, that the greater apostle and expounder of philosophic loyalty, Josiah Royce, would have been deeply moved by it.

In this altruism, Tucker incarnated and illustrated what has been called the "corporate consciousness" of the college. This consciousness is both institutional and personal. The college is an institution which is so vital, so related to officer and student and the community, that it ceases to be institutional merely, and becomes a personality. For, the college is indeed a legal personality: it is a corporation. But there is in the college a personality far more important than the legal. In this one personality are included personalities of several sorts. There is the personality intellectual. It represents the forces of understanding. There is the personality emotional. It stands for love, given and received, as a lasting power. There is a personality volitional. It means the will, the determination, the choice, to serve, and to be associated with, a college. There is the personality historic which represents and transmutes the past, and projects the past through the present into the lasting future. There is the personality, both visible and invisible, like the personality of the individual man himself. The personality depends upon both elements,—the invisible and the visible,—but more, and preëminently, on rather what is unseen than on what is seen. Even a new college easily takes on a personality through the devotion of its students, teachers, and trustees. The personality of Leland Stanford has already become dominant and fragrant. In the first days of the occupancy of the dormitories of the Harkness Quadrangle at Yale, I heard graduates sing "Dear Old Harkness!" Colleges differ tremendously in respect to the fact, and to the impression of the fact, of their personality. Four

American colleges seem to have the quality pre-eminently, three of them possibly, in particular, by reason of their age. They are Harvard, Yale, Princeton. Dartmouth, because of age and for other reasons, remains also personal. Of all the universities of the world, perhaps Oxford stands forth as being a personality,—a personality of generations numbering unnumbered dons, professors, and youths, of impossible beliefs, of undying prejudices, of beautiful enchantments, of ridiculous traditions, of victories and of disasters, of progresses and regresses, of comical tragedies and of tragical comedies, manifest in crumbling walls, in clinging ivies, and in triumphant towers. It is as Mackenzie says in "Sinister Street," an "uncapturable quintessence of human desire and human vision,"[6] a "mysterious material . . . grown through the Middle Ages."[7]

The president of a college is to feel the personality of his college, to feel it more deeply than others can feel it, and yet to be able to cause others to feel it also. Knowledge and reflection upon, sacrifice for, and union with, a college develops such an appreciation. It creates the corporate, collegiate consciousness. This feeling of and for Dartmouth as a personality is incarnated in Tucker himself.

This corporate personality represents what, for lack of a better term, might be called college spirit. No phrase is more common on the lips of the student, no lack is more evident to the heart of the under-

[6] p. 84.   [7] p. 147.

graduate, no lamentation is more common or more appealing as printed in the college paper or voiced at the football rally, than the cry for college spirit. It is heard in the great university of ten thousand, it is heard in the college of five hundred, students. It is often like the cry of Tennyson's "infant," a meaningless cry. But in its evident meaning, it expresses the contrast which obtains between the world inside, and the world outside, the academic gateway. It is an emphasis on the importance and imperativeness of college training and life, an emphasis which too close association with the great life beyond and outside would vitiate. It is an emphasis on the significance of the words, "Enter and learn wisdom," found inscribed on the outer side of the college gateways, at Cornell and elsewhere, for the guidance of the incoming freshmen. As such, college spirit voices a worthy sentiment, a sentiment which should be understood, appreciated, and made full and proper use of. In its essence, it is really a blossoming or a fruitage of academic self-respect.

United with this sense of the "corporate consciousness" of the college and of college spirit, was found in Tucker a mighty appreciation of the college itself. The college itself had, he believed, possibilities which it did not itself realize. Most colleges do not properly appreciate themselves as institutions and agencies of scholarship and of human betterment. They do not transform their potentialities into potencies. Like individuals, they have capacities of which they do not dream. They live a life of limitations, when they might enjoy enlargements,—and of poverties when wealth, and wealth of many sorts, awaits them. Tucker helped Dartmouth to realize its unconscious ideal. He quickened it unto the capitalizing of its history. It had indeed as he said, "no advantage in the transmission of culture. Her advantage, and it was very great, was in the well-nigh unrivaled possession of an originating spirit at once creative, adventurous, and charged with spiritual power."[8] Tucker helped the College to find its mind. He gave to the College out of his own fine enthusiasms a rich and noble sentiment for itself. The College had been inclined to think of itself as a rural college of a rural State. He gave to it a spirit at once modern and national.

This result was not won by a movement for expansion. Such a movement might have been proper for an urban university. But for Dartmouth, the movement, on the contrary, was a movement toward contraction. Along with the contraction went concentration. The university idea, which filled the mind of President Smith, was entirely eliminated. The College of Agriculture and Mechanic Arts was removed to Durham, where it has since greatly prospered. A bequest, made for the foundation of a Law School, was, in Bartlett's term, transferred to the foundation of a professorship of Law and Political Science. The Medical School was concentrated, like

[8] "My Generation." p. 269.

many other medical schools thus situated, into a course covering the first two years of professional training. The new Tuck School of Administration and Finance, and the older Thayer School of Engineering, became essentially a postgraduate course or department of the College. Thus, the ideal of the College as a college was both narrowed and broadened. Dartmouth was, is, and apparently will remain, as it ought in my judgment, an agency of liberal learning and culture. In respect to the fundamental element of undergraduate scholarship and its promotion, Tucker said:

"I sometimes think that the system of requirements and exactions, carried out as it must be, to be effective, into careful details, creates an environment distinctly unfavorable to the best scholarship. The allotted task is apt to fix the standard, which simply means that the average scholar gradually brings the better men down to his own commonplace. Here and there a man does his best out of respect to his own ability. Here and there a man pushes out beyond the commonplace to reach the fresh or seemingly inaccessible result. But the fact remains that the enforcements which are applied to the lower men do not prevent lapses on the part of men far above. And yet no college can exist in self-respect without the clear and sharp enforcement of scholarship. Grant that these do not stimulate, grant that required work lacks zest in the process and joy in the result, grant that the man who is sent to the library seldom if ever goes there on his own accord, what shall be done with the vast mass of students in all our colleges who have not the instinct nor the ambition of the scholar? Shall colleges be reduced to the number which can properly be labeled scholars? That test would reduce them to at most one-fourth of their present numbers. Shall colleges be changed into technical or professional schools? The change would doubtless double the amount of work now done, regardless of the quality. But the college is in the educational system to represent the spirit of amateur scholarship. College students are amateurs, not professionals. I think that a present danger, which in time may suggest a remedy, lies in the fact that instruction in our colleges is chiefly by professionals, who unconsciously or purposely strive to reproduce the methods of the graduate school. The scholarship of the undergraduate cannot be of the same type with that of the graduate unless it is prematurely professionalized. We must have professionals for college instructors. The graduate school is the only authorized and sufficient source of supply. We cannot ask these schools to change their standards or their methods. What we have the right to ask is that men who graduate from these schools, who seek positions as teachers in colleges, shall straightway proceed to study the student as they continue to study the subject. Not, however, by the same methods, but rather by learning, or perhaps relearning how to appreciate the mind of the undergraduate, so that in due time they may create the spirit of amateur scholarship."[9]

In all these services, so diverse, so fundamental, so immediate in application, Tucker,—a very human being himself,—never forgot that college administration is chiefly a human affair. Rules, prohibitions, statements of duties and of rights, precedents, written or unwritten, are only forms and forces for the use and usefulness of the human part. The failing to remember and to apply so obvious a truth is the cause of most college collisions, disagreements, disturbances. Tucker has himself said, "Nine tenths of all that pertains to a college is human, perhaps one tenth is material."[10] This human interpretation has made co-operation with faculty, students, graduates, and trustees natural, easy, and efficient.

Respecting the relations with the central body, the faculty, he has wisely and beautifully said:

"The changes here noted could not have been effected without the ready and even hearty coöperation of the Faculty. Nothing, for example, could have been more delightfully helpful than the hospitality of the older members not only toward the incoming members, but also toward the new subjects introduced into the curriculum, and toward the new methods of instruction and administration. The utter absence of friction in the transition from the

[9] The Report of President Tucker Covering His Administration: Issued to the Alumni. June 7, 1909. pp. 17-19.
[10] "My Generation." p. 410.

old to the new, or from simple to more complicated ways, was due entirely to the spirit of the Faculty, which was not that of acquiescence but of enthusiastic support. The hospitality of the older members was matched by the tactful adjustment of the incoming members to existing conditions, most of whom were strangers to Dartmouth.'' [11]

Such a spirit of co-operation means, above all else, what Walter Hines Page has written, regarding the use and the method of securing peaceful co-operation and co-operative peace, between the nations of the world, and between English-speaking nations in particular. ''I have found out,'' he says, ''that the first step toward that end is courtesy; that the second step is courtesy, and the third step—such a fine and high courtesy (which includes courage) as the President showed in the Panama tolls controversy. We have— we and the British—common aims and character. Only a continuous and sincere courtesy—over periods of strain as well as of calm—is necessary for as complete an understanding as will be required for the automatic guidance of the world in peaceful ways.'' [12] Courtesy is as creative in college administration as in international ambassadorships.

A similar humanity likewise characterized Tucker's relationship to that co-ordinate body, the students. No college president of his time more

[11] *Ibid.*, p. 316.
[12] ''The Life and Letters of Walter Hines Page.'' By Burton J. Hendrick. Vol. II, p. 71.

completely incarnated the undergraduate sentiment
of respect, of reverence, of love, and of loyalty. For
Tucker entered into the very real life and living of
the students. No interest of theirs, either as a body
or as individuals, was foreign to him. He saw into
them, as well as looked upon them. He also was less
a missionary than a diagnostician, less a spectator
than a comrade, less an auditor than a sympathetic
speaker, at their gatherings, and, be it added com-
prehensively, an interpreter of themselves to themselves. He was both honest and kind, uniting an
understanding of their immediate condition with a
prophetic vision of what they ought and might and
wanted to become. In ringing paragraphs, he talked
to them, week by week. He once said to them:

"Is it not worth a man's while to set up in the
days of his immaturity a self-government which will
give him some assurance of maturity? Time can
give us no such assurance. It may only make one's
immaturity more obvious and painful. But it was
not in God's intention, nor is it writ in the destiny
of any man, that he should fail to arrive at full-
grown manhood. I know the tremendous obstacles,
I know the temptations which line the way, and the
greater temptation within, but still I see the goal
clear and shining, yes, transfigured . . . I would not
have you forget for a moment that the possibilities
of our humanity have been realized in Christ, that
every man of us may find in Him his own possible destiny. This is what Christianity means. This is its

task. It does not shrink from its task nor stop short of its end. It proposes to deal with us according to our capacity if we will give it room in our lives for its work. It promises nothing, absolutely nothing, to indifferent or careless, or to calculating and bargaining souls. But to men who speak to God in the terms of manhood He gives answer in the terms of manhood. You want to come to a full-grown man. You shall come, and when you shall have come, you will see for the first time the measure of your manhood, 'the measure of the stature of the fullness of Christ.' " [13]

Also he gave the students, objects of his love, such commandments as these which are also beatitudes, and these beatitudes which are also commandments:

"Do not sell your minds. Self-respecting independence is above price. A man is of no value to himself who is not free.

"Be consistent in the use of mental power. Never discharge your minds of their obligation to the truth. At whatever stage you deal with material values, deal honestly.

"Do not live in the selfish employment of the present. Think, plan, work, sacrifice for the future. Be sure that something about you that you have said, or done, or suffered goes over into the service and remembrance of men." [14]

Such interpretations quicken young men unto at-

[13] "Personal Power: Counsels to College Men." pp. 13-14.
[14] *Ibid.*, p. 44.

taining their highest ideals by wisest methods, in the midst of ennobling conditions and through the lordliest powers. His Sunday vesper services have a lasting and grateful place in the memory of thousands of students.

The undergraduate soon becomes a graduate. The transient relation passes, and passes so easily, into the permanent. It is not, however, to the alumni represented in the board of trustees, nor to the alumni giving to a fund bearing the name of a dear teacher or president, to which they make annual contributions, nor to the efficient alumni council, important as all these conditions and forces are, but it is to the whole body of graduates, to which I now refer. For the Dartmouth body is, above most similar bodies, distinguished by its loyalty to Alma Mater. It is a noble company indeed, as Tucker's predecessor, Bartlett, says, a "magnificent roll of alumni unsurpassed in its average of good manhood and excellent work, and bright with names of transcendent lustre." [15] The grounds of the loyalty of graduates to Alma Mater form one of the most interesting of academic questions. Often have I asked myself if the following facts do not offer suggestions for an analysis of these grounds as applied to Dartmouth? First: the location of the College in a beautiful village, in the country of hill and valley, of river and

[15] "The Chief Elements of a Manly Culture" (Inaugural Oration). By Samuel Colcord Bartlett. Anniversary Addresses, p. 36.

wood, remote from conditions and forces drawing away attention from college life and fun. Second: the origin of the College as an adventure in faith, as a missionary foundation, as an appeal to the religious imagination. The "Wheelock succession" has not been limited to the presidential office, but has appealed to Dartmouth men who are apostles of the highest. All Dartmouth graduates drink of the quickening wine of the Wheelock cup. Third: the wise nursing of the historic tradition and personal conditions of the College. Daniel Webster has been a great asset and the College has constantly given heed to this worth. Fourth: may it not be added that the loyalty has been made deeper and of more meaning because of Tucker himself? The College and he came and went on, together, as horse and rider, till the end. The boys loved him, and loved him so much that they loved the College,—as they loved him,—the more.

Though Tucker was president of Dartmouth, yet because he was president, he was—as every college president should be, according to his ability and opportunity—much more than president. He was an interpreter of the whole people to themselves, their shepherd and their guide. Such service he gave during his more active administration, and he gave it in his retirement till his last day. Through speech, sermon, oration, and essay, was this service ever rendered. A service rich in content, diverse and apt in subject, persuasive and quickening, has it proved to be. In illustration let me quote from a paper "On the Control of Modern Civilization":

"A civilization of power cannot be shared without due regard to its liabilities. These, however, are discernible. In this respect it has a moral advantage over most civilizations of culture or of faith. Its dangers are less insidious. They are never disguised. At times they challenge attention. The distinction of living under a civilization of power is heightened by the acceptance of the responsibility involved. When this responsibility takes the form of control, whether by restraint or by direction, the generation entrusted with the task may find itself accorded an unusual place in the records of civilization." [16]

Likewise, in the address on "The New Movement in Humanity," a movement from liberty to unity, it is broadly and suggestively pointed out:

"But why should one at such a time content himself, in the joy of the intellectual life, with the reflective, or even, expectant attitude? In this movement from liberty to unity, who would not surrender himself to it, and become a part of it? The appeal of liberty was to men of action. The appeal of unity is to men of thought. The figure of the scholar on the field of battle was always inspiring, but he was seldom a leader there. In the new fields of service the scholar leads the way. The spirit of unity cannot be served as the spirit of liberty was served, except in regard to a like consecration. The new

[16] "The New Reservation of Time." p. 191.

kingdom of heaven may not suffer violence; the violent will not take it by force. The social unity must come through patient study, wise invention, identification with men, sympathy, and sacrifice; force will have no part in its accomplishment.'' [17]

These paragraphs provide evidence of the manifest truth that this president of an historic American college gave himself in a public-mindedness unto public services in shepherding of the people, which neither the towers of Oxford nor the ''backs'' of Cambridge can better memorialize or prophesy. Eliot of Harvard and Tucker of Dartmouth, contemporaries in life and not long divided in death, of all New England college presidents, represent most fully and deeply the American tradition.

Were I to go further afield, or to dig deeper, to find the origins of the power of Tucker, I should find myself brought face to face with certain contradictory elements of character,—contradictions, however, which are usually found in great men. In Tucker, one understands and feels the fineness of intellectual discrimination joined with swiftness of intellectual movement, delicacy of organization and temperament united with forcefulness of endeavor, fairness and a keen sense of justice welded with a capacity for intense moral indignation, the principles of the democrat lying close to the tastes of the patrician, virility and tenderness made one with persuasiveness and patience, geniality linked with self-

[17] *Ibid.*, pp. 212-213.

respect, open-mindedness vitalized with loyalty to one's own principles, contempt for cheapness and a despising of vulgarity interwoven with deepest human sympathies and, above all, a genuine love, both of heart and of will, for God and for man. And yet, even if the most thorough interpretation were possible, one has a feeling that one may not have cast the plumb line down deep enough. Perhaps one, after all, has not got hold of the real man. In one of the last paragraphs of the immortal Phaedo, Plato makes Socrates say to Crito[18], "Only you must get hold of me, and take care that I do not walk away from you." Socrates himself had the feeling that the real Socrates could not be caught; surely Crito could not catch him. As one contemplates men to-day, both great and small, one has somewhat the same feeling. But, go as far as we may, in all directions and relations, we know that there was essential greatness in this college president. This essential greatness co-existed, too, with a certain fineness which was also constructive and essential in his whole being. For, Tucker was a noble gentleman.

[18] Jowett's translation

XXII

GEORGE HERBERT PALMER

GEORGE HERBERT PALMER was born in Boston, March 19, 1842. Received A.B. degree, Harvard, 1864; A.M., 1867; University of Tübingen, 1867-69; graduated, Andover Theological Seminary, 1870; tutor in Greek, Harvard, 1870-72; instructor in Philosophy, 1872-73; assistant professor, 1873-83; professor, 1883-89; Alford professor of Natural Religion, Moral Philosophy and Civil Polity, 1889-1913; professor emeritus, 1913.

Author: An English translation of The Odyssey in rhythmic prose; The New Education; The Antigone of Sophocles; The Glory of the Imperfect; Self-Cultivation in English; The Field of Ethics; The Nature of Goodness; The Life and Works of George Herbert; The Life of Alice Freeman Palmer; The Teacher; Intimations of Immortality in the Sonnets of Shakespeare; The Problem of Freedom; Trades and Professions; Formative Types of English Poetry; Altruism—Its Nature and Varieties; Catalogue of English Poetry, etc.

XXII

GEORGE HERBERT PALMER

SCHOLAR, TEACHER, AUTHOR,
INTERPRETER OF HOMER

THE early home was formative, as the later one has been filled with contentment. Of the early home, he writes in an autobiographic sketch, entitled "The Puritan Home": "That was the most fundamental of Puritan institutions. Its effects were prodigious. It formed New England. Out of it came much of the mind and character of the entire country. Many of the older among us have felt its invigorating influence. Yet it is now in decay, where it has not altogether disappeared. Its usages are largely unknown, its strength and weaknesses have seldom been coolly studied. Often has it served as picturesque material for our novelists; but only to be held up to scorn as an oppressor of youth and a fosterer of gloom and hypocrisy,"[1] "I owe to it," he adds, "more than half of all that has made my life beautiful and rewarding."[2]

The essence of that home was religion. "We had

[1] "The Puritan Home." *Atlantic Monthly.* Vol. 128, 1921. p. 589.   [2] *Ibid.*

all that was needed for comfort and dignity,'' he writes, ''and on all that we possessed and did religion set its mark.''[3] The Bible was its Magna Charta. The Scriptures formed its rule of discipline and behavior:

''On rising I read a chapter of the Bible and had a prayer by myself. Then to breakfast, where each of the family repeated a verse of scripture, my father afterward asking a blessing on the meal. No meal was taken without this benediction. When breakfast was ended, the servants were summoned to family prayers, which ended with the Lord's Prayer, repeated together.

''Then we children were off to school, which was opened with Bible-reading and prayer. Of school there were two sessions, one in the morning and one in the afternoon; so that our principal play-time was between four-thirty and six o'clock, with study around the family table after supper. Later in the evening, when the servants' work was done, they joined us once more at family prayers; after which we children kissed each member of the family and departed to bed, always, however, before undressing, reading a chapter of the Bible by ourselves and offering an accompanying prayer. Each day, therefore, I had six seasons of Bible-reading and prayer—two in the family, two by myself, and two at school; and this in addition to the threefold blessing of the food. No part of the day was without consecration. The

[3] *Ibid.*

secular and the sacred were completely inter-twined." [4]

The religion that was presented in and through the Bible was a very personal experience. The old question, "Have you experienced religion?" had a real meaning. Religion was not a ritual. It looked askance upon a liturgy. It was not a communal affair. It did not embody a group-consciousness. Its ceremonies were few, and its sacraments were limited to two. Religion, standing for God, also quickened the sense of duty. Obligation was meas-ured by ability, and ability was stretched to its full length and lifted to its highest power. Life was a battle against sin. Happiness was often interpreted as a cloak for indulgence, and joyous indulgence was looked at askance as first cousin to evil. The virtues of courage, hardihood, perseverance, were empha-sized. Temperance was lost in prohibition, the songs of the pilgrim in statutes, and the beatitudes in the commandments.

Yet it is not to be inferred by this present law-less, pleasure-seeking generation, that the typical Puritan home was a home of unhappiness. If it lacked pleasures, it had joys. If it was without joys, —as it was not,—it had Christian peace. Its con-solations were not small. The ministries of the stars helped to overcome the roughnesses of the daily path. A strength, which seemed more than human, was given for the common round. It was thus a home

[4] *Ibid.*, p. 590.

which disciplined character, which gave to manhood purity, and to womanhood quiet strength and calm beauty. The eulogies pronounced upon it are more deserved than are the condemnations of which it has been the unanswering victim. If one cannot wish to restore it, one can wish that the virtues which it possessed, and incarnated in its members, might be given back to an age tempted through luxury unto softness, through the greater resources of the outer world unto materialism, and through the fullness of living to the forgetting of the infinite importance of life.

The religious element and atmosphere naturally, one might almost say inevitably, led Palmer, as it also led his brother, Frederic, to study for that profession which is the expression of supreme interest in religion, the ministry. The study included Tübingen, at that time one of the centers of rationalistic theology, and also, later, Andover Theological Seminary, where he graduated in the year 1870. At that time, Park was its professor of theology, as he was the leading new-school theologian in the United States. The influence of Park over his students has been diverse. Most students have found in him quickening intellectual forces, as well as comprehensive interpretations of presumed truth. Others have found his teaching wooden and his system of theology dry, meaningless, mechanical, unhuman. Palmer is one of those men to whom Park made little appeal. The reason is not far to seek. For, Park's system is, as I have said in a preceding chapter, formal, its logical divisions are exact, its proportions and relations, of Roman numerals and Arabic, of X's, Y's, and Z's, are forbidding to some, even if helpful to other, minds. Palmer could not find in Park's lectures, even if they were uniquely able, that human and humanistic nurture and nourishment which he himself later gave to thousands of men.

But the graduate of Andover did not follow his classmates into the acceptance of formal clerical service. Among the students of his time were several who became the great ministers of Congregational Churches, but he was not of them. Yet, be it added, Palmer has always preached. One does not forget the story of Lamb and Coleridge. His addresses on Sunday at Appleton, or other, chapel, his addresses at Wellesley, numerous and apt, represent what a sermon should be. His talks at morning prayers and elsewhere form the best type of preaching.

For, in his writing and teaching, as well as environment and character, religion is integral. It is at this point that one touches the key of personality. In the writing of each of these paragraphs, I am alone to blame, but I am especially to blame if, in interpreting this most intimate matter, my hand be particularly clumsy. For, to him religion is not so much a matter of creed—although I am sure he has his creed—not so much the adoption of articles of faith, as a matter of faith itself. Religion is an atmosphere, a mood, a point of view, as well as an assent of the intellect, a loyalty of the will and an enthusiasm of the heart. It is not a concern of liturgies, much less of litanies— although I am sure he joins in each—as it is of common obedience, trustfulness, and a contented ongoing. It is not catechetical, but meditative. It is not so much logical and argumentative, although this element is not lacking, as intuitive. It has the imagination of Newman, without mysticism, more of prayerfulness than of prayer, a sense of infinite relationships which does not yet sacrifice the vision for the nearest, and which strengthens the will for the immediate tasks. It represents the beauty of holiness. The aspirations fly Godward, but the wings are noiseless. The fire of devotion burns, yet silently.

Palmer's life and character has always seemed to me to be a unit, or unity. It flows on like a river, impossible of division. His devotion to religion easily becomes devotion to philosophy, as his philosophy in turn takes on religious relations and affiliations. As a philosopher, his teaching and his writing have been largely given, especially in the last years, to the cultivation of the ethical field. His final consummate office, the Alford Professorship, is officially named, as concerned with Natural Religion, Moral Philosophy and Civil Polity. His predecessor, a broad scholar and writer on many themes, Francis Bowen, did not decline, for at least a part of his long term of almost two score years, to cover these manifold relations. But Palmer, both before his accept-

ance of the historic professorship, as well as for the
twenty-four years of his holding it, gave himself
largely, though not wholly, to its moral philosophy.
I apprehend that his more durable contributions to
philosophy will be found to lie in ethics. If we
associate William James with psychology, and Royce
with certain historical and personal metaphysical
problems, do we not associate Palmer with ethics?[5]
In the ethical field, covered largely by three volumes,
are found at least two deeply significant interpretations. The first, and more important is "The Problem of Freedom." The interpretation of this doctrine is the profoundest of his writings, and a certain chapter of the discussion, the formative center
of the interpretation. If the doctrine of freedom is
the most intellectually profound, the interpretation
of goodness, found in the volume "The Nature of

[5] "Although I absolutely reject the platonism of it [San-
tayana's "Interpretations of Poetry and Religion"], I have
literally squealed with delight at the imperturbable perfection
with which the position is laid down on page after page; and
grunted with delight at such a thickening up of our Harvard
atmosphere. If our students now could begin really to understand what Royce means with his voluntaristic-pluralistic
monism, what Münsterberg means with his dualistic scientifi-
cism and platonism, what Santayana means by his pessimistic
platonism (I wonder if he and Mg. have had any close mutu-
ally encouraging intercourse in this line?), what I mean by my
crass pluralism, what you mean by your ethereal idealism,
that these are so many religions, ways of fronting life, and
worth fighting for, we should have a genuine philosophic universe at Harvard. The best condition of it would be an open
conflict and rivalry of the diverse systems." Letter to George
H. Palmer, "The Letters of William James." Edited by his
son, Henry James. Vol. II, p. 122.

Goodness,'' is the most emotionally moving. Chapter VII of the first-named book, and Chapter VI of the second, like the two books of which they are an important part, give forth Palmer at his best,—just, discriminating, learned, appreciative of the idea, happy in phrase and sympathic in feeling.

In the field of both theoretical ethics and practical morals, as in every other form of philosophy, Palmer is the embodiment of synthesis. Like Hegel he recognizes the antitheses of thinking, and like Kant the antinomies of reason. In these opposites, he finds elements of agreement and, out of the unlikenesses, evolves a yet higher principle, the principle of unity. The uniting element, or quality, is evidence of the insight and power of the mind. Both the insight and the force are intimated in such remarks as:—

"Each event is linked with that which went before. But while I see sequential causation everywhere, I see free action also. Accordingly I am obliged to defend something so paradoxical as chance or an ambiguous future in a world where all is causally connected." [6]

The comprehending element is set forth in such an interpretation as:

"There is no one doctrine of either freedom or determinism. Each presents diversities. Over and above those which spring from the nature of the subject are those grounded in the multiplicity of human

[6] "The Problem of Freedom." p. 131.

temperaments. Coleridge imagined that every man is born a Platonist or an Aristotelian. But there are cross divisions. Some Platonize in Aristotelic fashion, and some who follow Aristotle in general prefer Plato as their guide in certain exalted regions."[7]

Likewise in respect to practical affairs, antitheses are ever to become syntheses. Opposites are to be united in the highest principles. In writing of the three stages of goodness, he says:

"It is meaningless, then, to ask whether we should be intuitive and spontaneous, or considerate and deliberate. There is no such alternative. We need both dispositions. We should seek to attain a condition of swift spontaneity, of abounding freedom, of the absence of all restraint, and should not rest satisfied with the conditions in which we were born. But we must not suffer that even the new nature should be allowed to become altogether natural. It should be but the natural engine for spiritual ends, itself repeatedly scrutinized with a view to their better fulfillment."[8]

In happy sentences, too, is pictured the completeness of the ideal of good conduct:

"Human life is a complex and demanding affair, requiring for its ever-enlarging good whatever strength can be summoned from every side. Probably we must abandon that magnificent conception of our ancestors, that spirit is all in all and nature

[7] *Ibid.*, pp. 182-183.
[8] "The Nature of Goodness." p. 240.

unimportant. But must we, in deference to the temper of our time, eliminate conscious guidance altogether? May not the disparagement of recent ages have arisen in reaction against attempts to push conscious guidance into regions where it is unsuitable? Conceivably the two agencies may be supplementary. Possibly we may call on our fellow of the natural world for aid in spiritual work. The complete ideal, at any rate, of good conduct unites the swiftness, certainty, and ease of natural action with the selective progressiveness of spiritual.''[9]

In both the theoretical and practical relations, it is important for the thinker and for the reader to appreciate and to apply to himself the doctrine of opposites:

''What strikes me as important is that my readers should become acquainted with some other doctrine than the one advanced here, or at least some other than the doctrine to which their mind at present inclines. Until we understand the objections to any line of thought we do not understand that thought; nor can we feel the full force of such objections until we have them urged upon us by one who believes them.''[10]

It is because of this synthetic, or higher irenical, quality of his mind that it is difficult to put Palmer into any class of philosophers. In the early years he was interpreted by his colleague, William James,

[9] *Ibid.*, p. 223.
[10] ''The Problem of Freedom.''   pp. 207-208.

as an Hegelian. In the later years, I think of him as confined to no school. Call him, if one will, a synthetic idealist, or an irenical idealist. For one, I have little care: he is himself. I believe he would decline any such classified reference; and I, of all men, am the least willing to venture any such classification. Yet, one picks up, in many separated paragraphs, intimations of the essential philosophic principles. In writing of Kant, for instance, he says:

"I owe him a deep personal debt. After struggling for many years with the arbitrary limitations of English Empiricism, I found in him my liberator. I never became a Kantian. Few are that. But I gained an idealistic method, I learned the primacy of the Practical Reason, and I acquired a lifelong admiration for the man 'who broke the bands of circumstance and grappled with his evil star.' " [11]

As Palmer's interpretation of religion leads into philosophy, and philosophy into ethics, so both ethics and philosophy open a wide door to literature. For, though his books on philosophy and ethics are a part of literature, yet literature, as a constructive element and formative atmosphere, represents no small share of his contribution to human enlightenment and appreciation.

In literature, the most important part is style. Style is a term liable to mislead, and is quite too broad, representing either a quality or a fact, for exact and just understanding. Palmer's style has

[11] "Immanuel Kant, 1724-1924: Opening Words." p. 15.

many notes and emphases. It is a style which continues the Greek tradition and embodies French
lucidity and other excellences. In its fundamental
element of the sentence, it usually adopts shortness of
form, and into this shortness, it puts a single idea.
Style also makes much of the connective. His
sentences are well wrought together, as are the paragraphs fittingly linked. It might, therefore, be called
a simple style. In, and perhaps because of, this
simplicity, it is definite. It expresses adequately
and accurately the idea. It is prose, yet touched in
many parts by a simple rhythm, as in his Odyssey,
—"unobtrusively touched," be it added,—as he
says. It is a lavish style, perhaps at times too lavish.
Its words overflow the cup of ideas. Yet the Greek
self-restraint usually rescues. But more, and perhaps most, important, an "underglow of joy" moves
through sentence, paragraph, page. In it all is a
constant sense of vitality, arising, of course, from the
life-force of his thinking, and also qualified by the
custom of oral speech which seems to inspire and
quicken the written word. For the utterance of the
teacher is ever moving in the on-flowing pages of
written interpretation. I was about to call it a
pursuing style. For, it follows an idea into its relations, fundamental, superficial, lasting, timely, testing the idea's worth, weighing, measuring, assessing,
applying. In his essay on "Style" Pater writes of
prose:

"Prose is actually found to be a coloured thing with

Bacon, picturesque with Livy and Carlyle, musical with Cicero and Newman, mystical and intimate with Plato and Michelet and Sir Thomas Browne, exalted or florid, it may be, with Milton and Taylor.''[12] When one selects and lays down Pater's epithets on Palmer's style, one is obliged to say, it is not colored as is Bacon's, or picturesque like Livy's, or Carlyle's, but it is musical like Newman's, and it is mystical and intimate like Plato's. It is exalted, but not florid, like Milton's.

The style has Gibbon's luminousness, but not Gibbon's stateliness. It has more than Stevenson's charm, *plus* a cultivated richness, but without Stevenson's picturesqueness. It has the volume and fullness of Clarendon, as seen in his portraits, with more than Clarendon's nicety of word and phrase. It is as remote from the moving declamatoriness of Macaulay, as it is free from the extravagant lawlessness and ecstatic eccentricities of Carlyle. It is the embodiment of nobility in thought and expression, and it is the embodiment of this supreme quality because of the fineness and nobleness of the man himself. For, as Goethe said, if one is to write a noble style, let him have a noble soul. Gibbon also said that the style is the image of the man—base, base; majestic, majestic. Certain of Palmer's pages remind one of the richly illustrated manuscripts of the medieval monk in which intellectual delicacy and appreciation are

[12] ''Selections from Walter Pater.'' Edited by Edward Everett Hale, Jr. p. 123.

united with reverent devotion. They have indeed
some atmospheres which belong to highest inspiration.

I feel like comparing his style in particular to
that of three writers whose lives and service overlap
his own,—Pater, Arnold, Newman. They too, like
Palmer, deal in ideas, high, exalted, dignified. The
four are bathed in the aesthetic sense and sentiment.
They are devoted to the noblest and richest purposes.
They are gospelers of literature, or of religion, or
of both. They, too, move with youth, on terms of
quickening and of quickened comradeship. But how
unlike! In Palmer is a moral simplicity, a sublime,
a high, and constant devotion which the author of
"Marius" seldom manifests. In Palmer, too, is a
realness which one misses in Arnold. In the essay,
"The Glory of the Imperfect," first given as a college commencement address,—at the first commencement of a new college, he says of Arnold:

"Through him we have learned the charm of
simplicity, the refinement of exactitude, the strength
of finished form; we have learned calmness in trial
too, the patience of duty, ability to wait when in
doubt; in short, we have learned dignity, and he
who teaches us dignity is not a man lightly to be
forgotten or disparaged." [13]

In Palmer, we have the same great offerings.
But also we have a vivid and human intimation, a oneness with the reader or the hearer,
which is missed in the prose of the Oxford Pro-
        [13] "The Teacher." p. 145.

fessor of Poetry, and which one feels only in certain of his poems, as "Rugby Chapel." The closest comparison, with vast contrasts, lies in the style of Newman. In each, lavishness abounds. Discrimination is constant, and discrimination exact and persuasive. A definiteness and assurance of mental touch is seen, heard, felt. A sense of on-going is ever present. A heaven of optimism bends, radiant with the sunshine of high thinking and with the stellar light of fine feeling. In Newman, however, be it said, is a music which Palmer lacks, a music in both written discourse and in sermon which we know was not written, a music which exults in *glorias*, or sobs in *misereres*,—strains indeed which seem to breathe from his violin interpreting Palestrina, music which belongs to the other far-off or near-by world wherein Newman seemed to dwell. Herein, too, lies the difference. Palmer has less of music, far less; but he has more of this world, like Thoreau in the well-known story. His style fits into the hour, into the imperfect in which he yet sees glory, into the immediate duty which he realizes, into the obligation of the present life, in which, nevertheless, he feels the compulsions and the attractions of Wordsworth's Intimations.

Of the origin of this style, or at least of one of its origins, Palmer gives some knowledge, and this knowledge sheds light on personal character itself:

"Puritan children . . . were likely to read or hear six passages of the English Bible every day. That book, without regard to its religious value, is acknowledged to be the consummate masterpiece of our language. Here are primitive folk-lore, national history, personal anecdote, racy portraiture, incisive reflection, rapturous poetry, weighty argument, individual appeal, the whole presenting a wider range of interests than any other book affords. Throughout our version, too, runs a style of matchless simplicity, precision, animation, and dignity—a style exquisitely changing color to match its diverse subject-matter. What school-training in English can compare with year-long reading of this volume?

"Literary taste cannot well be directly taught. It comes best unconsciously, while the attention is given to something else. The Puritan child went through his many Bible-readings with a religious aim, the extraordinary beauty of the literature affecting him incidentally as something which could not well be otherwise. In that holy hush it was most naturally incorporated into his structure.

"I understate the case, however, in saying that the matchless English was daily read. Almost every week considerable portions were committed to memory. Before I was fifteen I had learned half the Psalms, and whole Gospel of John, three of Paul's Epistles, and large sections of Job and Isaiah. And this personal study was undertaken, not in obedience to commands, but because frequent contact with noble thought begets of itself a desire for more intimate acquaintance. Any man with half an ear, living in the company of musicians, is sure to think music beautiful and important. Just so the Puritan youth was drawn, not driven, to the study of the Bible through association with the biblically minded. Before he was aware what processes were going on, he found himself in possession of something priceless. He understood good English, and pretty generally spoke it." [14]

The testimony thus given is quite akin to the testimony of another master, John Ruskin, regarding the formative worth, for writing and for education, of the learning of the chapters of the Bible:

"I have next with deeper gratitude to chronicle what I owed to my mother for the resolutely consistent lessons which so exercised me in the Scriptures as to make every word of them familiar to my ear in habitual music,—yet in that familiarity reverenced, as transcending all thought, and ordaining all conduct.

"This she effected, not by her own sayings or personal authority; but simply by compelling me to read the book thoroughly, for myself. As soon as I was able to read with fluency, she began a course of Bible work with me, which never ceased till I went to Oxford. She read alternate verses with me, watching, at first, every intonation of my voice, and correcting the false ones, till she made me understand the verse, if within my reach, rightly, and energetically. It might be beyond me altogether; that

[14] "The Puritan Home." *Atlantic Monthly Magazine,* Vol. 128, 1921, pp. 594-595.

she did not care about; but she made sure that as soon as I got hold of it at all, I should get hold of it by the right end.

"In this way she began with the first verse of Genesis, and went straight through, to the last verse of the Apocalypse; hard names, numbers, Levitical law, and all; and began again at Genesis the next day. If a name was hard, the better the exercise in pronunciation,—if a chapter was tiresome, the better lesson in patience,—if loathsome, the better lesson in faith that there was some use in its being so outspoken. After our chapters, (from two to three a day, according to their length, the first thing after breakfast, and no interruption from servants allowed,—none from visitors, who either joined in the reading or had to stay upstairs,—and none from any visitings or excursions, except real traveling,) I had to learn a few verses by heart, or repeat, to make sure I had not lost, something of what was already known; and, with the chapters thus gradually possessed from the first word to the last, I had to learn the whole body of the fine old Scottish paraphrases, which are good, melodious, and forceful verse; and to which, together with the Bible itself, I owe the first cultivation of my ear in sound . . .

"And truly, though I have picked up the elements of a little further knowledge—in mathematics, meteorology, and the like, in after life—and owe not a little to the teaching of many people, the maternal installation of my mind in that property of chapters [a score of selections from the Old Testament and the New], I count very confidently the most precious, and, on the whole, the one *essential* part of all my education." [15]

With the influence of the English Bible as the source and resource of good style, one associates the Greek itself. My first meeting with Palmer was over the pages of the Apology. Plato and Homer helped to create and to nourish the form and method of his writing. In the Preface to the translation of the Odyssey, he speaks of his "debt of gratitude to the great friend who for twenty-five years has been showing me the beauty of himself and of the world." [16] For, Palmer is still the Hellenist, the Platonist, the humanist, in relations wider, and deeper, and higher than style, however expository the style is of the man himself.

This style, however, was not born, neither was it quite made in any artificial sense, nor is it primarily a growth. It is, probably, a pool into which both inheritances, reflections, and normal developments have flowed and mingled together. It is indeed the result of laboriousness, without being at all labored. It represents studying, weighing, balancing, considering. It has, I am sure, a certain slowness of growth, as it has, also, absolutely the rich ripeness of full maturity. "I sweat blood when I write," he once

[15] "Preaterita." By John Ruskin. pp. 35-37.
[16] P. vi.

said to a friend of his and of mine. He re-wrote his Odyssey thirteen times.

I was preparing to say that, as Palmer's interpretation of religion leads into philosophy, of philosophy into ethics, and of both, ethics and philosophy, into literature, so also literature, in its quality and style opens the door leading immediately to aesthetics. For, aesthetics, either as a quality of life, of writing, and of teaching, or as a body of doctrine, belongs intimately to the understanding of Palmer. In a narrow application, it is not wholly forgotten that he was curator of the Gray Collection of engravings; and that his students, of the early '70's, under his counsel, bought heliotype reproductions of some of these works, hanging them on their bare walls in Weld and Hollis. For one, I do not cease being grateful for his advising me, in answer to a question, to read "Modern Painters." Ruskin himself may have discarded many of the theories of these five volumes, but their ethical, as well as their aesthetic, quickenings still have meanings for one who is no longer a growing boy. In the priceless edition of Herbert, Palmer uses interpretations of Flemish and German paintings and of Dürer's wood-cuts to illustrate the poems of one who, as a pietist, gave himself to the interpretation of the beautiful in verses of beauty. His precious "Catalogue of English Poetry" also, in what it is and more. in what it intimates, offers full proof of his devotion to the beautiful as a literature, as a gospel and as a life.

What I have so far written, significant as it may or may not be, is merely an introduction to the great life and to the real service. For, Palmer has been and is a teacher. He has given himself constantly, severely, gloriously, remuneratively, to the work of education. The college has been his domain, the class-room his throne. There he has instructed and ruled, by the one wand of learning and of love, the generations of his students, to the number of fifteen thousand, for more than two score years. Is not the number greater than has been instructed by any teacher since Abélard?

As a teacher, I want to contrast him with his predecessor in the historic professorship, one who was also, for a time, his contemporary, Francis Bowen, and also, further, with his contemporary, William James.

Bowen was an admirable teacher of philosophy. He had the virtue of making the complex simple, the obscure plain, and his exposition was given with an earnestness not belonging usually to teachers of philosophy. His Yale contemporary, Porter, was a theologian as well as a philosopher, and became a president, following Woolsey. Bowen had less learning by much, and a far greater assurance, than his successor. For, Bowen seemed to reason to a conclusion to which he had made up his mind in advance, usually sound in logic and rich in ethical principle. Palmer seemed, and seems, to be a voyager with many companions on board, having a clear view of the

general course of the craft, but having also a seeming
doubtfulness of the port at which they all shall finally
land. Bowen argued a subject with a sense of finality
in reasoning and mood, a finality determined by himself. Palmer argued pro and con, and the student,
not Palmer, and the general sense of things, not
the *ipse dixit* of the teacher, determined conclusions.
To change a phrase, used in the Introduction to his
"Antigone," the verdict was made at the bidding of
the student, and not at the arbitrary command of
the teacher. Bowen was irritated at the "crass
materialists," always sniffing at them,—the outer be-
haviour, too, seeming to be an index of the inner
mood. He refers to the writings of one of these
"dirt materialists" as "an attempt to reconcile
materialism with spiritualism, realism with idealism,
optimism with pessimism, atheism with the belief in
a divine Providence, and monism with common
sense." [17] Palmer would find, even in thinkers as
opposite as Plato and John Locke, as Aristotle and
Berkeley, as Descartes and Rousseau, as Spinoza and
Herbert Spencer, as Kant and John Stuart Mill, as
Hegel and Schopenhauer, a common philosophic and
ethical good, most worthy of understanding, and, to
a degree, of adoption. He also would find weaknesses,
or limitations, in each, and he would further help
the student to discover truth and to discriminate
between truths.

[17] "Modern Philosophy, from Descartes to Schopenhauer and
Hartmann." By Francis Bowen. P. 479.

The contrast with the later colleague is quite as marked as with the earlier. For, Hocking, comparing Palmer and James, says:

"Professor Palmer was clear to a fault: for his transparency often concealed the actual profundity and scope of his thought: it deceived by its apparent ease. To him clearness was a matter of duty; he believed that he ought not to inflict on students the traces of personal struggle with his thought. In this respect he was at the opposite pole from William James, who often made his courses his laboratories —I was about to say the hospitals in which his thoughts were brought to birth. But the result was that while Palmer showed us the master, James showed us the process of mastering." [18]

In his essay, "The Ideal Teacher," used first as an address, Palmer lays down four fundamental elements of the teacher. They are, first, "an aptitude for vicariousness; and second, an already accumulated wealth; and third, an ability to invigorate life through knowledge; and fourth, a readiness to be forgotten." [19] He himself embodies all these elements and also others,—at least three,—to which I shall presently come.

By the first named, "vicariousness," he means a sense of intellectual altruism *plus* affection. He has

---

[18] "Professor Palmer at Eighty." By William Ernest Hocking. *Harvard Graduates' Magazine.* Vol. XXX, 1922, No. CXX, p. 518.
[19] "The Teacher." p. 8.

a passion to make scholars, scholars more scholarly than himself. But he also, and more, has a passion to make men, men large, true, fine, men better than himself, through scholarship. He has the imagination necessary to consummate this pious substitution, and he has also the aptness to secure the richest result. This aptness has become to him almost an instinct. It began with a sense of unsacrificing sacrifice, and has grown in priceless worth, unto unconscious, calm forcefulness.

Such vicariousness belongs to literature, as well as to pedagogy. The other person, the reader, is to be remembered. Palmer says: "Every utterance really concerns two. Its aim is social. Its object is communication; and while unquestionably prompted halfway by the desire to ease our mind through self-expression, it still finds its only justification in the advantage somebody else will draw from what is said. Speaking or writing is, therefore, everywhere a double-ended process. It springs from me, it penetrates him; and both of these ends need watching. . . . We are so full of ourselves that we do not remember the other person. Helter-skelter we pour forth our unaimed words merely for our personal relief, heedless whether they help or hinder him whom they still purport to address. For most of us are grievously lacking in imagination, which is the ability to go outside ourselves and take on the conditions of another mind. Yet this is what the literary artist is always doing. He has at once the ability to see for himself and the ability to see as others see him. He can lead two lives as easily as one life; or rather, he has trained himself to consider that other life as of more importance than his, and to reckon his comfort, likings and labors as quite subordinated to the service of that other. All serious literary work contains within it this readiness to bear another's burden. I must write with pains, that he may read with ease.'' [20]

In both the teaching and the writing, the sense of intellectual and emotional altruism is deep. It began early in his experience. It has continued, and it shall endure.

The second element, which Palmer presents and represents, is accumulated intellectual wealth. Such wealth is quite invariably hidden from the unobservant member of the class-room. But to the observing and to the responsive, it is a rich treasure upon which he draws consciously or unconsciously. To the observant student, gleams are given from time to time:

"The teacher should be the big bounteous being of the community. Other people may get along tolerably by holding whatever small knowledge comes their way. A moderate stock will pretty well serve their private turn. But that is not our case. Supplying a multitude, we need wealth sufficient for a multitude. We should then be clutching at knowledge on every side. Nothing must escape us. It is

[20] *Ibid.*, pp. 94-95.

a mistake to reject a bit of truth because it lies outside our province. Some day we shall need it all. All knowledge is our province. . . .

"I cannot teach right up to the edge of my knowledge without a fear of falling off. My pupils discover this fear, and my words are ineffective. They feel the influence of what I do not say. One cannot precisely explain it; but when I move freely across my subject as if it mattered little on what part of it I rest, they get a sense of assured power which is compulsive and fructifying." [21]

In Palmer's category of the elements of good teaching, the third, the invigorating of life through learning, is his indeed. I am asking myself if such quickening is not Palmer's supreme contribution? For, he is gifted in intellectual and emotional altruism. His intellectual wealth, accumulated through wide and high gatherings, is great. Vicariousness is the constant and pervading atmosphere, and rich learning the tool, or force, used to quicken the life of his fellows and followers. I was about to put before life, the epithet, intellectual. It would, however, be a false narrowing, and one which he would stay my pen from making. For, all life, not one side of it only, however inclusive, commands him. Excellence is both his mood and achievement. He is "productive," as say the academicians. His books are many. His courses of lectures, formal and informal, abound. But he is more, and most, "productive" in men, and

[21] *Ibid.*, pp. 16-17.

to men, he has given more life, and fuller. This consummation and general result have been gotten primarily by calling on students to use their own powers of understanding and of reflection. His students are not docile. They are not recipients. They are remote from being intellectual buckets into which he constantly pumps sweet, metaphysical waters. They are, by his wish or command, fellow-climbers on steep and stiff mountain trails of thinking. To change the figure into a timely metaphor, they are fellow-flyers in the air-planes of metaphysics. He is the directing aviator. But his students he takes into his confidence, and with them he holds conferences, both before and on the voyage. They have, or at least they think they have, some share in the management and direction of the craft. They are thus made alert, observant, reflective, directive. Life becomes enlarged, enriched, dignified.

Palmer also represents, in his teaching, another element which he theoretically names "readiness to be forgotten." In this interpretation, "readiness" should be emphasized. I should prefer, however, the word willingness. For, "readiness" connotes almost a certain eagerness. The teacher need not, and should not, be guilty of any such Lethean inclination or disposition. Yet it is proper for him to be willing. That is both Calvinistic and gentlemanly! Palmer is one of the great teachers of Harvard College of his generation who will be remembered as long as the life of his students, or of the children, or grandchildren, of his students, continues. Indeed, one might omit the narrowing limitations of Harvard. The depth and debt of lasting appreciation which his students feel for him, suggest, both by comparison and by contrast, the wideness of his grateful following. For, his line has gone out through all the earth, and his words to the end of the world. As he says:

"Let us display our subjects as lucidly as possible, allow our pupils considerable license in apprehension, and be content ourselves to escape observation. But though what we do remains unknown, its results often awake deep affection. Few in the community receive love more abundantly than we. Wherever we go, we meet a smiling face. Throughout the world, by some good fortune, the period of learning is the period of romance. . . . It is better to be loved than to be understood." [22]

But to this quartette of elements, theoretical and incarnated, I want to add three which belong to the mind and work of our man, (1) his power of analysis, (2) the quality of discrimination, and (3) the element of fairness.

These three things go together, making up a certain force for weighing evidence which Palmer's colleague, Henry Adams, used to tell his students constituted education. Yet, they are to be separated for this present interpretation.

The power of analysis is formative and fruitful. If it relate to the separation of the like from the

[22] *Ibid.*, pp. 28-29.

unlike, and of unlikes from each other, it also leads out and into unique processes and results of rich worth. Philosophy has a name for confusion, for complexity, for obscurity, for both blindness and blindingness. Palmer has a way of unsnarling the snarled. He has a sense of relations. His gift is one of interpretation. He understands proportions. Under his quiet, almost monotonous voice, of the class-room, what was obscure is made clear, and what was complex, simple. What was disturbing in perspective is brought out into just relationships. This power on its literary side is made manifest in his priceless edition of Herbert, in the interpretations,— "sweet sounds, and delicate diction,"—of Shakespeare's sonnets, in his philosophic and ethical essay on freedom, and in the personal biography of his wife.

This power of analysis has close relation to his method of discrimination. For, what is analysis but discrimination writ large? But, for my present purpose, by discrimination, I mean a quality which distinguishes, in the meaning of words, in the connotation of phrase, verse, sentence, in the significance of moods, tenses, tendencies, and voices. Herein is seen again his likeness to John Henry Newman. He disentangles the skein of thought. He detects what is sophistical. He discards what is irrelevant.[23] He is the discoverer and the apostle of the hidden essen-

[23] See "The Idea of a University." By John Henry Newman. (Longman's Edition.) p. 178.

tial. I might call his discrimination delicate and
dainty, did not these epithets war against his robust-
ness and pugnacity. For, I have heard him censure
men of close relations to himself, in strong language,
and, at times, his earnestness and seriousness, though
quiet, in condemning the unworthy would have won
the approval of Jonathan Edwards. His mind seems
to me, not infrequently, like Ambrose Swasey's
machine which cuts a million lines within the space
of an inch. Yet, one does not forget that these almost
infinitely minute discriminations do not war against
essential strength and forcefulness. He is still
dynamic; and again he seems to be dogmatic.

Such a quality and power are quite akin to a certain intellectual balance, or judicialness, or fairness,
which some might say is chiefly dominant and characteristic. William James writes, apropos of a letter
of Palmer's, commenting on one of James' books,
"A Pluralistic Universe":

" 'The finest critical mind of our time!' No one
can mix the honey and the gall as you do! My con-
ceit appropriates the honey—for the gall it makes
indulgent allowance, as the inevitable watering of
a pair of aged rationalist eyes at the effulgent sun-
rise of a new philosophic day! Thanks! thanks! for
the honey." [24] Palmer might be called the disciple
and apostle of the opposite, as I have already intimated,—not, of course, in the sense of cantanker-

[24] "The Letters of William James." Edited by his son,
Henry James. Vol. II, p. 322.

ousness, but in the sense of a desire to give a proper interpretation and a just hearing and defense to the side in which he does not believe:

"All who read should differ from me as deeply as they can. I have tried to differ from myself, and fundamentally questioned how to escape from the conclusions I here present. Just such questioning I desire from my readers; for my aim is not to impose my opinions on others, but to stimulate them to vigorous and connected thought of their own. Let us then together enter this repellent region and scrutinize the obstacles which hedge it in." [25] Thus he often seems to give more than a fair chance to his antagonist.

This most manifest quality not unjustly lays Palmer open to charges, and charges, too, of a serious nature: first, of being sophistical, and, second, of being guilty of insincerity or of something akin. These charges are essentially one. They arise simply from the force and fullness of his appreciation of a proposition or movement to which he is intellectually repellent. For, many a time, as I have listened to, or read, his interpretations of causes, I have found my mind accepting his interpretation. Within a half-hour, or a few pages, I have also found my mind adopting the opposite conclusion. The fact is, he seeks to present both, or several of many, sides of a question as fully and as strongly as possible. He knows, too, and his reader or hearer finally recognizes,

[25] "The Problem of Freedom." p. 129.

that "fairness does not necessitate absence of conviction." [26]   Judicialness does not spell indifference, either intellectual or ethical.

There is one element in Palmer less frequently found in the teachers of American colleges than in the dons of Oxford and Cambridge. It is the element of picking out undergraduate friends, joining one's self to them, and them to one's self, unto the common benefit and happiness. His wife, Alice Freeman, likewise possessed the precious gift. Of course, Jowett or Green is the most distinguished instance to be found at Oxford. This student association, entered into in undergraduate days, was continued, in the case of Palmer, into the graduate years. He became a special friend with George Edward Woodberry and with Theodore Chickering Williams in their undergraduate years, and in the years immediately following. In fact, he and Williams were, in a sense, chums for a time, in one of the Harvard halls. Of Williams, too, and soon after his lamented death, in introducing his translation of "The Georgics and Eclogues of Virgil," Palmer wrote:

"This open-mindedness, intellectual refinement, and disposition to create his own modes of speech made poetry, and indeed Fine Art of all sorts, a constant ingredient of his daily life. It never became an artificial pastime. He looked out upon a glad world with the unwearied eyes of a child, seized its human values with rejoicing, sensitively harmonized

[26] *Ibid.*, p. 90.

its discords, and swiftly created appropriate forms for depicting its incidents. . . .

"All who met him felt his unselfish character and were fascinated by its blending of virility and loveliness. Religion went all through him. He might be said to live with the Eternal and to be ever engaged in tracking its presence through temporal things." [27]

With Woodberry, too, similar graduate and undergraduate relationships were maintained. On the occasion of Woodberry's seventieth birthday, Palmer wrote, saying:

"Just fifty years ago in one of my classes I noticed a young fellow of exceptional promise. As I had in my house at 3 Garden Street more rooms than I needed, I offered one to him and he became a member of my household. Mrs. Palmer as well as I became warmly attached to him. His literary interests were then forming and he was reaching out toward that perfection of style in prose and verse which has ever since distinguished him. Often we three read together the masterpieces of English poetry, and in the discussions which followed he took an active part." [28]

Such intimacies of friendship, begun in undergraduate years and enriched in all the following times, represent the best in method and means and result of all education and other relationships. It is,

[27] pp. 18-19.
[28] "Letters: The Woodberry Dinner," 1925. p. 3.

in a sense, even better than the more equal relationships obtaining between Tennyson and Arthur Hallam.

These fundamental and conservative elements, and these great qualities, form, and serve to interpret, his idea of education. It is to education that he has given his life and his learning, and it is through education, largely understood, that he makes his richest contribution. Education is teaching seen from the teacher's point of view. In phrases far more apt than I can coin, and in interpretations much wiser and weightier than I can give, I want to present his understanding of this living process and endeavor:

"Education should unfold us and truth together; and to enable it to do so the learner must never be allowed to sink into a mere recipient. He should be called on to think, to observe, to form his own judgments, even at the risk of error and crudity. Temporary one-sidedness and extravagance is not too high a price to pay for originality. And this development of personal vigor . . . is the great aim of education . . ."[29]

"What, then, is the central aim of teaching? Confessedly it is the impartation of knowledge. Whatever furthers this should be eagerly pursued; and all that hinders it, rejected. . . ."[30]

"Both education and morality set themselves to rationalize the moody, lawless, transient, isolated, self-assertive, and impatient aspects of things, in-

[29] "The Teacher."   p. 24.   [30] *Ibid.,* p. 50.

troducing the wondering scholar to the inherent necessities which surround him . . .[31]

"Education may well be defined as the banishment of moods at the bidding of the permanently real . . .[32]

"What we should like to impart is that earnestness, accuracy, unselfishness, candor, reverence for God's laws, and sturdiness through hardship, toward which we aspire—matters in reality only half ours and which spring up with fresh and original beauty in every soul where they once take root . . .[33]

"More than health, wealth, and beauty, literary style may be called the man, good judges have found in it the final test of culture and have said that he, and he alone, is a well-educated person who uses his language with power and beauty . . .[34]

"The culture of these weak wills is the problem of every college. Here are unintentional boys waiting to be turned into intentional men. What limitations on intellectual and moral vagrancy will help them forward? . . .[35]

"Now in college a boy should learn perpetually to think; and an excellent way of helping him to learn is to ask him often what he is thinking about. The object of the questioning should not be to thwart the boy's aims, rather to insure that they are in reality his own. Essentially his to the last they should remain, even though intrinsically they may not be the best. . . .[36]

[31] *Ibid.*, p. 54. [32] *Ibid.*, p. 55. [33] *Ibid.*, p. 65.
[34] *Ibid.*, p. 75. [35] *Ibid.*, p. 247. [36] *Ibid.*, p. 250.

"George Herbert, praising God for the physical world which He has made, says that in it 'all things have their will, yet none but thine.' Such a free harmony between thinking man and a Lord of his thought it is the office of education to bring about.[37]

"The aim of education, as I conceive it, is to spiritualize the largest possible number of persons, that is, to teach them how to do their own thinking and willing and to do it well.[38]

"Wise ways of training boys are of more consequence . . . we want to hear of a constructive policy which can take a young man of nineteen and so train him in self-direction that four years later he may venture out alone into a perplexing, and for the most part hostile, world. The thing to be done is to teach boys how to manage themselves . . . We stand with this aim of self-guidance in our hands. What are we going to do with it? It is as dangerous as a bomb. But we cannot drop it. It is too late to objurgate. It is better to think calmly what possible modes of treatment are still open. When railroads were found dangerous, men did not take to stage-coaches again; they only studied railroading the more. . . . In the mass of negative criticism . . . I detest these positive suggestions."[39]

"It is a long time before we come to the great discovery that every object in the world is dependent on every other. The moment we have mastered this thought and know that we cannot understand one

[37] *Ibid.*, p. 269.   [38] *Ibid.*, p. 239.   [39] *Ibid.*, p. 213.

thing until we have understood all, incipiently at least we are scientific men." [40]

"For most of us the period of learning is a period of romance. We are young, and all things are possible. Every circumstance is novel, calculated in some way to serve our growth and happiness. Even those of us who have spent our early years in toil learn at last how to profit by play. We make a few intimate friends and a wide circle of acquaintances. We fashion our ideals, compare them with those about us, and have them sharply criticised. The physical world more deeply discloses its wonder. Through many avenues we enter into the heritage of the race. Whatever is precious in the past and has been thought worth preserving in the caskets called books is offered for our enrichment. And in our teachers we have wise guides who not only conduct us to these treasures, but point out their human significance . . ." [41]

"But of at least equal importance with the knowledge acquired in college is the influence on a student of the personality of his teachers. Some of these, it is true, will always be mere purveyors of knowledge; others, more insignificant still, inspectors of what has been learned already. But in every college faculty there are pretty sure to be certain men of mark, from whom—sometimes in the course of in-

[40] "The Field of Ethics": The William Belden Noble Lectures for 1899. pp. 122-123.
[41] "The Life of Alice Freeman Palmer." p. 46.

struction, sometimes through personal acquaintance
—a student half-imperceptibly carries off impressions
and impulses of incalculable worth . . .[42]

"In college the aims of culture and enjoyment are
dominant; in the world outside there is the necessity
of watching others' wants; our own preferences drop
a good deal out of sight. Accordingly it is often said
that a college unfits one for practical life. Though it
gives the means of becoming broadly serviceable, it
does not necessarily bring the desire, and certainly
does not form the requisite habits. What we gain
in college is apt enough to stick fast within us, and not
easily to pass beyond. Before we can succeed in the
new and dutiful ways our aims need readjusting.
For most persons there comes something of a jolt in
turning from the period of acquisition to that of
distribution."[43]

These interpretations, written or spoken, made
under diverse conditions, for diverse purposes, and
belonging to periods of time widely separated, invite
remarks. They reveal the man, and it is the man in
whom I want the reader to be interested, as dominant
over the teacher, or writer, or artist. They indicate
that the human quality is immeasurably superior to
the professorial, the vital to the formal, the personal
to the professional, even if the professional and professorial be uniquely interpretative and formative.
They prove that this man is the foe of the artificial,
of the superficial, of the narrow; that he is the pro-

[42] *Ibid.*, p. 49.   [43] *Ibid.*, p. 72.

moter, the defender, the apostle of the instinctively noble and the natural. He believes in the individual as a subject and force in education. The individual is the center and source of the social order.

But Palmer also believes in institutions: "I mean by institutions those fairly permanent relations between persons which past experience has established for the promotion of human welfare and successive generations have approved." [44]

He has lived his life, and is living it. He has done his work and is still doing it, as a member of an institution, an institution the most historic in America. There are advantages and disadvantages in such institutional association. On the whole, however, the advantages are far richer. If an institution limits the individual, it also magnifies him. If it is a monarch, it is a constitutional one. If it commands, it also obeys. If it lays down requirements which determine life's daily regimen, it also aids in making systems for one's self which spell efficiency. If it takes away a certain sense of responsibility for one's self, it also dignifies and enlarges this sense, carrying it over into an appreciation of responsibility for the whole institution or movement. If it seems to minimize individuality, it also, and more, magnifies personality unto richer content and more harmonious relationships. Be it also added, if one desire lasting fame, and I am sure that Palmer seldom if ever feels

[44] "Altruism: Its Nature and Varieties." The Ely Lectures for 1917-18. p. 132.

such a desire, let him link his service and his life with an institution. The individual dies and is usually, and presently, forgotten. The institution lives, and, therefore, he, its associate, lives.

This personal service and institutional association have taken on a definite and a most fruitful relation. For a generation, the philosophical department of Harvard was recognized as the ablest in the world. It is to Palmer that its origin is in no small degree due. As a successor of Palmer, in the Alford Professorship, has said:

"It was Palmer who showed us James, securing his attachment to the philosophical staff at Harvard. And it was Palmer with James who discovered Royce; and these three acquired Münsterberg and produced Santayana. The building of that great department of philosophy was thus in substance Palmer's work. And this achievement is an illustration of one of his most notable powers, a connoisseurship of life capable of meeting the supreme test, that of recognizing greatness in its awkward and immature stages." [45]

He is free and as happy as he is free to recognize the good fortune, or fortunes, belonging to himself as a college man and teacher:

"Harvard is a complex and august institution, possessed of all the attractions which can be lent by age, tradition, learning, continually renewed re-

[45] "Professor Palmer at Eighty." By William Ernest Hocking. *Harvard Graduates' Magazine,* Vol. XXX, 1922, No. 120, p. 518.

sources, fortunate situation, wide-spread clientage, enthusiastic loyalty, and forceful guidance. She is the intellectual mother of us all, honored certainly by me, and I believe by thousands of others, for a multiplicity of subtle influences which stretch far outside her special modes of instruction.'' [46]

Much that I have been trying to say, and saying, I know, so inadequately, comes to certain conclusions which are indicated in various *dicta obiter* which are found scattered in his dozen volumes. I am picking up some of these nuggets broken off from their surrounding mass. For they are, in their singleness even, weighty and precious in substance as they are discriminating and delicate in form:

''Instruction must go all through. We are obliged to treat each little human being as a whole if we would have our treatment wholesome . . .'' [47]

''It is safest not to meddle much with the insides of our pupils. An occasional weighty word is more compulsive than frequent talk . . .'' [48]

''Something like what we mean must never be counted equivalent to what we mean. And if we are not sure of our meaning or of our word, we must pause until we are sure. Accuracy does not come of itself . . .'' [49]

''We must give our thought its head, and not drive it with too tight a rein, nor grow timid when it begins to prance a bit . . . Pedantry is worse than blunder-

[46] ''The Teacher.'' p. 203.   [47] *Ibid.*, p. 34.
[48] *Ibid.*, p. 67.   [49] *Ibid.*, p. 82.

ing. If we care for grace and flexible beauty of language, we must learn to let our thought run . . .[50]

"What stamps a man as great is not freedom from faults, but abundance of powers . . .[51]

"Religion is only enlarged good sense, and the words of Jesus apply as well to the things of earth as of heaven . . .[52]

"Let us make ourselves as large as possible, in order that we may contribute our little something to that to which all others are contributing . . .[53]

"The joy of perfecting is beyond the joy of perfection . . .[54]

"To permit choice is dangerous; but not to permit it is more dangerous; for it renders dependency habitual, places outside the character those springs of action which should be set within it, treats personal adhesion as of little account, and through anxiety to shield a young life from evil cuts it off from opportunities of virile good . . .[55]

"He [Professor Sophocles] was long a notable figure in university life, one of those picturesque characters who by their very being give impulse to aspiring mortals and check the ever-encroaching commonplace." [56]

"Hardihood in goodness is as desirable as in bodily matters. We need to discriminate in evil and to foster the habit of distinguishing great things from

[50] *Ibid.*, p. 84. [51] *Ibid.*, p. 86. [52] *Ibid.*, p. 101.
[53] *Ibid.*, p. 141. [54] *Ibid.*, p. 153. [55] *Ibid.*, p. 183.
[56] *Ibid.*, pp. 284-285.

small. Men stoutly righteous seek to fill conduct
with excellence rather than to keep it free from
blemish . . .[57]

"A fact without a law is as nonsensical as a law
without a fact." [58]

"Religion roots best in isolation . . .[59]

"Either master nature or be mastered by her . . .[60]

"It is a heroic moment for any one of us
when, face to face with God, we formally announce
that henceforth we are accountable to Him alone.
It marks the attainment of full self-consciousness . . .[61]

"She was a hardened optimist . . .[62]

"Where little money is, there often appears a kind
of compensatory devotion . . .[63]

"The law of good manners is dictated by the pos-
sibility of sympathy . . .[64]

"Civilization rests upon dedicated lives, lives which
acknowledge obligation not to themselves or to other
single persons, but to the community, to science, to
art, to a cause . . .[65]

"The worth of public leadership is pretty exactly proportioned to the wealth of the personal
nature . . .[66]

"Great causes and great institutions are generally

[57] "The Field of Ethics" (Noble Lectures). p. 62.
[58] *Ibid.*, p. 185.
[59] "The Life of Alice Freeman Palmer." p. 23.
[60] *Ibid.*, p. 26. [61] *Ibid.*, p. 38. [62] *Ibid.*, p. 82.
[63] *Ibid.*, p. 128. [64] *Ibid.*, p. 168. [65] *Ibid.*, p. 172.
[66] *Ibid.*, p. 177.

best founded, or guided through crises, by a single leader." [67]

"Delight in discovering difficulties is a good preservative against error." [68]

"One cannot contemplate long such exalted themes without receiving an impulse, and being lifted into a region where doing wrong becomes a little strange. When, too, we reflect how many human ills spring from misunderstanding and intellectual obscurity, we see that whatever tends to illuminate mental problems is of large consequence in the practical issues of life . . ." [69]

"Richness of character is as important as correctness. The world's benefactors have often been one-sided and faulty men. None of us can be complete; and we had better not be much disturbed over the fact, but rather set ourselves to grow strong enough to carry off our defects." [70]

If I were to seek a counterpart to Palmer, I should go to Oxford, and should find that counterpart in T. H. Green,—Green, who died as long ago as 1882, and at the early age of forty-six. Of Green, one who knew him well,—Lord Bryce,—says:

"He was the most powerful ethical influence, and perhaps also the most stimulative intellectual influence, that in those years played upon the minds of the ablest youth of the University . . ." [71]

[67] *Ibid.*, p. 180.   [68] "The Problem of Freedom." p. 7.
[69] "The Nature of Goodness." p. 9.   [70] *Ibid.*, p. 43.
[71] "Studies in Contemporary Biography." p. 95.

"From the first he had won the confidence and affection of his pupils. Many of them used long afterwards to say that his conduct and his teaching had been the one great example or one great influence they had found and felt in Oxford . . .[72]

"To him metaphysics were not only the basis of theology, but also the basis of politics. Everything was to converge on the free life of the individual in a free State; rational faith and reason inspired by emotion were to have their perfect work in making the good citizen . . .[73]

"Green will be long remembered in the English Universities as the strongest force in the sphere of ethical philosophy that they have seen in the second half of the nineteenth century."[74]

The correspondences thus intimated are indeed far closer than can be found in most biographical parallels.[75]

Palmer is still young, for life to him is a process, a lasting youthfulness, not a finality. It is a syllogism with a major premise of universal law, a minor premise of application, and without the drawing of a conclusion. It is to him, this life, a wonderful and gracious system of indeterminates and determinates. It began, like Emerson's, without firm hope for its length of years. It has continued for four score and more, without haste and without rest, with the flexi-

---

[72] *Ibid.*, p. 96.   [73] *Ibid.*, p. 97.   [74] *Ibid.*, p. 99.
[75] For further resemblances, see "Memoir," Works of T. H. Green. Vol. III, pp. xi-clxi.

bility of steel, and with far more than the steel's strength. He has himself said:

"Those whose early years were feeble often outlive the strong. Knowing that sound bodies are rare and that much of the hard work of the world has been done by semi-invalids, they are ready to take their infirmities soberly and gradually to discover how to dispose of them in their system with the least harm." [76]

When Palmer had been a teacher at Harvard forty years, a portrait of him was given to the University. [Later a second portrait was presented by his associates.] On the occasion, his colleague, Royce, at a gathering of his former students, said:

"I deeply regret that I was not in the ordinary sense his pupil. You who have been his pupils know that herein I have lost much. But this I know, that we can none of us ever lose him or his influence so long as we continue either to reflect or to love." [77]

At the same time, another colleague, Professor Edward K. Rand, addressed him in Greek verse, of which the following is a translation:

"Hail, wise in counsel! Over many seas
Of thought thou ridest, and shalt ride, at ease.
Modern and ancient, thou, for whom agree
The imperfect glory and fair symmetry." [78]

[76] "Immanuel Kant, 1724-1924: Opening Words." p. 11.
[77] "In Honor of Professor Palmer." By Joseph Royce, *Harvard Graduates' Magazine*, Vol. XIX, 1911, No. 76, p. 578.
[78] *Harvard Graduates' Magazine*, Vol. XIX, No. 76, p. 579.

After the death of Royce, Palmer wrote of him, saying: "Happy the University that had for a long time so vitalizing a presence!" [79] The simple eulogy one may transfer to Palmer himself, and in the transferring make the interpretation wider. Happy the man and the men who have had for so long a time a presence so vitalizing, a teacher so wise, a companion of the way so quickening, and a friend so true and so dear! If in a single word I could compress what I have been trying to write,—and ever with a sense of failure,—I should make a threefold compound, adding to the Greek compound, standing for beauty and for goodness, a part which stands also for wisdom: beauty *plus* goodness *plus* wisdom. Each is great; all are greatest.

[79] Josiah Royce, *Ibid.*, Vol. XXV, 1916, No. 96, p. 170.

INDEX

PRESIDENT THWING'S BOOKS ON COLLEGE SUBJECTS

GUIDES, PHILOSOPHERS, AND FRIENDS
STUDIES OF COLLEGE MEN

DATE DUE
